CITIES AND URBAN LIVING

Cities and Urban Living

MARK BALDASSARE, Editor

Columbia University Press
NEW YORK
1983

Library of Congress Cataloging in Publication Data
Main entry under title:
Cities and urban living.
  Includes bibliographies.
  1. Sociology, Urban—United States—Addresses,
essays, lectures. 2. Cities and towns—United
States—Addresses, essays, lectures. I. Baldassare,
Mark.
HT123.C4965 1983   307.7′64′0973   82-19875
ISBN 0-231-05502-1
ISBN 0-231-05503-X (pbk.)

Columbia University Press
New York   Guildford, Surrey

Contents

Acknowledgments

I THANK ALL of the contributors for their assistance in ma¹ ing this collection possible. Participation in various conferences and informal contacts with urban sociologists too numerous to mention were influential in my choice of topics and specific selections. The idea of editing a reader evolved while teaching urban sociology at Berkeley, UCLA, UC Irvine and Columbia. My students clearly convinced me of the need for a new urban reader. Helen Danner prepared the index, Margaret Thomlinson typed the entire manuscript, and Wendy Steinberg assisted in proofreading. I also wish to thank Charles Webel of Columbia University Press for his support for the project and useful advice about the book's content.

CITIES AND URBAN LIVING

Introduction:
Urban Change
and Continuity

MARK BALDASSARE

THIS READER BRINGS together recent articles on the sociology of urban life. It is organized by topical areas that, since 1970, have sustained careful attention. The essays offer a broad statement about modern America's social and demographic realities. Each considers how such facts affect the urban resident and most review present policy options.

New topics in urban sociology, and older issues that have regained relevance, are represented in this collection. Both have raised questions about the usefulness of traditional urban sociology and the need for a newly formed discipline. The critics claim that traditional urban sociology, which is described in detail later, lacks relevance to modern problems, is politically conservative, is not attuned to the most significant socioeconomic factors, disregards cultural and historical considerations, and refuses to admit the importance of the resident's actions and beliefs. The defenders claim that their urban paradigm presents the most holistic and integrated study of urban conditions and that it can inform urban practitioners of policy options, and thus they see no need for incorporating other perspectives. The reader is therefore warned that urban sociology has been shaped by disciplinary controversy in addition to actual city events. The collection seeks to represent these varying perspectives, in the introductory chapter and in the essays themselves, offering an opportunity to assess the present and future state of urban sociology.

This book, however, does not seek an exhaustive treatment of all substantive areas in urban sociology today. Nor does it offer a complete review of the modern urban setting. Areas of concern usually highlighted in urban collections, such as deviance, crime, poverty, suburbs, social problems, comparative urbanization, and race do not specifically comprise this volume's selections. There are several reasons for organizing the book in this manner. Many topics usually considered "urban" are excluded because, in my judgment, they are sociological events coincidentally occurring in cities which deserve separate attention. Recent developments in urban sociology outside the United States and reviews of worldwide urban trends are thoroughly considered in existing collections (Abu Lughod and Hay 1977; Berry 1976; Pickvance 1976). Most importantly, I have chosen articles that represent intensive and interrelated work on what seems to be the most significant development in modern urban America.

A major theme in today's urban sociology, and this reader's focus, is the emergence of a new social life due to fundamental changes in land use and movement. While the transformation of American society has been underway for many years, it is my position that various changes reached an advanced state in the past decade. This allows us, for the first time, fully to realize the impact of revolutionary improvements in transportation and communication. In short, Americans' notions of geographical constraints, the importance of social territories, and the expansiveness of urban boundaries have taken on new meanings. This has caused urban sociologists to reexamine how urban space is used and conceptualized, both in terms of the "fixed features" of community development and the "fluid features" of residents' daily activities.

There are several documented population shifts that confirm radical changes in acceptable locations for residence, work, and leisure. The 1970 census noted that, for the first time, most Americans resided in suburbs instead of central cities. The 1980 census indicates that cities in the so-called "Frostbelt" region have declined as jobs and residents relocated to the new cities of the Sunbelt region. Older high-rise settlements are quickly giving way to life in low-density and centerless "boomtowns." In general, new developments in suburbs and "sun cities" are based on the availability of automobiles and telecommunications. These factors encourage urban sprawl and frequent, long commutes. Not only has urban population spread into previously underdeveloped regions and expanded metropolitan boundaries, but the latest evidence suggests that even adjacent and remote rural areas have experienced urbanization. One task of urban sociology is to understand the causes of these new patterns; another is to comprehend the consequences of recent trends for communities, individuals, and special resident groups.

This book's purpose is thus to present evidence of new urban patterns, and to examine sociological essays that are concerned with the roots and implications of these changes. This is an introduction to the subject matter of the collection. The following two sections provide detailed descriptions of recent trends in urban sociology and American urban settings. Then follow commentaries about the topical areas represented in this collection.

Recent Trends in Urban Sociology

Urban sociology is having an identity crisis. For more than half a century the "Chicago School" has dominated intellectual conversations about how the city developed, what constitutes the city's daily operations, and how city living affects residents. But to some its framework has failed recently to predict or to explain important urban phenomena. The riots and crime waves that flared in large cities during the 1960s seem immune to traditional sociological interpretations. Fiscal crises of municipal governments during the 1970s are not the typical subject matter of urban sociology. The recent

emergence of inner-city revitalization and a rural repopulation run counter to most theories' premises about urban expansion. Consistent evidence that tightly knit communities
exist in the most unexpected places, such as urban slums and
immigrant settlements, has raised doubts about the assumptions made about city living. Yet these events comprise the
reality of America's modern cities and call for serious analyses. The discipline is increasingly being asked, along with
questions of relevance, what "urban" sociology is in a highly
urban nation.

The history of the traditional urban paradigm should be
reviewed, in order to place the present controversy in perspective. A century of sociology has tried to comprehend the
effects of modern urban society on social organization and on
individuals' lives. Early theorists assumed that industrialization resulted in radical social changes. As agricultural production became partially replaced by manufacturing, society's economic activities became more organizationally
complex and socially interdependent. The drift away from
rural communal existence toward urban specialized labor also
placed new pressures on the individual. Rather than increasing "happiness," modernization stripped people of a meaningful social and economic existence and forced them into
purely functional tasks and transient relationships. Feelings
of alienation, normlessness, social isolation, worthlessness,
and opportunities for deviance were to emerge (see Durkheim 1893). University of Chicago sociologists imported these
ideas and used them in studying the fast-growing, heterogeneous, and economically booming American cities. Much of
the foundation was laid between the two world wars. They
considered their work an "ecological analysis," since they
were interested in how humans organized their cities, adapted
to urban surroundings, and, ultimately, gained collective
sustenance from the city environment. They followed Durkheim's strict definition of sociological inquiry, which excluded from study such nonsocial factors as the physical
world and individual psychology.

An early concentration of the Chicago School was urban

social organization. Robert Park viewed the city landscape as a set of distinct communities, each highly specialized in function, which were dependent for survival on one another's contributions. The urban areas were conceived as "moral worlds" with their own internal dynamics, and the city was viewed as a functioning whole composed of these separate but intertwined organic parts (Park 1925, 1926). The empirical studies, the classic example being Burgess' elaboration of the concentric zone model, described in detail the urban world's internal structure. Burgess (1925) used maps and census data from Chicago to illustrate that five concentric areas with distinct social features, yet integrated functions, existed: the central business district, a transition zone, a workingmen's zone, a middle-class zone, and a commuters' zone. Case studies that sought to describe the social order in different sections of the city were thereafter launched (Wirth 1928; Zorbaugh 1929). While the observations seemed to validate the ecological perspective, empirical researchers disagreed about the concentric zone model's usefulness (Quinn 1940) and criticized the Chicago School's seeming obsession with geography. Theories about city structure that considered multiple factors, including transportation and industrial activities, eventually gained in popularity (Harris and Ullman 1945; Hoyt 1943; Shevky and Bell 1955).

There was also an effort to understand why "personal disorganization" was rampant in American cities. This concern is due to Durkheim's influence, reported earlier, and also because of the Chicago School's connection with Georg Simmel. In an essay entitled "The Metropolis and Mental Life," Simmel (1905) suggested that city living can be psychologically overstimulating and thus harmful. The individual must compensate for too many social encounters by adopting a protective life-style, which includes social withdrawal, a reserved nature, and blasé attitudes toward other people. Overstimulation at worst causes psychic problems and, at best, leads to many impersonal contacts. Robert Park, a student of Simmel's, suggested in an essay "The City" (1925) that the social structure of cities distorted human values and actions.

Since daily activities (such as work, shopping, leisure) are often conducted away from home, in unfamiliar areas, people can lead private and socially unrestricted lives. Loneliness, despair, deviance, conflict, and confusion are all by-products of the new-found freedom.

In the Chicago School's most important statement, Louis Wirth's "Urbanism as a Way of Life" (1938) developed further the themes of the Park and Simmel essays. One of Wirth's major tasks was to define urbanism. He selected three factors that distinguish city from countryside: population size, population density, and social heterogeneity. Wirth postulated that these attributes affect the urbanite's personal life. Social diversity in the context of limited space and astronomical personal contacts combine to reduce intimate relationships, cause social conflict, and create mental stress. Wirth drew such a powerful and convincing picture of urban life that few questioned the essay's validity.

The ecological studies of personal disorganization, which were few in number, collected community deviance rates and associated these data with community census statistics. The evidence was mixed. Faris and Dunham (1939) found that mental hospital admissions were more frequent in dense and socially diverse central districts than in the city's outlying areas. Shaw (1929) reported the same pattern in rates of juvenile delinquency, confirming the Chicago School's hypothesis that variations in social organization affect residents' well-being. However, studies that sought to link rapid urbanization to social disruption (McKenzie 1925) in American cities were less conclusive. Ogburn (1935) found no association between city growth rates and city crime rates, while Wechsler (1961) reported a moderate relationship between population growth and poor mental health. Personal disorganization was also examined through field studies, since the social factors causing communities to malfunction should be obvious. Close observations also yielded inconsistent results.

A slow but building resistance to the ecological approach developed. Clausen and Kohn (1954) argued that the methodology was flawed, the findings were regularly misinterpreted, and the government statistics on deviance rates were of questionable validity. Critics argued that the "ecological fallacy" was too often committed, meaning that average statistics on groups were used to impute the causes of behavior in separate individuals. The "drift hypothesis"—the idea that deviant persons gravitated to inner-city areas rather than that such districts caused disorganization—placed many of the researchers' conclusions in doubt. Still others claimed that human ecology theory left too much substance outside the realm of urban sociology. Prime omissions included culture, values, politics, and personal attitudes (Firey 1945).

It was the field studies of the 1950s and 1960s, once encouraged by the Chicago School, that posed the greatest threat to the ecological perspective. Herbert Gans's studies (1962, 1967) of a Boston neighborhood and a Philadelphia suburb suggested that class position and stage of life were social factors that transcended the importance of any "urban" characteristics. Oscar Lewis' observations of Mexico City migrants (1952) led to the conclusion that people live in small circles of friends and family, and thus any city-wide variables are irrelevant. Gerald Suttles (1969) found that a Chicago multiethnic slum offered an orderly life-style for its residents, perhaps not perceived by most outside observers, which was effective in helping residents cope with inner-city conditions. Another study discovered that ecological factors influenced friendship patterns but perhaps only in highly homogeneous neighborhoods (Festinger et al. 1950; see also Newman 1973).

More complete opposition to the ecological perspective is expressed by urban sociologists today. Michelson (1976:17–21) lists the following shortcomings of the ecological approach: incomplete conceptualization of the environment; fixation on aggregates; and erection of disciplinary boundaries. In place of traditional concerns, Michelson suggests a focus on individuals' preferences and their interactions with the actual residential setting. A lack of "congruence" between ideal and reality thus explains personal problems. Michelson (1977) finds examples through personal interviews concerning recent moves, personal adjustments, daily schedules, transportation patterns, reported satisfaction, and present housing conditions. Thus, an emerging approach is to study the urban context in which the individual lives, with the belief of the ecologists that urban environments affect people, but with a new realization that people cope, manipulate, and change environments (Stokols 1972). This perspective avoids the extremes of "environmental determinism" and the total denial of the urban environment's importance.

Some recent researchers insist that the Chicago School's devotion to the ecological method has left many of their important ideas untested. Claude Fischer has merged survey data with census information to examine Wirth's hypothesis that a more "urban" setting has meaningful social and psychological consequences. The conclusion is that greater social complexity, more deviance, and higher tolerance for diversity emerges in large cities. Urbanites are not, however, more psychologically troubled or socially isolated as originally conceived. It appears that large population concentrations or "critical masses" allow for the development of social groupings, be they called networks or subcultures, to emerge around special interests. Thus, the existence of "different ways of life" in the city is explained by greater, not lesser, social organization (Fischer 1976). Such a discovery has led to revised conclusions about why social uprisings in many historical periods began in large cities (Lodhi and Tilly 1973). Researchers are now also encouraged to study the workings of elites, in order to determine the roots of urban political decision making. In general, new urban inquiries are emerging through the study of urban social networks. The effects personal constraints have on friendship choices and tightly knit communities is one example of new research. To what extent "social supports" help newcomers cope with the problems of urban life is another area of interest.

Other shortcomings in ecological work, which have surfaced recently, result in a broadening of the social variables deemed crucial to urban analyses. Abu Lughod (1964) found that the demographic changes that are supposed to occur with society's rural-to-urban transformation do not apply to newly developing countries. This is because past theories are based on western cultural values and economic conditions. A city's political system, which is often shaped by peculiar historical incidents and charismatic leaders, can clearly influence the quality of residents' lives (Clark and Ferguson 1981). Political-economic factors, which are national and international in scope, can account for important events in American cities and neighborhoods (Tabb and Sawers 1978).

Still, the ecological paradigm is defended as a relevant tool for understanding the modern city. Its users point to successes in describing the fundamental demographic changes that are forming new urban communities in America (see Kasarda 1980). A recent review of ecological research (Frisbie 1980) points to the impressive body of knowledge regarding metropolitanization, the city's internal structure, suburbanization, residential segregation, and national city systems (see also Berry and Kasarda 1977). There has also been a resurgence of its application in the studies of residential crowding and the recent phenomenon of inner-city revitalization, to be treated later. Urban sociology, however, has perhaps permanently entered a stage in which no one theory or method will dominate. Instead, a growing number of researchers choose approaches to match substantive issues. Urban sociology also considers more topics than ever before.

Recent Trends in Urban America

The way of life in urban America has changed dramatically during the twentieth century. While the nation was experiencing rapid industrialization a hundred years ago, dense cities were built mostly along the major waterways of the eastern and midwestern states. People walked or took short rides from their homes to work, shopping, and leisure sites. Most city residents rented apartments in multifamily buildings. Large numbers of foreign immigrants entered port cities, seeking manufacturing jobs and crowding into ethnically segregated neighborhoods. City government did not plan for the future, was minimally involved in safety standards, and provided few basic services. Outside of these dense urban clusters were farmlands and estates.

The electric trolley offered the first possibilities for change, allowing some people to move away from crowded downtown districts and commute to work. It was the introduction of the automobile and trucking, however, that led to the eventual decline of the past urban form. Once automobiles were available to the masses, the urbanite's choice of residential location need no longer be constrained by walking distance or access to mass transit. Likewise, manufacturing firms could use trucking to get supplies and distribute to retailers, thus avoiding crowded commercial-industrial zone locations. The widespread distribution of telephones enhanced urban deconcentration, since communication about work matters and personal affairs no longer required face-to-face contact on a regular basis.

The changeover from high-density cities to large-scale metropolises was slowed by two world wars and the Great Depression. But in the 1940s the suburban movement of business and residents took hold. Federal government subsidies in housing and roadways, available capital for private developers, rising expectations of the middle class, and the community conditions offered by localities outside the city were all incentives to build suburbs composed of one-family homes and interspersed with commercial-industrial facilities. The cities that matured in the automobile era, in the South and West, mirror this low-density, large-area metropolitan structure.

Since the 1960s a series of urban crises have acted as stimuli to discourage residence in older central cities: the influx of poor migrants, racial violence, crime waves, tax burdens, and shortages of decent and affordable housing are among the considerations. It is also true that urban Americans today have expectations about local governments' tasks and residential quality that are, by world and historical standards, very high, and that the economic resources to make nearer-optimal choices are available to many individuals. In short, the nation is now in the advanced stages of reordering urban life, with sizable numbers of "old city" residents and enterprises exercising their ability to locate elsewhere. Some are choosing the surrounding suburbs, others opt for cities in other regions, and a sizable number are now relocating in nonmetropolitan areas. The extent of change in where and how most Americans live is evident in the recent census statistics.

The 1980 census statistics on city populations offer evidence of these urban trends. In view of all the arguments about undercounting offered by mayors and legislators, such figures cannot be taken literally. Yet they are representative, when viewed across numerous urban areas, of the gross changes in work and habitat that have occurred. Central-city population declined by almost 2 percent during the 1970s. The older large cities of this nation, which were population losers during the 1960s, are now experiencing dramatic declines. New York and Chicago each lost 10 percent of their populations between 1970 and 1980, translating into losses of 700,000 and 300,000, respectively. In fact, among the five largest American cities only Los Angeles had a net gain, since Philadelphia and Detroit each lost around 300,000 residents. Three major industrial centers lost nearly 25 percent of their 1970 populations, or around 150,000 residents—Buffalo, St. Louis, and Cleveland. The central cities in the Midwest and Northeast, in sum, lost 10 percent of the residents they had ten years ago (Long and DeAre 1981).

A primary destination of outmigrants is the metropolitan region surrounding the "old city" boundaries. From these suburban locations, residents commute to their central-city jobs or to the suburban businesses, which have also found new settings desirable. Suburban population increased by nearly 20 percent during the 1970s. Metropolitan growth can be seen in the rapidly growing counties outside declining central cities' boundaries. Lake County in the Chicago Standard Metropolitan Statistical Area (SMSA) grew by 15 percent in the last decade and the Philadelphia SMSA's county of Chester increased its population size by 11 percent. Examples of more extreme proportional changes in suburban county population are found in the following statistics: Jefferson County, St. Louis SMSA, 40 percent; Clermon County, Cincinnati SMSA, 35 percent; Fairfax County, District of Columbia SMSA, 31 percent. Continued suburban population increases in the Northeast (4 percent) and Midwest (13 percent), despite large regional losses, indicate this pattern's strength. Suburbanization continues nationwide despite dramatically increased housing costs and the fact that many young Americans are postponing family formation.

The other important population shift is the movement of Frostbelt residents to the Sunbelt. The Northeast and North Central regions had little growth in the last decade, while the South and West grew by 20 percent (the national rate was 11 percent). The migration is primarily composed of "old city" residents who follow industrial relocation or seek jobs in the nation's "new cities," thus forgoing settlements in the North's metropolitan areas. Central-city population increases in the South (11 percent) and West (3 percent) occurred despite national trends. There are big gainers, just as there are big losers, in the modern-day economic "war between the states." Houston grew by 29 percent in the past decade and gained over 350,000 residents. Two other Texas cities, Dallas and San Antonio, also had sizable population increases. San Jose and San Diego in California each added about 200,000 residents and grew at a rate exceeding 25 percent. In general, these central cities regularly expanded their municipal boundaries. Still, suburban populations increased by more than 40 percent in the West and South. Annexation and suburban migration suggest even further erosion in the Sunbelt's city-suburb distinctions.

There are several immediate repercussions of these demographic phenomena. The national population was divided equally in 1960 among central-city, suburban, and nonmetropolitan locations. By 1970, the numbers showed for the first time a plurality for suburbs (37 percent), which around 1980 increased further to 40 percent of the total United States population. The country began the 1970s with a majority of its population living in the Northeast and North Central states and ended the decade with the majority found in the South and West. More subtle yet equally powerful statistics speak to related changes in urban life. The densities (persons per square mile) have declined in all large cities, whether they grew or not, while suburban densities have increased. Thus, while residential crowding may have been somewhat reduced for inner-city populations, the individuals inhabiting massive metropolitan areas now feel the pressure of a rather evenly distributed dense urban form. Since employment has also decentralized, urban problems such as traffic congestion and air pollution have now taken on metropolitan implications rather than being confined to the city limits.

The emergence of an urban-to-rural migration in the 1970s suggests that even the expanded boundaries will soon be redrawn. The nonmetropolitan counties increased by 15 percent in the 1970s, while metropolitan areas showed only a 10 percent increase. Nonmetropolitan growth occurred in all regions of the country though, as with other trends, the increase was most pronounced in the South and West. The growth cannot be accounted for merely as an expansion of metropolitan boundaries into adjacent areas. Remote areas also gained residents and, significantly, the proportion of the United States population designated as "metropolitan" actually declined for the first time in recorded history (Long and DeAre 1981). The future may thus bring an even more dramatic reordering of urban life.

The most troubling aspect of "old city" population loss is that the migrant stream to the suburbs and the Sunbelt is not random. After a decade and a half of civil-rights efforts it is still difficult for blacks to move into white suburban neighborhoods. In addition, the cities of the South and West are largely attracting whites to new jobs. The combination of middle-class white flight, a high black birth rate, and a substantial Hispanic immigration is creating an apartheidlike situation in older cities, with poor minorities in the center and whites on the outskirts. A larger proportion of the remaining white central-city residents, as evidenced by a growth in persons living alone and a large elderly population, is composed of dependent persons, individuals with few housing options, and those who cannot participate in an automobile-oriented society. There is high unemployment among young adult minorities, because blue-collar jobs have long since left the city. Jobs for which they are qualified are inaccessible, either in distant suburbs or in the Sunbelt. Fear of victimization is rampant among the whites who must share transitional neighborhoods with poor minorities.

Older cities are taking on new tasks and "symbolic meanings" in the era of easy travel and communication. There has been a boom in commercial office building, as international and national corporations have been lured into the downtown by tax incentives and their special needs for central locations. New York City has become a tourist mecca for Americans who want to experience the theaters, museums, restaurants, and hustle of midtown. Philadelphia became a "nice place to visit" after its historical value was accentuated by the bicentennial celebration. In fact, suburbanites still gravitate toward city centers to obtain certain services, recreational or otherwise, and even the centerless cities of the Sunbelt are constructing new symphony halls and museums to instill civic pride. Perhaps the increasing administrative role and tourism have added municipal revenues, revitalized a few neighborhoods, and encouraged some retailers to stay in business. But changes in the private sector have done little to improve job and housing prospects for most blacks, or to offer training to the new Hispanic and Asian immigrants, or to upgrade residential conditions for the elderly who must live outside prime inner-city neighborhoods. The climate of local budget deficits and federal budget cuts offers little hope that improvements will be stimulated by government.

In the remainder of this chapter, the six topical areas around which this collection is organized are reviewed. The first and last sections contain sociological ideas about the "form" of modern urban life. One reconsiders the classic community question and the other is concerned with the emerging political economy perspective. Neighborhood revitalization, rural growth, and residential crowding are then reviewed in terms of their known causes and consequences. Since special groups are adversely affected by present urban trends, another section examines vulnerable populations in the city.

Recent Ideas About Modern Urban Communities

Special types of communities have evolved in the late twentieth century and, as already noted, they are quite different from earlier settlement patterns. Urban areas are larger in population size and land area than ever before. Older cities have seen their residents and businesses spread out into surrounding areas, forming suburbs that now comprise the bulk of metropolitan areas. New cities have drawn migrants and jobs from previously dominant regions and have created massive but thinly populated developments. The emerging urban patterns have placed work further from residence, demanding that most individuals make long daily commutes. There are more specialized activities available to metropolitanites, but they are not usually found in one's local area or in a single commercial district. We know that even the central business districts have special functions in modern urban communities, serving as regional cultural centers and the headquarters for international and regional businesses.

Some examine these trends and find the modern community in America structurally flawed. Is it wasteful, for example, to exert energy resources on long automobile commutes? Low densities also rule out mass transit alternatives. A mismatch exists between the unemployed and new blue-collar jobs. Underskilled minorities are in the older inner cities while the manufacturers have moved to the Sunbelt and the suburbs. Central-city jobs are becoming more predominantly white-collar, offering work to the suburban commuter.

Central cities in the Frostbelt seem destined to suffer budgetary problems. They have had an erosion of the tax base as businesses and residents have migrated. They must pay for services needed by suburban daytime users and their own increasingly poor and elderly population. In the midst of decline are a decaying physical plant, a housing shortage, and a demand for more police protection. Solutions are hampered by our political system's unwillingness to engage in metropolitan-wide planning, that is, to shift the fiscal burden to suburban residents and businesses dependent on the city. While the prospects for central-city recovery, overall, are dim, during this era some municipalities have adjusted to fiscal problems quite well. With many local governments likely to face deficit spending, new community studies that elaborate on the factors predicting fiscal strain and recovery are much needed.

Elsewhere in the nation the old-style civic boosterism of counting new residents and building permits is under attack. Even the self-proclaimed "golden buckle of the Sunbelt," the city government of Houston, is questioning unrestrained growth. Problems such as congested roads, inadequate services, and high crime rates are increasingly noted in southern and western cities and suburban localities. Despite the complexity of predicting the actual consequences of local growth (Baldassare 1981), many communities "close the door" on unwanted residents. Cities have placed severe restrictions on future growth through purchases of vacant land, planning pauses, permit moratoria, population ceilings, and annual permit limitations. Local policies that encourage decline in one area or growth in another have begun to cause public outcries. Alonso (1973) argues that no-growth policies may reduce local problems in the short run, but the expense of unwanted newcomers is merely passed on to the surrounding localities. Eventually, the difficulties will come back to haunt the community acting in its immediate self-interest. Logan (1978) contends that cities within metropolitan areas vary in status, and that those with initial advantages act in self-interest to maintain their relative standing. Some information even suggests that socioeconomic inequalities among metropolitan communities have increased in recent decades (Logan and

Schneider 1981). In a recent study, growth control policies in northern California were more stringent in cities with white-collar residents and notable opposition by business and citizens. "Growth control" residents were found to be no more satisfied with their localities (Baldassare and Protash 1982). A need to understand the factors that explain growth, local responses, and actual outcomes has necessitated new community studies. The evidence to date indicates that effective and equitable local policies must include metropolitan, state, and even national considerations.

The above trends and other recent events have reopened the general issue of whether people feel "attached" or personally committed to their communities. Many argue that the local area now has little meaning since people spend so much of their time in activities away from home (see Suttles 1972). Others contend that local residents get involved with each other only if an external threat (such as a crime wave, new developments) dictates that they collectively mobilize in order to protect their individual interests. The lack of importance given to "place" is sometimes viewed as a positive event, interpreted as residents being freed from the constraints of having to choose friends and services from a small local area (Webber 1970).

While there has undoubtedly been a growing independence from the residential area, there is still evidence of the importance of local community. In most major cities there are ethnic and racial neighborhoods that are composed of intense local friendships, strong feelings of commitment to the area, and community shops and services geared toward the locality's needs. It should be remembered that some, but certainly not all, residents live in such communities not because they lack mobility opportunities but from choice. Further, while many residents have long since left the "old neighborhood" in the city, there are the weekend pilgrimages to the downtown's Little Italies and Chinatowns. Even in a less spatially bound environment, metropolitanites value places with stored "symbolic meanings" that allow them to reexperience their culture and heritages.

What about the possibilities for people developing their own "communities" in an urban world in which people frequently change residence and daily go their own ways? In an important review of the "community question," Wellman and Leighton (1979) consider whether interpersonal ties are attenuated (community lost), persisting (community saved), or found outside the neighborhood (community liberated) in the modern urban setting. They argue that neighborhood ties exist for most urban residents, but in the context of larger social networks. Contrary to what we have been led to believe about city life and modern anonymity, most recent studies suggest that the vast majority of urbanites today have "social networks" or personal associations that fulfill their intimate needs. The question is not whether or not people have social networks, but rather what types of social networks are encouraged by the urban structure. For example, do our friends know one another, do we depend on different people for different needs, and where do our acquaintances live and work?

It was once believed that urbanism left the individual socially isolated, and that this resulted in personal disorganization. The latest thoughts on this subject are that large populations provide the "critical masses" of people to form subcultures around special interests or collective threats (see Fischer 1976, 1977, 1982). Urban life thus presents unique opportunities for communities of artists, scholars, sportspersons, criminals, and political activists. If urban life is associated with more deviance, it is not because communities are more disorganized, but rather because social organization is more possible (see also Tilly 1974).

Neighborhood Revitalization in the Inner City

In the mid 1970s, urban watchers began to observe what was once considered an unlikely pattern of events. Neighborhoods long deserted by middle-class families were being reoccupied by young professionals. Housing that had experienced decades of neglect or abandonment was now the object of intense rehabilitation efforts. There were scattered reports of so-called "inner-city revitalization" in many large cities (London 1978). For example, New York, San Francisco, Boston, Philadelphia, Baltimore, and Washington, D.C., were all net losers of population in the 1960s, yet had neighborhoods that were clearly showing signs of physical and social improvement. This trend seemed all the more surprising since private initiatives rather than public policies per se accounted for the specific neighborhood changes. The revival in central-city neighborhoods is such a new and unexpected event that, until the 1980 census is fully analyzed, much of the systematic research will remain at a primitive stage.

There is controversy about how much "revitalization" has occurred largely because there is no agreed-on definition or measurement of this phenomenon (see also Laska and Spain 1980). An Urban Land Institute survey found that local officials in three-fourths of all cities over 500,000 in population reported the incidence of significant private rehabilitation (Black et al. 1977). Spain (1980) investigated neighborhood revitalization through statistics of whites moving into housing previously occupied by blacks. Housing turnovers of this sort are on the increase according to data derived from the Annual Housing Survey. Still, these trends represent only a small proportion of all housing moves in central cities. Increased housing investments and social "upgrading" have been noticed in some inner-city areas. Whether or not such cases represent a significant trend, how to weight the importance of various social factors in assessing change and how to describe what has actually occurred are still in question.

Many explanations have been offered for neighborhood revitalization. No one factor seems crucial. Perhaps higher energy costs have induced people to live nearer to their central-city jobs. The skyrocketing housing prices may have also dampened potential buyers' interests in new suburban housing. This, in turn, has caused them to consider rehabilitating lower-cost, inner-city housing. Several demographic and economic variables also seem to have converged recently. These factors seem to explain why the "typical revitalizer" is young, professional, white, and without children. The post World War II baby boom generation has flooded housing markets and, given the conditions of inadequate supply, has sought out once ignored residential locations. Younger persons are delaying marriage and childbearing, and thus are for now less concerned with public schools and the neighborhood safety issues that discouraged previous middle-class residents. This cohort has also produced many professionals and managers, now the growth occupations of the inner-city businesses (Kasarda 1972). Some also contend that the revitalizers are choosing a different life-style, notably one emphasizing cultural amenities, though the evidence is less than conclusive (Long 1980).

It is too early to judge the consequences of inner-city revitalization. Since inner cities' futures are at stake, however, such predictions are difficult to avoid. Some claim that the "back to the city" movement will save our cities from bankruptcy and obsolescence. Population decline will be halted, commercial business will return, the streets will again be safe, and tax dollars will begin to flow into city treasuries. Gross statistics from the 1980 census indicating continued population decline are already dimming these hopes. This is also evidence, from information I collected in Manhattan, that neighborhood revitalization is exceptional. A few areas are improving within the context of overall decline. Further, much of what we have come to call "revitalization" is actually the expanding boundaries of already attractive areas or the consolidation of middle-class enclaves. A dramatic turnaround in the whole inner city is highly unlikely.

A different concern with neighborhood revitalization is its effect on poor residents. Some worry that those with few housing options are being displaced by the middle class. As their rental leases expire or housing costs increase, the minorities and elderly are forced to relocate to even more undesirable areas. Others insist that involuntary moving of this sort has not occurred on a large scale. Further, some city officials believe that the benefits of revitalization outweigh the costs of displacement. This topic will undoubtedly attract heated debate, and perhaps result in policy paralysis, until more evidence is available.

Population Growth in Rural Localities

Americans in modern times have usually moved from the country to the city, leaving small places and farm areas depopulated. However, the 1970s saw an end to that trend (Long 1980). Perhaps the most surprising recent event of all to social demographers is the increasing movement of urban Americans to rural areas. At first, this seemed to be another sign of metropolitan "spillover" into undeveloped surrounding territories. A closer look at the statistics indicated, though, that this was not the only form of rural growth. Remote areas were also attracting newcomers. Some have described the urban-to-rural migration as a "rural renaissance" offering new hope to unpopulated and economically depressed areas. Others see new crises arising as cities lose more residents and small places experience rapid growth (Morrison and Wheeler 1976).

Why was there growth in three-fourths of all nonmetropolitan counties during the 1970s and a net migration of over four million during the decade? Why has this pattern continued, more recently, despite housing slumps and energy shortages? In all probability, many converging factors account for the "population turnaround." Nonmetropolitan areas have become accessible to metropolitan counties (McCarthy and Morrison 1978) due to the completion of interstate highway systems, more air travel routes, and advances in telecommunications. Industries are thus able to decentralize and urban residents can seek leisure, homes, and work in nonmetropolitan areas. A "graying" of the United States has also meant that a larger population of retired people can live away from the urban employment centers. Since Americans on fixed incomes find lower costs of living in rural places they are, in fact, moving to nonmetropolitan areas. Also, price increases in domestic coal and petroleum have led to energy extraction installations in remote areas of the country.

There is another variable that has played a role in the movement from city to countryside. For decades, Americans have expressed preferences in public opinion polls for living in small localities rather than big cities (Zuiches and Fuguitt 1972). People had previously settled for suburban environments as a compromise. Now, with the demographic and economic events mentioned above, this is no longer necessary. Americans' stated desire for a nonmetropolitan residence is usually related to a romantic image of the social and physical qualities of rural places. Recent surveys in turnaround areas suggest that people are moving out of cities at least in part due to such antiurban and prorural biases.

Many studies are now being conducted to learn if urban-to-rural migrants are achieving the desired amenities. Perhaps instead an influx of new population has ruined the good qualities of small places. The early reports from newspapers and field studies suggested that serious problems were emerging in growing areas. New residents clashed with old residents about future growth, school systems, and what public services should be provided. Small local governments seemed unable to keep up with the demand for new services, more police protection, and the need for planning (Gilmore 1976). But as more evidence emerged, it appears that such problems were exceptional. Northern Michigan surveys found little association between antigrowth sentiments and local population change (Marans and Wellman 1978). A national survey of nonmetropolitan residents found that, in comparison with population loss, there were advantages of rural growth with few notable disadvantages (Baldassare 1981). Most growth-area respondents were highly satisfied with their social lives and well-being. They were also distinctly positive in their reports of their community's services and physical attributes, which is not always the case in rural areas.

Studies such as Long and DeAre (1980) clearly document the existence and persistence of nonmetropolitan growth. While industrial deconcentration and metropolitan spillover are important factors, nonemployment reasons for moving and growth in remote regions suggest the diversity of the turn-around. No reversal in the urban-to-rural move begun in the early 1970s is expected. Original worries about rural growth problems seem unwarranted, but still many localities will engage in controversial policies to "close the door" on new-comers. Nevertheless, careful and coordinated planning is needed in certain community contexts. Industrial develop-ment sites, retirement communities, previously impoverished areas, and rapidly expanding localities will deserve special attention.

Renewed Interest in Residential Crowding

Researchers in the 1960s found remarkable abnormalities among animals exposed to high population densities. In a highly publicized study of overcrowded caged rats, Calhoun (1962) observed that high densities destroyed the normal so-cial fabric and produced cannibalism, infant mortality, ex-treme aggressiveness, social withdrawal, hypersexuality, and psychotic behavior. At that time, American cities were faced with high crime rates, antiwar riots, and racial disturbances. It was tempting to name "automatic" responses to residential crowding as the cause of our troubles as well. Social scien-tists were offered federal research support to examine the wide-ranging effects of overpopulation. Urban sociologists were called on once again to investigate the possibility that urbanism spawned a deviant "way of life."

The first studies tried to reproduce the animal findings by observing small groups of college students in rooms of varying densities. These experiments did not provide defini-tive evidence of crowding's adverse consequences. Some-times there were higher reports of interpersonal hostility, competitiveness, unease, and measurable stress in dense rooms. But these problems were not replicated in further ex-periments that slightly changed the group's composition or tasks (see Freedman 1975). Saegert et al. (1975) conducted field studies to examine overcrowding in urban public settings. They noted the need for design and planning interventions to avoid problems such as negative affect, poor memory, reduced movement, and difficulties in completing simple tasks. Some claimed that research on humans in temporary and out-of-the-ordinary circumstances, no matter how well conceived, was of little value to understanding the effects of residential crowding.

A different line of investigation developed through the sociologists trained in the ecological approach. Published government statistics on urban neighborhoods were used to correlate rates of social problems (such as crime, mental health) with local densities (persons per square mile, percent of overcrowded homes). The classic study of crowding conducted in Chicago (Galle et al. 1972) found that it was almost impossible to sort out the effects of high density from the effects of poverty. In all American cities, these two variables tend to be highly associated. Additionally, high density and low income are both correlated with the prevalence of urban problems. This fact has made conclusive evidence on the effects of crowding to be more elusive than originally expected.

In a break from the traditional methodology of urban sociology, resident surveys were conducted. These attitudinal data were then correlated with information concerning housing density. Booth (1976) interviewed Toronto residents and could find no evidence that household overcrowding or high neighborhood density adversely affected health, family life, mental health, or friendships, Gove et al. (1979), in contrast, reported that Chicago residents living in crowded conditions had more psychological stress and family problems. These two researchers have criticized each other's work and have defended their own conclusions. Their differences are probably explained by sampling variations. Using national surveys, which provide the broadest representations of housing and individuals, I found that household density and neighborhood crowding are associated with specific complaints about the residence but do not affect personal well-being

(Baldassare 1979). The results regarding social life and family relations suggest that there are means of adjusting to dense environments. Individuals develop "selective withdrawal" from less primary encounters in their neighborhoods and reduce frictions in the home among family members through organizing space and activities (see also Milgram 1970).

The salient issues for humans experiencing crowding thus seem different from those initially raised by the animal studies. Crowding does not always have dire consequences. Observational studies and the closer analyses of recent surveys point to the need to understand how people adjust to urban crowding. The "costs" of these adaptations for urban residents, such as anonymity, feelings of powerlessness, blasé attitudes toward others in trouble, also take on greater significance. A recently emerging perspective is that crowding demands resources for successful coping. Thus, some persons experiencing high density may have social and personal characteristics that place them in more difficulty than others. The real issue, then, is not whether low status or residential crowding better predict social problems. The important question for future research is whether the combination of social and spatial deficit factors is an especially troublesome situation.

Vulnerable Populations in the City

In the last two decades, various groups have organized and expressed discontent about their disadvantaged status in American society. More and more, sociological studies are indicating that the new urban form has done nothing to alleviate the problems of the elderly, minorities, women, children, and the disabled. Rather, it increasingly appears that existing inequalities have been aggravated.

Social scientists pondering the effects of mass society on the individual have often viewed events such as industrialization or urbanization as having similar repercussions on all people. Empirical research suggests, in fact, that the social

context in which the individual lives mediates the consequences of "macroscale" events on the person's "microscale"
attitudes and behavior. There are glaring indications that even
the most dramatic demographic changes do not equally affect
all Americans. For three decades there has been a massive
movement of central-city residents to the suburbs. More recently there has been a large shift of persons and industries
from the "frostbelt" or older northern cities to the "Sunbelt"
or newly built southern cities. The differential rates of participation, however, are too often overlooked. Few minorities or
unskilled workers, and mostly Anglos and the middle class,
are involved in the movement of high-technology industries
to the South and West (Farley 1976; Frey 1980). Those left
behind in the older central cities are especially the elderly
and minority groups. Demographic trends, even of the present magnitude, thus cannot be comprehended without
knowledge of vulnerable populations, which may or may not
be participating in them. Factors such as socioeconomic
characteristics clearly influence attitudes toward a changing
urban scene. Personal reactions to ongoing problems are also
affected by social resources and special needs.

Even widely diffused technology is not accessible to all
urban residents. In the United States, the number of privately
owned automobiles per 1,000 persons climbed from 77 to 440
between the years 1920 and 1970. Choice of residence, possibilities for employment, and human services utilization have
all become heavily dependent on the availability of automobiles. However, ownership of automobiles varies dramatically among subpopulations. The ratio of cars per household
for the nation was 1.09 in 1970, but it was 0.64 for black
households, 0.64 for elderly households, and 0.15 for poverty
households in the old, large cities. Further, a San Francisco
survey by Foley (1975) indicates that lacking direct access to
automobiles is more prevalent among females than males (43
percent versus 19 percent) and among ethnic-racial minorities than Anglos (47 percent versus 26 percent). Mass transit
systems are a necessity, rather than a luxury, needed to re-
move the mobility deficits facing some "special" populations

that already experience discrimination. However, prospects for adequate provisions seem remote given the fiscal and geographical realities of providing nonautomobile transportation in large metropolitan regions (Webber 1976; Ortner and Wachs 1979). Nonetheless, academic research, policy decisions, and public attitudes are too often blinded by not recognizing transportation-deficient subgroups (Wachs 1979). Knowing which populations lack automobiles, why this is so, the behavioral outcomes of such deficits, and the existence of alternative transportation modalities is obviously in order.

Recent discoveries of the social complexity of large societal events can be supplemented with documentation concerning many substantive urban issues. Empirical studies of long-distance moves suggest that migrants vary in disorientation because some groups have relatives or friends at their destinations while other groups do not (Fischer 1976; Lewis 1952). Research conducted in communities experiencing growth has found that differences in community type and socioeconomic characteristics result in varying perceived impacts and collective responses (Baldassare 1981). The experience of overcrowding, instead of having uniformly harmful effects, seems to depend on individuals' circumstances, such as social position in the home and rights to privacy (Baldassare 1979). Rather than residential conditions per se having importance, the effects of physical environments seem contingent on groups' resources and abilities to obtain optimal settings (Michelson 1976). Such findings are beginning to have an impact on academic thinking and should eventually be heard in planning and policy making circles.

The "vulnerable populations" thus far receiving the most attention are distinguished by ethnic-racial status, age, and gender. Perhaps the most dramatic studies concern racial and ethnic minorities. Since sociologists have monitored neighborhood segregation there has been no sign of increased integration between blacks and whites. Moreover, studies now indicate that economic differences only partly explain the residential separation (Frisbie 1980). Not only does this pattern limit minorities' housing and employment opportunities, but there is substantial evidence that their actual housing conditions are worse than the national average. Abandoned housing in New York City and elsewhere is mostly populated by blacks and Latin American immigrants. Private lending policies ensure that minority neighborhoods remain more dilapidated and more devoid of local services than others (Morris and Winter 1978). Even among ethnic and racial minorities, however, there are significant variations. There are examples of Hispanic groups, such as the Cubans, who have developed "ethnic enclaves" which pool available labor and capital to upgrade the immigrants' neighborhoods (Wilson and Portes 1980). Likewise, success in educational institutions and the occupational setting vary among ethnic minorities.

Important age differences are now being considered, much to the betterment of academic research (Michelson 1980). The older person, for example, is more dependent on local facilities and social support from neighbors. The elderly do not drive cars as often as other adults and, because of health and safety reasons, rarely manage long commutes. Since they often must walk to local facilities, they are more subject to dangerous conditions. As a result, fear of crime is higher among the elderly than among other adults (Clemente and Kleinman 1976; Lawton 1980). The elderly are less likely to change housing than other adult groups (Morris and Winter 1978); they have remained in inner-city areas despite neighborhood decay and racial succession. Older persons, in addition, experience more health risks due to urban pollutants. Although these facts are increasingly evident, planning and policies continue to be shaped by knowledge of middle-aged adult patterns and preferences.

There is growing evidence that the traditional roles occupied by men and women lead to different urban activities and psychological outcomes. Depression is usually more common among women, but new research suggests that this is mediated by whether women leave the house for the workplace (Rosenfield 1980). Considerable debate is now emerging regarding the effects of long-distance migration—which often improves the husband's employment circumstances and the family's finances—on the wife's well-being and career opportunities (Freudenberg 1981). There is some evidence that women who move with their families to suburban homes spend more time caring for their houses, may become "taxi drivers" for children and, importantly, are often careless and isolated from amenities and job opportunities (Michelson 1973).

The basic issue in studying vulnerable populations is that subgroups, differentiated by explicit social criteria, vary in their local dependency, problems with specific changes, mobility, daily activities, personal attitudes, and health outcomes. New research should consider how vulnerable groups differ from the general population; how vulnerable groups differ from one another; and the unique effects of combined vulnerable statuses. Such studies will enhance general urban knowledge and policy debates.

New Perspectives in Urban Sociology

How did the urban landscape come to be the way it is today? Most urban sociologists have avoided this question altogether, choosing instead merely to describe the urban form. The seemingly neutral forces of the "free market" have traditionally been used in ecological discussions. Others have relied on "technology" to explain urbanization, assuming that specific land uses are accidental. A growing number of urban sociologists argue that such a question is relevant. Further, they claim to know the causal agents that are responsible for today's urban crisis. Their approach is generally called the study of urban "political economy" (Walton 1979). It represents a paradigm of growing popularity, great potential, and, as yet, little systematic research.

The basic idea behind urban political economy is simple. It has perhaps been most elegantly stated in the works of Castells (1973) and Harvey (1973). The organization of urban life is determined by the forces that have power in our society.

All decisions are guided by capitalist attempts to achieve greater wealth and advantages against competitors. The "political-economic" forces that determine urban shape and form emanate from multinational corporations, local, national, and regional firms, and individual capitalists. The world system of cities, national urban networks, metropolitan exchanges, intracity activities, and resident groups' welfare are all subject to the political economy's influence. Two major concerns are expressed in the new urban sociology: how urban space is organized and how collective consumption—that is, housing, transportation, and education—operates in the city (O'Connor 1973).

One of the most widely read applications of the political economy perspective is Perry and Watkins' (1977) analysis of Sunbelt growth. They argue for a historical interpretation of the population shifts from North to South. The Northeast had developed a regional economy that "dominated" the nation for many decades, resulting in "uneven economic development" and a wealth transfer (capital accumulation) that solidified its supremacy. But as an industrial era dominated by light manufacturing gave way to high technology and post-industrial service industries, urban areas that are "locked into" an old economic stage are no longer in a strong position. In fact, the obsolescence of some urban forms has not only paved the way for southward business migrations, but has severely limited the location of "growth industries" in the North. The thrust of the argument is thus that neither demography, nor market tendencies, nor technology is the real protagonist in the decline of the Frostbelt. The outcome of power struggles among capitalists, and its consequences for the nation's cities, are best predicted by historical and economic forces (see also Gordon 1978).

There are also political struggles within metropolitan or city limits that account for specific urban forms. Land speculators have a great influence on what types of housing developments and residents are found in a particular area (Feagin 1980). Their influence on government may explain what transportation systems and human services become publicly available. Urban social policies are determined by the struggle between opposing groups. Those interests best organized for "collective action" are in the most powerful structural position to influence events (Walton 1976).

The state receives close scrutiny through the political economy approach. All American governments are viewed as capitalist agents, developing policies that benefit industry and landowners (Mollenkopf 1978). City planning is not seen as representing public interests, but as concentrating instead on the mediation of capitalist conflicts and the promotion of profit-making (Castells 1978). The fiscal crisis experienced by today's governments, according to the political economic framework, is brought about because state expenditures and tax policies are geared toward saving a failing economic system (O'Connor 1973; Tabb 1978).

An analysis that ignores the political-economic realm is, in the opinion of the "new" urban sociologists, espousing a conservative ideology regarding the causes and salient consequences of urban phenomena (Castells 1976). Theories and descriptive examples obviously comprise much of the new urban sociology. As yet, there are few quantitative studies to indicate the causal influence of political economy (see for example Lyon et al. 1981). To establish the existence of business elites, corporate networks, and state cooptation may prove to be a tedious task for those convinced that such factors explain all. If, however, the urban political-economy paradigm is to challenge traditional sociology, with its present emphases on sophisticated techniques and statistical significance, a concerted empirical research effort must soon begin.

Some Thoughts About the Urban Future

Guesswork is not a favorite task of any sociologist, myself included, but the reader obviously has a right to know if the concerns of this book apply to the future. Barring unforseen and dramatic changes in technological capabilities or in the political economic system, I would have to conclude that the issues of urban sociology today are not severely timebound. In the next few paragraphs I will extrapolate from some recent facts and offer a few predictions about the urban future.

With a low birth rate perhaps permanently in place, migration will be a determining factor in local growth, and ought to generate further controversy in sending and receiving communities. Some cities will develop incentives and attempt to keep their residents, while others will block new migrants' entry. Still others will encourage people to join their community. The competition among places will be fierce as the nation approaches zero population growth, since municipal revenues and residential quality are ultimately at stake.

The regional shifts and metropolitanization process will not be halted. Urban services in older cities cannot improve without massive federal assistance, which is unlikely, and the chronic social problems associated with these urban centers will not disappear. As the nation moves away from manufacturing and toward a service-oriented and high-technology economy, businesses will seek outer fringes and new metropolises as sites for new plants. People will follow the movement of industry. "Rural repopulation" will be a continued trend since it is directly related to the deconcentration of urban activities and residents. There will be instances of middle-class resettlement in older cities because of housing prices and availability, but these will remain insignificant exceptions.

What types of urban communities are possible in the future? Housing costs and spatial competition will undoubtedly drive up metropolitan densities. Cluster developments and multiple-family dwellings will become more commonplace. However, the automobile's dominance ensures that overcrowding will not exceed levels reached in earlier historical eras. For affluent Americans, telephones and geographical mobility will make aspatial "communities of interests" a reality. This will outweigh inconveniences brought about by the lack of local amenities.

These predictions are largely relevant to affluent Americans and not to the central cities' vulnerable populations. Nationwide economic growth will not be strong enough to greatly improve the plight of the poor. New white-collar employment opportunities will not be relevant to the chronically unemployed. Therefore, residential and geographical mobility will be no more available to America's underclass tomorrow than it is today. Ethnic and racial minorities and stranded clusters of the elderly will, as a result, inhabit apartheidlike inner cities. Subcultures and locally-based social lives may flourish in some of these high-density settings; by and large, however, one can expect only their further isolation from the opportunity structure and dominant urban life in America.

Summary and Conclusions

This introduction has presented an overview of urban sociology and urban trends. Evidence of change and continuity has been documented in each case. Urban sociology's roots are traced to Europe, nearly a century ago, where sociologists wrote about the dawn of an urban-industrial world. Initial concerns with new community forms, and their consequences for residents, were transplanted to and flourished in the Chicago School. Of late there has been a less orthodox approach to urban sociology than that which dominated theory and methods especially prior to World War II. Traditional analyses that concentrate on the social relationships among different parts of the city, or the neighborhood statistics that best predict group rates of deviance, still persist. But today there is no consensus that urban "ecology" is the most useful paradigm. Some argue that overlooked political and economic factors best explain macro urban patterns. Others contend that middle-range features, such as subcultures and social networks, are needed to comprehend urban life and its consequences. Yet others have focused on the more minute, personal details of urbanites as a means to understand residential attitudes and behaviors. Important new ideas that make use of older and more recent approaches, are documented. The likelihood of synthesis seems remote, and perhaps not desirable, in view of the exciting developments that have occurred in this symbiotic intellectual environment.

At least some of the shifts in urban sociology can be traced to urban demographic realities. The facts have brought into focus new issues and raised some old unanswered questions. A century ago people were moving from the countryside to densely populated industrial cities. Over the past few decades those cities have progressively lost residents and employers. Transportation and communication improvements produced new freedom of movement. Suburbs developed, low-density Sunbelt cities grew, and now even rural areas are becoming urbanized. What were once considered "city problems" (such as crime, pollution, traffic congestion) are now metropolitan or regional in scope. Northeastern and midwestern cities are faced with budget deficits, decaying buildings and streets, high unemployment, and a growing dependent population. Cities elsewhere in the nation, and the suburbs and beyond, are struggling to keep pace with population growth and new service demands. The urban transformation of the mid twentieth century is now reaching its advanced stage, with no signs of imminent change. Sociologists monitoring these trends are now directing their attention to relatively ignored urban areas and residents. Questions about community structure and life-styles are being reanalyzed in light of the present urban context.

I have chosen six topical areas to reflect recent developments in urban sociology and concerns with the new urban form. These interrelated themes comprise community, inner-city revitalization, rural population growth, residential crowding, vulnerable city populations, and the political-economy perspective. The remainder of the book contains fifteen articles, arranged in six sections, that represent the major recent pieces on these topics. In front of each section I have summarized the contribution of the articles that follow.

References

Abu Lughod, J. 1964. "Urban–Rural Differences as a Function of the Demographic Transition." *American Journal of Sociology,* 69:476–490.

Abu Lughod, J. and R. Hay, eds. 1977. *Third World Urbanization.* Chicago: Maaroufa Press.

Alonso, W. 1973. "Urban Zero Population Growth." *Daedalus,* 102:191–206.

Baldassare, M. 1979. *Residential Crowding in Urban America.* Berkeley: University of California Press.

—— 1981. *The Growth Dilemma: Residents' Views and Local Population Change in the United States.* Berkeley: University of California Press.

Baldassare, M. and W. Protash. 1982. "Growth Controls, Population Growth, and Community Satisfaction." *American Sociological Review,* forthcoming.

Berry, B. J. L. and J. D. Kasarda. 1977. *Contemporary Urban Ecology.* New York: Macmillan.

Berry, B. J. L., ed. 1976. *Urbanization and Counterurbanization.* Beverly Hills, Calif.: Sage.

Black, J., A. Borut, and R. Dubinsky. 1977. "Private Market Housing Renovation in Older Urban Areas." Washington, D.C.: Urban Land Institute Research Report no. 26.

Booth, A. 1976. *Urban Crowding and Its Consequences.* New York: Praeger.

Burgess, E. W. (1925) 1967. "The Growth of the City: An Introduction to a Research Project." In R. E. Park, E. W. Burgess, and R. D. McKenzie, eds., *The City,* pp. 47–62. Chicago: University of Chicago Press.

Calhoun, J. 1962. "Population Density and Social Pathology." *Scientific American,* 206:138–148.

Castells, M. 1973. *The Urban Question.* Boston: M.I.T. Press.

—— 1976. "Theory and Ideology in Urban Sociology." In C. G. Pickvance, ed., *Urban Sociology: Critical Essays,* pp. 60–84. New York: St. Martin's.

—— 1978. *City, Class, and Power.* New York: St. Martin's.

Clark, T. N. and L. Ferguson. 1981. "The Middle Class: New Fiscal Population and the Taxpayers' Revolt," in "Political Processes and Urban Fiscal Strain," ch. 7. Manuscript, University of Chicago, Department of Sociology.

Clausen, J. and M. Kohn. 1954. "The Ecological Approach in Social Psychiatry." *American Journal of Sociology,* 60:140–151.

Clemente, F. and M. Kleinman. 1976. "Fear of Crime Among the Aged." *Gerontologist,* 16(3):207–210.

Durkheim, E. 1893 (1964). *The Division of Labor in Society.* New York: Free Press.

Faris, R. and H. Dunham. 1939. *Mental Disorders in Urban Areas.* Chicago: University of Chicago Press.

Farley, R. 1976. "Components of Suburban Population Growth." In B. Schwartz, ed., *The Changing Face of the Suburbs,* pp. 3–38. Chicago: University of Chicago Press.

Feagin, J. 1980. "Urban Real Estate Speculation." Paper presented at the American Sociological Association meetings, New York.

Festinger, L., S. Schacter, and K. Back. 1950. *Social Pressures in Informal Groups.* New York: Harper & Row.

Firey, W. 1945. "Sentiment and Symbolism and Ecological Variables." *American Sociological Review,* 10:140–148.

Fischer, C. S. 1976. *The Urban Experience.* New York: Harcourt Brace Jovanovich.

—— 1977. *Networks and Places.* New York: Free Press.

—— 1982. *To Dwell Among Friends.* Chicago: University of Chicago Press.

Foley, D. 1975. "Accessibility for Residents in the Metropolitan Environment." In A. Hawley and V. Rock, eds., *Metropolitan America in Contemporary Perspective.* New York: Wiley.

Freedman, J. 1975. *Crowding and Behavior.* San Francisco: Freeman.

Freudenberg, W. 1981. "Women and Men in an Energy Boomtown." *Rural Sociology,* 46(2):220–244.

Frey, W. 1980. "Black in Migration and White Flight: Economic Effects." *American Journal of Sociology,* 85(6):1396–1417.

Frisbie, W. P. 1980. "U.S. Urban Sociology." *American Behavioral Scientist,* 24(2):177–214.

Galle, O., W. Gove, and J. McPherson. 1972. "Population Density and Pathology: What Are the Relations for Man?" *Science,* 176:23–30.

Gans, H. 1962. *The Urban Villagers.* New York: Free Press.

—— 1967. *The Levittowners.* New York: Pantheon.

Gilmore, J. 1976. "Boom Towns May Hinder Energy Resource Development." *Science,* 191:535–540.

Gordon, D. 1978. "Capitalist Development and the History of American Cities." In W. Tabb and L. Sawers, eds., *Marxism and the Metropolis,* pp. 25–63. New York: Oxford University Press.

Gove, W., O. Galle, and M. Hughes. 1979. "Overcrowding in the Home." *American Sociological Review,* 44:58–80.

Harris, C. and E. Ullman. 1945. "The Nature of Cities." *The Annals,* 242:7–17.

Harvey, D. 1973. *Social Justice and the City.* Baltimore: Johns Hopkins University Press.

Hoyt, H. 1943. "The Structure of American Cities in the Post-War Era." *American Journal of Sociology,* 48:475–481.

Kasarda, J. D. 1972. "The Impact of Suburban Population Growth on Central City Service Functions." *American Journal of Sociology,* 77:1111–1124.

—— 1980. "The Implications of Contemporary Distribution Trends for National Urban Policy." *Social Science Quarterly,* 61:373–400.

Laska, S. and D. Spain. 1980. *Back to the City: Issues in Neighborhood Revitalization.* New York: Pergamon Press.

Lawton, M. 1980. "Housing the Elderly." *Research on Aging,* 2:309–328.

Lewis, O. 1952. "Urbanization Without Breakdown." *Scientific Monthly,* 75:31–41.

Lodhi, A. and C. Tilly. 1973. "Urbanization, Crime, and Collective Violence." *American Journal of Sociology,* 79:296–317.

Logan, J. 1978. "Growth, Politics, and the Stratification of Places." *American Journal of Sociology,* 84:404–416.

Logan, J. and M. Schneider. 1981. "The Stratification of Metropolitan Suburbs: 1960–1970." *American Sociological Review,* 46:175–186.

London, B. 1978. "The Revitalization of Inner City Neighborhoods: A Preliminary Bibliography." Vance Bibliographies (October), P-90.

Long, L. 1980. "Back to the Countryside and Back to the City in the Same Decade." In S. Laska and D. Spain, eds., *Back to the City: Issues in Neighborhood Renovation,* pp. 61–76. New York: Pergamon Press.

Long, L. and D. DeAre. 1980. "Migration to Nonmetropolitan Areas: Appraising the Trends and Reasons for Moving." Washington, D.C.: U.S. Bureau of the Census, CDS-80.

—— 1981. "Population Redistribution: 1960 to 1980." U.S. Bureau of the Census. Unpublished.

Lyon, L., L. Felice, and M. Perryman. 1981. "Community Power and Population Increase: An Empirical Test of the Growth Machine Model." *American Journal of Sociology,* 86(6):1387–1400.

McCarthy, K. and P. Morrison. 1978. "The Changing Demographic and Economic Structure of Nonmetropolitan Areas in the 1970s." Rand Series P-6062. Santa Monica, Calif.: Rand.

McKenzie, R. D. 1925 (1967). "The Ecological Approach to the Study of the Human Community." In R. E. Park, E. W. Burgess, and R. D. McKenzie, eds., *The City,* pp. 63–69. Chicago: University of Chicago Press.

Marans, R. W. and J. Wellman. 1978. *The Quality of Nonmetropolitan Living.* Ann Arbor: Institute for Social Research.

Michelson, W. 1973. "The Place of Time in the Longitudinal Evaluation of Spatial Structures by Women." Toronto: Center for Urban and Community Studies, University of Toronto, Research paper no. 61.

—— 1976. *Man and His Urban Environment.* Reading, Mass.: Addison-Wesley.

—— 1977. *Environmental Choice, Human Behavior, and Residential Satisfaction.* New York: Oxford University Press.

—— 1980. *The Child in the City.* Toronto: University of Toronto Press.

Milgram, S. 1970. "The Experience of Living in Cities." *Science,* 167:1461–1468.

Mollenkopf, J. 1978. "The Postwar Politics of Urban Development." In W. Tabb and L. Sawers, eds., *Marxism and the Metropolis*, pp. 117–152. New York: Oxford University Press.

Morris, E. and M. Winter. 1978. *Housing, Family, and Society*. New York: Wiley.

Morrison, P. and J. Wheeler. 1976. "Rural Renaissance in America?" *Population Bulletin* (October), 31:2–26.

Newman, O. 1973. *Defensible Space*. New York: Macmillan.

O'Connor, J. 1973. *The Fiscal Crisis of the State*. New York: St. Martin's.

Ogburn, W. 1935. "Factors in the Variation of Crime Among Cities." *Journal of the American Statistical Association* (March), 30:12–34.

Ortner, J. and M. Wachs. 1979. "The Cost-Revenue Squeeze in American Public Transit." *Journal of the American Planning Association*, 45:10–21.

Park, R. E. 1925 (1967). "The City: Suggestions for the Investigation of Human Behavior in the Urban Environment." In R. E. Park, E. W. Burgess, and R. D. McKenzie, eds., *The City*, pp. 1–46. Chicago: University of Chicago Press.

—— 1926 (1967). "The Urban Community as a Spatial Pattern and a Moral Order." In R. H. Turner, ed., *Robert E. Park on Social Control and Collective Behavior*, pp. 55–68. Chicago: University of Chicago Press.

Perry, D. and A. Watkins, eds. 1977. *The Rise of the Sunbelt Cities*. Beverly Hills, Calif.: Sage.

Pickvance, C. G. 1976. *Urban Sociology: Critical Essays*. New York: St. Martin's.

Quinn, J. 1940. "The Burgess Zonal Hypothesis and Its Critics." *American Sociological Review*, 5:210–218.

Rosenfield, S. 1980. "Sex Differences in Depression: Do Women Always Have Higher Rates?" *Journal of Health and Social Behavior*, 21:33–42.

Saegert, S., E. MacKintosh, and S. West. 1975. "Two Studies of Crowding in Urban Public Spaces." *Environment and Behavior*, 7:159–185.

Shaw, C. R. 1929. *Delinquency Areas*. Chicago: University of Chicago Press.

Shevky, E. and W. Bell. 1955. *Social Area Analysis*. Berkeley: University of California Press.

Simmel, G. 1905 (1969). "The Metropolis and Mental Life." In R. Sennett, ed., *Classic Essays on the Culture of Cities*, pp. 47–60. New York: Appleton.

Spain, D. 1980. "Black-to-White Successions in Central City Housing: Limited Evidence of Urban Revitalization." *Urban Affairs Quarterly*, 15:381–396.

Stokols, D. 1972. "A Social Psychological Model of Human Crowding." *Journal of the American Institute of Planners*, 38:72–84.

Suttles, G. 1969. *The Social Order of the Slum*. Chicago: University of Chicago Press.

—— 1972. *The Social Construction of Communities.* Chicago: University of Chicago Press.

Tabb, W. 1978. "The New York City Fiscal Crisis." In W. Tabb and L. Sawers, eds., *Marxism and the Metropolis,* pp. 241–266. New York: Oxford University Press.

Tabb, W. and L. Sawers. 1978. *Marxism and the Metropolis.* New York: Oxford University Press.

Tilly, C. 1974. "The Chaos of the Living City." In C. Tilly, ed., *An Urban World,* pp. 86–108. Boston: Little, Brown.

Wachs, M. 1979. *Transportation for the Elderly.* Berkeley: University of California Press.

Walton, J. 1976. "Community Power and the Retreat from Politics: Full Circle After 20 Years?" *Social Problems,* 124:292–303.

—— 1979. "Urban Political Economy: A New Paradigm." *Comparative Urban Research,* 7(1):5–17.

Webber, M. M. 1970. "Order in Diversity: Community Without Propinquity." In R. Gutman and D. Poponoe, eds., *Neighborhood, City, and Metropolis,* pp. 792–811. New York: Random House.

—— 1976. "The BART Experience: What Have We Learned?" Berkeley: Institute of Urban and Regional Development, Monograph no. 26.

Wechsler, H. 1961. "Community Growth, Depressive Disorders, and Suicide." *American Journal of Sociology,* 67:9–16.

Wellman, B. and B. Leighton. 1979. "Networks, Neighborhoods, and Communities: Approaches to the Study of the Community Question." *Urban Affairs Quarterly,* 14:363–390.

Wilson, K. and A. Portes. 1980. "Immigrant Enclaves: An Analysis of the Labor Market Experiences of Cubans in Miami." *American Journal of Sociology,* 86(2):295–319.

Wirth, L. 1928. *The Ghetto.* Chicago: University of Chicago Press.

—— 1938. "Urbanism as a Way of Life." *American Journal of Sociology,* 44:1–24.

Zorbaugh, H. W. 1929. *The Gold Coast and the Slum.* Chicago: University of Chicago Press.

Zuiches, F. and G. Fuguitt. 1972. "Residential Preferences: Implications for Population Redistribution in Nonmetropolitan Areas." In S. Mazie, ed., *Population, Distribution, and Policy,* pp. 617–630. Commission on Population Growth and the American Future, vol. 5. Washington, D.C.: GPO.

PART ONE

Recent Ideas About Modern Urban Communities

EDITOR'S NOTE:

KASARDA REFLECTS ON the redistribution of population and industry which has resulted in the formation of metropolitan communities. The socioeconomic reorganization has involved among other things a shift of the downtown district to administrative functions, the deconcentration of manufacturing, and suburban white-collar localities. The article discusses problems this reorganization has caused and speculates about the metropolitan community's future. Clark examines the factors associated with fiscal strain in New York and other American cities. Our widely held belief of what causes municipal financial problems—such as the city's size, age, rate of population decline, or geographical region—are wrong. Instead, local political leadership and government organization seem to have the strongest influences on fiscal conditions. Fischer calls for a reconsideration of ecological factors as determinants of communities. In particular, he hypothesizes that greater population size results in diverse subcultures. A series of propositions follow, linking urbanism to social intensity, intergroup conflict, information diffusion, and unconventionality.

1

Urbanization, Community, and the Metropolitan Problem

JOHN D. KASARDA

ALTHOUGH ANALYTICALLY DISTINCT, the concepts of industry and community have become so interwoven in urban society that one concept is frequently defined in terms of the other. We talk about mining communities, manufacturing communities, college towns, administrative cities, and other functional types of territorial localities. At the same time, the increasing scale of urban units and growing mobility of their inhabitants have fostered numerous nonterritorial networks ("communities without propinquity"), where bonds of common identity and patterns of social interaction are determined more by professional or industrial affiliation than by residential locale (Webber 1963).

In this article, the focus is on communities as territorial entities with particular emphasis given to the dominant urban unit of today—the metropolitan community. I shall begin with an overview of the now classic ecological model of the industrial metropolis as formulated by Chicago sociologists Robert E. Park and Ernest W. Burgess. The expansion of the American metropolis will then be examined first in terms of

Reprinted with permission from David Street and Associates, eds., *Handbook of Contemporary Urban Life* (San Francisco: Jossey-Bass, 1978).

its technological stimuli and then from the vantage of the
redistribution of population and industrial activity. Next the
economic strains resulting from the expansion process will
be reviewed and their implications for employment opportunities and fiscal problems in central cities and suburbs discussed. I will conclude with a documentation of the post
World War II expansion of the industrial metropolis and assess its impact on the financial welfare of our central cities
and their inhabitants.

Classic Ecological Model of the Metropolis

The classic ecological model of the industrial metropolis
evolved during an era of massive concentrative migration in
the United States. As industrialization and urbanization operated concurrently, waves of foreign-born and rural immigrants converged on northern and midwestern cities in search
of improved social conditions and economic opportunities.
At the peak of this period (about 1893 to 1898), a young
newspaper reporter, Robert E. Park, was writing human interest stories for metropolitan dailies in New York, Chicago, Detroit, Denver, and Minneapolis about the problems facing the
newly arriving immigrant groups. Park, who had an engag-
ing mind and was well read in the biological sciences, was
struck with the amazing similarity between the immigrants'
"struggle for survival" in the expanding metropolis and Darwin's (1860) ecological-evolutionary mode. He was particularly impressed with the adaptation process (including conflicts, adjustments, accomodations, and assimilation) in the
local immigrant communities and how urban order seemed
to emerge naturally through unplanned processes of competition, invasion, succession, segregation, and dominance. Park
later became a member of the faculty of the department of
sociology at the University of Chicago, where along with his
colleague, Ernest Burgess, he formulated an ecological model
of the industrial metropolis.

   In essence, the Park-Burgess theory views the industrial

metropolis as a dynamic adaptive system that relates various population groups, commercial institutions, and local industries to one another and to the outside world (Park and Burgess 1921; Park 1952). Its internal structure (that is, its physical and social subareas, nodes, networks, and gradients of change with distance from the center) is seen as evolving not through any form of planning or design but through competition and the spontaneous operation of the marketplace. The effect is territorial differentiation and segregation of various ethnic groups, industrial facilities, and activity patterns into relatively homogeneous subareas, which Park and Burgess labeled "natural areas" because of their unplanned evolution. Such natural areas in the metropolis include the central business district, the rooming-house area, the slum, the ethnic ghetto, the "bright lights" area, and the industrial zone.

The underlying premise of the ecological model is that the overall spatial pattern of the urbanized area, including the location of specific natural areas, is also regulated by competition (Alihan 1938). This premise reflects the sociopolitical and economic milieu of nineteenth- and early twentieth-century America, where the dynamics of privatism and laissez-faire enterprise prevailed. Relatively unfettered by public intervention, industries and commercial institutions compete for strategic locations, which, once established, provide them with economic advantages (externalities) through which they can exercise control (dominance) over the functional use of land in other parts of the community (McKenzie 1933). This strategic location, or area of dominance, is found at the point of highest accessibility, the community's geographic center. It is at the center that the largest number of people converge daily to work, shop, and conduct their business. Consequently, land values are substantially higher in the central business district than in the surrounding area. Expecting to reap profits when the central business districts expand, speculators frequently acquire the land and buildings immediately adjacent to the central business districts. Since speculators are concerned primarily with the future value of the land per se rather than the buildings on it, the area surrounding the central business district deteriorates into a slum (the "zone-in-transition").

The zone-in-transition, including its slums and immigrant ghettos, performs an important function for the metropolitan community, however. Its relatively inexpensive (albeit crowded and deteriorating) housing and propinquity to expanding industries provide a convenient and affordable locus of settlement for newly arriving immigrants. Park, Burgess, and their students at the University of Chicago lucidly described how each migrant group initially concentrates in a highly segregated ethnic enclave within the deteriorating zone where they face suspicion, distrust, and discrimination from earlier ethnic arrivals; yet, with the passage of time, each group is able to adjust and assimilate into city life, slowly climb the socioeconomic ladder, and escape to better residences further removed from the ethnic ghettos and slums. They are then replaced by another wave of arriving immigrants, who replicate the spatial and temporal process of mobility and assimilation (Burgess and Bogue 1962; Cressey 1938; Freedman 1948; Hauser 1961; McKenzie 1929). It is these successive movements, first-generation settlement in the core followed by residential progression outward toward the periphery over time, that are responsible for the correspondence between length of residence of the immigrant group in the city, the group's socioeconomic status, and the distance that the group resides from the central business district. This interpretation constitutes the classic concentric zonal model of the expanding metropolis (Burgess 1925).

Transportation and the Evolution of Metropolitan Form

Of course, the expansion of the industrial metropolis into territorially differentiated residential, commercial, and industrial subareas would not have occurred to the extent that it did had it not been for revolutionary improvements in short-distance transportation and communication. Where transportation is primitive, inhabitants and their employing and service institutions must be in relatively close proximity (the distance in the local community typically determined by pedestrian movement). Territorial differentiation of urban areas is thereby limited, with each local community or neighborhood providing residence, employment, and sustenance goods and services. The urbanized area as an aggregate may grow, but it does so in a fissionlike manner, characteristic of early preindustrial cities, where there was limited functional interdependence among the various cellular subareas (Sjoberg 1955, 1960).

Such was the situation in the United States before 1870, when walking was the predominant mode of urban movement. Then came a sequence of public transportation innovations that completely restructured the metropolis. The first was the introduction of the horse-drawn streetcar (about 1870), which enabled substantial numbers of urban residents to live as far as five miles from their place of work and commute on a daily basis. The electric trolley lines and streetcars of the 1880s and 1890s extended the commuting radius to ten miles, and when rapid transit electric trains arrived at the turn of the century, the urban population was able to expand outward as far as twenty miles from the center of the city (Hawley 1950; Tobin 1976; Ward 1971). Radial strings of new suburban developments sprouted along these commuter rail lines, giving the city a star-shaped population pattern.

The commuter railways signified the beginning of widespread suburbanization and territorial differentiation in the metropolis. Places of residence and places of work became increasingly separated and segregated, as did the distances between the lowest- and highest-income neighborhoods. The poorest groups, who, as noted above, were typically first-generation migrants, simply could not afford commuting costs on a daily basis and therefore remained concentrated in the older, deteriorating residential units near innercity industrial zones. The wealthier third- and fourth-generation inhabitants, on the other hand, pushed outward to superior residential suburbs far removed from the dense city smoke, congestion, and decaying urban neighborhoods. With spatial mobility matching social mobility, a crystallized sociospatial residential distribution emerged attuning the income and status of residents to the exlusiveness and desirability of the neighborhood.

Commercial institutions likewise began a selective redistribution process, with convenience goods and service establishments following the middle- and upper-income groups outward, while administrative, communications, financial, and professional services increased in the city center to serve the entire metropolitan population. The central business district took on the form of a specialized financial and administrative hub, and as the population dispersed along the rail lines, the entire metropolis began to acquire a new physical structure.

The electric commuter trains were inflexible, however. They operated on fixed time schedules and tended to constrain urban expansion to those areas located near the rail arteries. It was the development of the motor vehicle in the late nineteenth century that overcame these limitations and substantially accelerated the expansion process. Between 1900 and 1930, motor-vehicle registration increased from 8,000 to 26,352,000, or from an average of one automobile for every ten thousand persons to an average of one for every household (U.S. Bureau of the Census, 1960). During the same period, extensive peripheral highway systems evolved, weaving a tight web of hard-surfaced roads throughout the suburban hinterland. The speed and convenience of the automobile, together with the hard-surfaced roads, brought many previously isolated towns and villages into routine contact with the central city. Some of those towns and villages were as far as fifty miles away.

Throughout this period, significant advances and improvements in short-distance communications technology occurred. Household and business telephones became ubiquitous; regularly scheduled radio broadcasts began from urban centers; and central-city newspapers were distributed daily to virtually all outlying communities. Such communications developments contributed immensely to the social and economic integration of the expanding urban complex (McKenzie 1933).

There was a price paid, however, by the outlying communities after they were absorbed into the expanding metropolis. Because of their semi-independent nature, these communities had previously provided and supported their own sustenance organizations, consumer services, and local institutions. After they were brought into daily contact with the urban centers, their small shops, stores, food producers, and semiprofessional service units could not compete effectively with their larger and more diversified counterparts in the central cities. Many of their movie theaters, newspapers, and banks closed entirely. A large number of their basic goods and service establishments, especially grocery stores and restaurants, were replaced by standardized services, distributed through chain outlets and branch offices of units headquartered in the urban centers (Hawley 1971:148). Some of these outlying communities were functionally transformed, becoming residential suburbs primarily housing a commuting population that worked either in the city or in the suburban ring. Others became retail centers, distributing convenience goods to nearby residential developments. Still others were transformed into industrial suburbs when manufacturers found that they could decentralize their production facilities from the congested core yet easily maintain daily contact with central-city institutions and draw on the new automobile-owning labor force.

In sum, late nineteenth- and early twentieth-century advances in transportation and communication not only were responsible for the spatial expansion of the metropolis but also eliminated the semiautonomy and heterogeneous work-residence-service structure of many outlying towns and villages. These communities were absorbed and integrated into a single diffuse community composed of territorially specialized subunits, linked together by a routinized system of daily social and economic interactions. This altogether new type of community became known as the metropolitan community (Gras 1922; McKenzie 1933; Bogue 1949).

Metropolitan Growth and Deconcentration

Not until 1910, however, did the Bureau of the Census recognize the inadequacy of the political boundaries of the city
as a territorial unit for measuring urban population. At that
time, the bureau introduced the category "metropolitan districts" to take into account the spread of the urban complex
well beyond the city limits. Since then the United States has
become increasingly metropolitan in scope. Despite recent
population increases in many nonmetropolitan counties (see
Beale 1975; Tucker 1976; Berry and Dahmann 1977), metropolitan areas as a whole have continually absorbed larger
shares of the national population increase. In 1900, less than
one third of the U.S. population resided in urban areas that
met present metropolitan criteria. By 1975, over 150 million
people, or nearly three quarters of the U.S. population, resided within 270 metropolitan units designated as Standard
Metropolitan Statistical Areas (SMSAs); over 95 percent resided within the labor shed, the zone of reasonable commu-
tation, of their central cities (Hawley and Rock 1975:14).

Population growth was only one demographic manifestation of metropolitan expansion, however. Another was deconcentration, or movement outward from the central cities.
Deconcentration, commonly known as suburbanization, is a
multifaceted phenomenon that has been measured for metropolitan areas as a whole in three ways: (1) relative decennial growth rates (percent change) of suburban ring population compared to central city population; (2) absolute
decennial growth in the suburban ring population, compared
to absolute decennial growth in the central cities; and
(3) comparative decennial changes in the population density
of the central cities and suburban rings. Deconcentration begins using the first measure when the suburban ring of a metropolitan community grows at a faster rate than the central
city. The 1920s have traditionally been considered a transitional decade for the deconcentration of the metropolitan
population using the relative growth rate method (see Bogue
1953; Hawley 1956). Such studies, however, did not consider

the fact that substantial annexation of suburban territory by central cities inflated central-city growth rates and artificially deflated suburban growth rates. When adjustments for annexation are made, the suburban rings of metropolitan areas are seen to have been growing at faster rates than the central cities in all regions of the country since at least 1900 (Kasarda and Redfearn 1975). As a result, by 1970 more people resided in the suburban rings of SMSAs (76 million) than in the central cities (64 million).

The second indicator of deconcentration measures the extent to which raw population increases in the suburban rings exceed increases in the central cities. This indicator measures the share of metropolitan growth accounted for by growth in the suburban rings. Adjusting for annexation, suburban rings as a whole exhibited larger absolute increases in population than did the central cities in every decade since 1930, with many individual suburban rings assuming a larger share of metropolitan growth a decade or so earlier. By the 1960s, essentially all metropolitan growth was accounted for by suburbanization, as absolute population declines in numerous central cities offset gains in others.

The third indicator of deconcentration measures the degree to which metropolitan centers have declined in population density while density in peripheries has increased. Most studies of urban population densities document successively lower density levels for those cities that evolved during periods of faster, more efficient local transportation (Duncan et al. 1961; Guest 1973; Mills 1970; Winsborough 1963). Nonetheless, with the exception of some of our oldest central cities, deconcentration, as measured by decennial density declines within constant city boundaries, is largely a post World War II phenomenon. Even after 1950, real central-city density declines (those not masked by annexation) were highly selective, occurring mostly in the larger, older central cities in the Northeast and North Central regions of the nation (Kasarda and Redfearn 1975). This finding calls into question the conventional wisdom that suburban commuter trains and the increase in mass automobile usage (from 1920 to 1950) were responsible for depopulating the cities—or even decreasing density patterns within existing central-city boundaries. Without doubt, the automobile and commuter trains, along with rising real incomes, federally insured home mortgages, and state and federally funded suburban highways, encouraged and facilitated the suburbanization of the middle and upper-middle classes in metropolitan America. However, as fast as these groups moved beyond central-city boundaries, they were replaced by lower-income groups in the typical Burgess concentric growth pattern. The outcome, of course, has been growing numbers of metropolitan poor concentrated in the central cities, while the suburban rings serve as the residential locus of the upwardly mobile social groups.

Commercial and Industrial Redistribution

The growth and selective deconcentration of metropolitan population were matched with a significant alteration in the commercial and industrial structure of both the central cities and the suburban rings. The dispersion of retail establishments and consumer services closely followed the suburbanization of middle- and upper-income groups. Between 1954 and 1977, over fifteen thousand suburban shopping centers and regional malls were constructed to serve the expanding metropolitan population. By 1978 these shopping centers and malls accounted for more than one-half the annual retail sales in the United States, and the trend shows no signs of abating. In documenting the suburban shopping center boom, *Fortune* magazine reported:

> The shopping center has become the piazza of America. In big metropolitan areas and smaller cities alike . . . indoor piazzas are reshaping much of American life. Giant regional shopping centers have risen by the hundreds across the nation and are still going up by the score. To an amazing degree, they are seizing the role once held by the central business district, not only in retailing but as the social, cultural, and recreational focal point of the entire community. Grim, formal, unwelcoming,

old cities scarcely fit the more relaxed lifestyle of the newly affluent middle class with considerable leisure. . . . In many cities middle class white shoppers are beginning to abandon the downtown to the poor and blacks except from nine to five, Monday through Friday. (Breckenfeld 1972:86)

Many commercial and service establishments that are located in suburban shopping centers and malls are outlets or branches of headquarter units remaining in the central business districts. Other headquarters migrated directly to the suburbs, closing their inner-city establishments entirely when middle-class clientele no longer resided in the vicinity. Their proprietors found that opening new stores in the suburban rings not only brought them closer to their traditional patrons but also enabled them to design their establishments much more compatibly with modern transportation, storage, and distribution technologies than was possible in the older inner-city sectors (Meyer, Kain, and Wohl 1965).

The shift of manufacturing industries to the suburbs paralleled the deconcentration of retail trade. Prior to the era of the automobile and truck, central cities provided distinct locational advantages to large manufacturing establishments. These advantages included superior rail and water transportation facilities, suited for receiving raw material and distributing finished products to regional and national markets; a large, diverse, and relatively cheap labor supply; and external economies, including complementary businesses and industries and the full range of public services (electricity, water, police and fire protection, and so on) that were more effectively provided there than in outlying communities.

During the past fifty years, changing modes of transportation and production technology altered the central cities' locational advantages. Industries soon discovered that early urban street patterns were not designed to handle the automobile and truck. Traffic congestion, lack of employee parking space, and problems of freight transfer greatly increased direct and indirect costs, particularly for those manufacturers located in the old, densely settled sections of the cities. On the other hand, the development of suburban highway systems, extensive automobile ownership, and increased dependence by manufacturers on trucking for receiving raw materials and supplies and shipping finished products made uncongested suburban sites more attractive. Manufacturers recognized that by locating on or near suburban expressways they could reduce their transportation costs, tap an adequate automobile-owning labor supply, and solve problems of employee parking and freight transfer.

A second factor that encouraged suburbanization of large industry was the changing mode of manufacturing technology from unit processing to mass production and assembly-line methods. Old central-city manufacturing facilities had been constructed as multistory, loftlike structures that are not adaptable to much of today's mass-production technology. The assembly line, in particular, has large horizontal space requirements that are more difficult and more costly to obtain in the central city than in the suburban rings. Just as did the retail and wholesale sectors, large manufacturers realized that it was more practical to build newly designed facilities on relatively inexpensive suburban ring land than to convert their obsolete inner-city structures. New metropolitan industries with large space requirements would rarely ever consider a central-city site, usually locating their production facilities directly in the suburban rings.

A third, equally important factor stimulating the suburbanization of industry was the widespread development of suburban public services and external economies, which as noted above had previously been concentrated in the central cities and their adjacent, built-up areas. The spread of electricity and gas lines, water utilities, sanitary waste systems, police and fire protection, and highway services throughout the suburban rings released manufacturers from their dependence on the central cities. Moreover, rapid suburban development after World War II also brought housing, local suppliers, subcontractors, and other complementary services to nearby areas, which provided manufacturers with additional suburban externalities.

With the push factors of obsolete inner-city structures,

lack of inexpensive space for expansion, increasing taxes, deteriorating public services, rising city crime rates, and vandalism operating concurrently with the suburban pull factors noted above, manufacturing industry fled to the suburban rings en masse. Between 1947 and 1972 metropolitan central cities in this country lost a net total of 1,146,845 manufacturing jobs while their suburban rings gained 4,178,230. Had it not been for substantial increases in post World War II manufacturing employment in younger, smaller SMSA central cities and cities in the South and West, the net employment decline in metropolitan central-city manufacturing would have been more than double the above figure.

In contrast to the deconcentration of the manufacture of standard goods and services, the number of establishments offering specialized goods and services has actually increased in the central business districts. The nature of these establishments still makes it advantageous for them to have a central location that maximizes their accessibility to the largest number of people and firms in the metropolis. Such establishments as airline ticket agencies, advertising firms, brokerage houses, consulting firms, financial institutions, and legal, government, and professional complexes have been accumulating in the central business districts, replacing many of the standardized goods and services establishments that were unable to afford the increasing land values of a central location.

The 1960s and 1970s also witnessed a remarkable growth of administrative office buildings in the central business districts of our biggest SMSAs. Administrative headquarters rely on large pools of clerical workers and the complement of legal, financial, communications, and specialized business services that are most readily available in central business districts. In downtown Manhattan, for example, over 75 million square feet of office space was added between 1965 and 1972—an increase of more than 50 percent. In other large central cities, the picture is much the same. Between 1960 and 1972, central office space increased by 52 percent in Chicago, 79 percent in San Francisco, 82 percent in Atlanta, and

100 percent in Houston (Manners 1974). Many central-city office structures are now experiencing high vacancy rates, however, and given the deteriorating externalities of an inner-city location, one must wonder whether the central business districts can continue to attract and hold administrative, professional, and financial functions while the rest of the U.S. economy suburbanizes. Almost weekly another corporation leaves a large central city for a suburban location. Thus, while white-collar employment has increased in the central cities, it has grown in the suburban rings at a rate four times faster (Kasarda 1976). There seems little reason to doubt that the central cities will capture smaller and smaller shares of metropolitan white-collar employment in the future. Moreover, as I shall document shortly, since white-collar employment growth in the administrative and professional services sectors in central cities is not nearly offsetting the huge losses of central-city jobs in other sectors, the overall employment base of the cities continues to decay.

Thus, the growth of administrative and professional office structures in the central business districts, together with the suburbanization in heavy industry, middle-income population, and establishments providing consumer goods and services, has spatially reorganized the modern metropolis. Population groups, land use, and activity patterns have been systematically redistributed, increasing both the degree of territorial specialization and the functional interdependence of localized areas within the metropolis. In the expanded metropolitan community, residential suburbs rely on other sectors of the metropolitan area for their daily supplies of food, clothing, news, entertainment, and other recurrent household needs. They also depend on other portions of the expanded community, some as far as sixty miles distant, for their employment opportunities. It is precisely this dependence on other portions of the metropolitan community that enables these suburbs to specialize in residential development (Bollens and Schmandt 1970:9).

Conversely, central-city institutions depend on the residential suburbs to provide a large proportion of employees, particularly professionals, clerical staff, and managers. And central business district department stores, speciality shops, and business and professional services draw their patrons and clientele from throughout the metropolitan community. Bollens and Schmandt (1970:9) comment on the great interdependence between the center and periphery of the expanded metropolis: in New York City, several million persons daily pour into Manhattan to work, man the executive suites, conduct business, shop, or be entertained. In other SMSAs across the nation, the pattern is the same; only the scale is smaller. The people of the metropolis, in short, share a common spatial area for their daily activities. Within this area, although its limits may be imprecisely defined, an intricate web of business and social interrelationships exists and a high degree of communication and interchange among residents, groups, and firms continually takes place.

Strains of Metropolitan Expansion

We see then that the centripetal and centrifugal movements of metropolitan expansion have absorbed all segments of the metropolitan community into a single, diffuse social and economic organization. In reshaping the metropolis, however, these movements have also introduced problems for its functioning as a coherent entity. Such problems have impinged most heavily on the economic viability of the central cities.

One fundamental problem is that the political reorganization of the metropolitan community has not adjusted to its socioeconomic reorganization. Absorbed into the metropolitan community is the myriad of originally autonomous villages, townships, small cities, special districts, and other administrative jurisdictions that have remained politically discrete. Metropolitan expansion itself produced additional governmental fragmentation as populations spreading into unincorporated suburban-ring territory inexorably sought some form of local rule. In 1972, nearly 23,000 local government units were operating within 264 metropolitan communities designated as SMSAs. The thirty-three largest SMSAs alone contained 8,847 local governments, or an average of 268.1 governmental units per SMSA (U.S. Bureau of the Census, 1973). This maze of heterogeneous and overlapping governments has resulted in fragmented taxing powers, public service inefficiencies, conflicting public policies, and administrative impotence in dealing with many of today's urban problems that have become metropolitan in scope.

Absence of political reorganization within the metropolitan community has placed particularly severe strains on the central cities' ability to finance adequate municipal services. Essentially, two factors lie behind these fiscal strains. First, the exodus of higher-income population, retail trade, and large industrial establishments to the politically autonomous suburban rings has substantially diminished central-city tax bases. Wealthy commercial, industrial, and residential suburbs are commonly found today adjacent to bankrupt central cities, with only an invisible administrative boundary separating the two.

The second factor is that much of the responsibility for financing municipal services, many of which are used by central-city and suburban residents alike, has fallen on central-city governments. In the expanded metropolitan community, suburban residents regularly use central-city streets, parks, zoos, museums, and other public facilities at no or nominal charges; the daily presence of large numbers of suburbanites in the central city creates problems for the sanitation and public health departments and poses additional fire risks, which are reflected in the allocation of funds for fire protection; and the routine movement into and out of the central city by the large and growing commuting population leads to traffic congestion on city arteries, which requires a major component in the budget for funding both the police and highway maintenance departments. These are only some of the costs that result from the services central-city governments provide to their suburban neighbors. The suburbanites, however, by residing in separate political jurisdictions are often sheltered from the fiscal burden of these municipal service costs.

Furthermore, numerous suburban jurisdictions have established zoning regulations, covenants, and extravagant housing quality standards to maintain their upper-income residential composition, while financial institutions, real estate agencies, and residents of middle-class white suburbs frequently practice overt housing discrimination against those perceived to be of lower social standing (Berry and Kasarda 1977; Mueller 1976). By these widespread practices, middle- and upper-income suburban communities ensure that the vast majority of minorities and urban poor are confined to the central cities, and they thus avoid the costs of public housing, public health, and social, rehabilitative, and other welfare services that impose a heavy burden on the operating budgets of many central cities.

Because of this combination of factors, public service demands on the central cities have dramatically increased while their fiscal ability to support additional public services is diminishing. The problem, it appears, is not that metropolitan resources are insufficient to support municipal services but that the largest portion of those resources has been redistributed to the politically autonomous suburban rings. In short, metropolitan expansion in the absence of political reorganization has created an unfair distribution of economic resources and service costs between the cities and suburbs and is a major cause of the financial crises facing our central cities today.

Residential-Employment Mismatches

Exacerbating the economic malady of the central cities is the growing mismatch between employment opportunities in the central cities and the skills of the resident labor force. Prior to 1950, central cities were the locus of large, diverse quantities of blue-collar jobs that required little education or training. These jobs provided ready employment opportunities for unskilled and semiskilled migrant groups, and because of their proximity to lower-income neighborhoods, they were easily accessible by either pedestrian movement or public transportation. With the expansion of the metropolitan community, lower-income groups continued to flow into the urban centers, while job opportunities appropriate to their education levels and skills were dispersed. Conversely, as middle- and upper-income white-collar workers moved to the suburban rings, central-city white-collar jobs increased substantially. Between 1960 and 1970, for example, central cities of 101 longitudinally comparable SMSAs lost a total of 828,257 blue-collar jobs while actually gaining 485,447 white-collar positions (Kasarda 1976).

The growth of administrative, financial, clerical, professional, and other specialized white-collar jobs in and around the central business districts, along with the suburbanization of blue-collar jobs, has had a major impact on the occupational structure of the central cities. The central cities have become increasingly specialized in jobs that have high educational prerequisites just at the time that their resident populations are increasingly composed of those with poor educational backgrounds (Chinitz 1964; Gold 1972; Kain 1970; Wilburn 1964). As a result, inner-city unemployment rates are more than twice the national average and even higher among inner-city residents who have traditionally found employment in blue-collar industries that have migrated to suburban locations (Downs 1973; Friedlander 1972; Harrison 1972, 1974; Hoskin 1973).

Another consequence of the mismatch between residence groups and employment opportunities is increased commuting between the suburbs and the central business districts of our larger SMSAs. In the mornings one observes large streams of white-collar workers commuting into the central business districts from their residential suburbs, while in the opposite lanes large streams of inner-city residents commute to their blue-collar jobs in industrial suburbs. In the evening the flows are reversed. One must contemplate the energy savings alone that would be obtained if the residences of these groups were adjacent to their workplaces.

The commuting necessitated by metropolitan expansion has been especially costly for minorities and blue-collar ethnic whites residing in the inner city. As blue-collar industries have deconcentrated, they have relocated on scattered sites along suburban beltways and expressways. Their dispersed nature makes public transportation from central-city neighborhoods to suburban industrial complexes impractical, requiring almost all city residents who work in the rings to commute by private automobile. The high and increasing costs of inner-city automobile ownership (including insurance and maintenance) imposes a heavy financial burden on these people. Moreover, a large portion of inner-city residents, particularly low-income minorities, cannot afford automobile ownership. In the Chicago metropolitan area, for example, four out of five inner-city adult blacks do not own automobiles (Zimmer 1975). One outcome is growing frictional as well as structural unemployment among city residents who lack access to cars (Foley 1975). (*Frictional* unemployment refers to the minimum unemployment that would exist even under conditions of "full employment," as workers move between jobs; *structural* unemployment refers to the lack of mobility in some sectors of the labor force and insufficient demand for some types of labor.) A second outcome, as indicated above, is that larger and larger portions of the take-home pay of many inner-city residents are consumed by the costs of commuting to suburban employment by automobile.

Hard pressed (and often overlooked) too are inner-city white ethnics who have historically been employed in the industries that are suburbanizing the fastest. Many of these people originally purchased their inner-city residences near their industrial jobs for relatively small sums of money. Because of racial transition in nearby neighborhoods, high crime rates, the deconcentration of industry, and an oversupply of inner-city housing created by the flight to the suburbs, housing values have risen much slower in their neighborhoods than in the suburbs. As their jobs have suburbanized, numerous inner-city white ethnics find themselves not only physically removed from employment opportunities but also residentially trapped by the high cost of suburban housing.[1] One solution that white ethnics have employed is to purchase mobile homes. As a result, thousands of mobile-home communities have sprouted in unincorporated peripheral areas of SMSAs during the past decade. No doubt, the mobile-home community binge will accelerate as suburban housing prices further exceed suburban workers' financial resources.

The deleterious effects of the residence-workplace mismatch have not been nearly so great for middle- and upper-income suburban residents who commute to the cities. Because of their higher incomes, automobile ownership and commuting costs do not absorb as large a portion of their income as do the same costs for the inner-city commuter. Moreover, because their jobs are concentrated at a central location, where public transportation lines converge, they may take advantage of this option and often reduce their real costs of transportation. In some of our largest SMSAs (New York City and San Francisco are the prime examples) suburban commuters who use public transportation are actually subsidized by the city, since the per-rider cost to the cities is greater than the purchase price of the transportation token. The general problem that suburban residents, through their routine use of central-city services and facilities, contribute to greater marginal service costs for the city than the marginal revenue they generate has become known as the "suburban exploitation thesis" (Neenan 1970; Kasarda 1972).

Drawing the foregoing sections together, I am arguing that the centrifugal and centripetal movements inherent in metropolitan expansion are at the root of the current economic and fiscal problems plaguing our large central cities. These movements, which are analytically distinct but interrelated, include (1) the exodus to the suburbs of middle- and upper-income families; (2) the huge influx into the central cities of poor minority groups, the chronically unemployed, the aged, social misfits, and others who tend to be more of a fiscal liability than an asset to central-city budgets; (3) the drift of commerce and industry beyond the taxing jurisdiction of the cities, which has eroded municipal tax bases and made needed blue-collar jobs physically inaccessible to many inner-city residents; (4) the buildup in central cities of administrative office structures, financial institutions, specialized professional and technical services, and other white-collar business complexes whose jobs require substantial education and training, and hence are inappropriate to the growing concentrations of unskilled and poorly educated inner-city residents; and (5) the daily flow into the central city of large numbers of suburbanites, who regularly use central-city public services and facilities as part of their working, shopping, and recreational activities. The combined effect of these movements is increased debt service for the central cities as their fiscal base contracts and their public service needs increase.

The Metropolitan Future

What can we say about the future of the metropolitan community? While our statements here are necessarily speculative, the trends appear well established. We should anticipate a continuing large absolute movement of whites compared with blacks and other minorities from the central cities, which will eventually lead the overall central-city residential composition to minority dominance. We should also anticipate a continued deterioration of blue-collar employment opportunities in the central cities and concurrent growth of those opportunities in the suburban rings, leading to expanding pockets of unemployment and poverty in the inner cities and the evolution of larger numbers of lower-income (working-class) suburban enclaves near industrial parks and other suburban blue-collar job complexes. Mobile home communities will proliferate in suburban ring areas, especially in the rural fringe portions.

The long-term process of lower-income populations migrating to the central cities and then moving outward to better residential zones as their socioeconomic status improves will remain strong, however. For example, the median family income of central-city blacks who migrated from nonmetropolitan areas between 1970 and 1975 was only $5,037—about one-half that of black families already residing in the central cities. The average family income of all those entering the central cities between 1970 and 1974 was $10,300, compared with $12,500 for those leaving the central cities (Berry and Dahmann 1977; U.S. Bureau of the Census, 1975a, 1975b). The aggregate income in 1973 of families and unrelated individuals who moved out of the central cities between 1970 and 1974 was $55.3 billion, whereas that for families and unrelated individuals who moved into the cities during this period was $25.7 billion. As a whole, central cities suffered a net loss of $29.6 billion in aggregate annual personal income between 1970 and 1974, resulting from differential migration and the wide gap in income levels between immigrants to and emigrants out of the central cities (U.S. Bureau of the Census, 1975b). Thus, while family income levels in the suburbs increased (in constant dollars) an average of 4.6 percent between 1970 and 1974, central-city income levels actually declined an average of 0.3 percent (Berry and Dahmann 1977). These ominous declines in the aggregate personal income and in the average family and unrelated individual income of central-city residents are a response to the basic structural transformations described in this chapter.

Some point to encouraging signs for the cities, such as the restoration and revival of inner-city high-income neighborhoods (for example, Georgetown in the District of Columbia and New Town on Chicago's north side) and the growth of luxury apartments and condominiums at prime locations in and around the central business districts of our large cities. However, these enclaves of inner-city residential wealth have attracted small numbers compared with the overall emigration to suburbia of middle- and upper-income families that has occurred since World War II. Poor public schools and high crime rates in the inner cities remain powerful repelling forces, which have tended to dissuade all but a unique set of middle- and upper-income persons from returning from suburbia to city residences. Most of those returning are not middle- and upper-income families with school-age children but adult singles, young professionals, newly married couples, and older, wealthier couples whose children have left the household. Many are semitransient, moving after short periods of time, while others are only part-time city residents who maintain vacation or recreational homes elsewhere. In almost all cases, they reside in highly segregated complexes (by age as well as by race and class), fortified by electric door locks, security guards, closed-circuit television, and what otherwise has come to be known as the "architecture of defense."

From a sociological perspective, racial, ethnic, and class polarization has replaced the old notion of the urban melting pot. Segregation rather than assimilation is the pervasive sociospatial feature in both city and suburb. What the White House Commission on Crimes of Violence predicted in 1969 is now approaching reality:

> We can expect further social fragmentation of the urban environment, formation of excessively parochial communities, greater segregation of different racial groups and economic classes . . . and polarization of attitudes on a variety of issues. It is logical to expect the establishment of the "defensive city," the modern counterpart of the fortified medieval city, consisting of an economically declining central business district in the inner city protected by people shopping or working in buildings during daylight hours and "sealed off" by police during nighttime hours. Highrise apartment buildings and residential "compounds" will be fortified "cells" for upper-, middle-, and high-income populations living at prime locations in the inner city. Suburban neighborhoods, geographically removed from the central city, will be "safe areas," protected mainly by racial and economic homogeneity and by distance from population groups with the highest propensities to commit crime. Many parts of central cities will witness frequent and widespread crime, perhaps out of police control. (Mulvihill, Tumin, and Curtis 1969)

These polarization patterns and consequent economic disparities between the central cities and suburban rings will likely grow as the deconcentration of white-collar jobs, professional and financial services, prestigious retail establishments, and cultural and entertainment facilities makes central-city services and facilities superfluous to the suburban masses. With core domination on the wane, even in the administrative and professional service sectors, central business districts are becoming just one specialized node in a multinodal, multiconnective metropolitan system of suburban office building complexes, industrial parks, and regional shopping centers and malls. Fueled by the interaction of social, economic, and technological forces, the reverse thrust of counterurbanization has transformed the fried-egg pattern of the old industrial metropolis into a pattern that now looks more like a scrambled egg. In the process, the bulk of this nation's urban wealth and tax resources has shifted from the cities to the suburbs and exurbs.

The outcome of all the above will likely be a new form of geopolitical welfare, as federal and state governments increasingly transfer funds on an area-by-area basis from more economically viable suburban and exurban communities to the less viable central cities. Postindustrial counterurbanization forces are so strong that only through growing infusions of intergovernmental transfer and subsidies, such as revenue sharing, block grants, and jobs programs, will large central-city governments be able to pay their bills and provide employment for their poor.

Notes

1. This idea was stimulated by William Yancey of Temple University, who is conducting research on the effects of industrial deconcentration on inner-city white ethnics.

References

Alihan, M. 1938. *Social Ecology: A Critical Analysis.* New York: Columbia University Press.

Beale, C. L. 1975. *The Revival of Population Growth in Nonmetropolitan America*, ERS-605. Washington, D.C.: U.S. Department of Agriculture, Economic Development Division, Economic Research Service.

Berry, B. J. L. and D. C. Dahmann. 1977. *Population Redistribution in the United States in the 1970s*. Washington, D.C.: Assembly of Behavioral and Social Sciences, National Research Council, National Academy of Sciences.

Berry, B. J. L. and J. D. Kasarda. 1977. *Contemporary Urban Ecology*. New York: Macmillan.

Bogue, D. J. 1949. *The Structure of the Metropolitan Community: A Study of Dominance and Subdominance*. Ann Arbor: University of Michigan Press.

—— 1953. *Population Growth in Standard Metropolitan Areas, 1900–1950*. Washington, D.C.: GPO.

Bollens, J. C. and H. J. Schmandt. 1970. *The Metropolis: Its People, Politics, and Economic Life*, 2d ed. New York: Harper & Row.

Breckenfeld, G. 1972. "Downtown Has Fled to the Suburbs." *Fortune* (October):80–87, 156, 158, 162.

Burgess, E. W. (1925) 1967. "The Growth of the City: An Introduction to a Research Project." In R. E. Park, E. W. Burgess, and R. D. McKenzie, eds., *The City*, pp. 47–62. Chicago: University of Chicago Press.

Burgess, E. W. and D. J. Bogue, eds. 1962. *Contributions to Urban Sociology*. Chicago: University of Chicago Press.

Chinitz, B., ed. 1964. *City and Suburb: The Economics of Urban Growth*. Englewood Cliffs, N.J.: Prentice-Hall.

Cressey, P. 1938. "Population Succession in Chicago: 1898–1930." *The American Journal of Sociology*, 44:59–69.

Darwin, C. R. 1860. *On the Origin of Species by Means of Natural Selection, or the Preservation of Favoured Races in the Struggle for Life*. London: Murray.

Downs, A. 1973. *Opening up the Suburbs: An Urban Strategy for America*. New Haven, Conn.: Yale University Press.

Duncan, O. D. et al. 1961. *Metropolis and Region*. Baltimore: Johns Hopkins University Press.

Foley, D. L. 1975. "Accessibility for Residents in the Metropolitan Environment." In A. H. Hawley and V. P. Rock, eds., *Metropolitan America in Contemporary Perspective*, pp. 157–198. New York: Halsted Press.

Freedman, R. 1948. "Distribution of Migrant Population in Chicago." *American Sociological Review*, 13:304–309.

Friedlander, S. 1972. *Unemployment in the Urban Core*. New York: Praeger.

Gold, N. N. 1972. "The Mismatch of Jobs and Low-Income People in Metropolitan Areas and Its Implications for the Central-City Poor." In S. M. Mazie, ed., *Population, Distribution, and Policy*, vol. 5. pp. 441–486. Commission on Population Growth and the American Future, Washington, D.C.

Gras, N. S. B. 1922. *Introduction to Economic History.* New York: Harper & Row.

Guest, A. M. 1973. "Urban Growth and Population Densities." *Demography,* 10:53–69.

Harrison, B. 1972. *Education, Training, and the Urban Ghetto.* Baltimore: Johns Hopkins University Press.

—— 1974. *Urban Economic Development.* Washington, D.C.: Urban Institute.

Hauser, P. M. 1961. *Population Perspectives.* New Brunswick, N.J.: Rutgers University Press.

Hawley, A. H. 1950. *Human Ecology: A Theory of Community Structure.* New York: Ronald Press.

—— 1956. *The Changing Shape of Metropolitan America.* New York: Free Press.

—— 1971. *Urban Society: An Ecological Approach.* New York: Ronald Press.

Hawley, A. H. and V. P. Rock, eds. 1975. *Metropolitan America in Contemporary Perspective.* New York: Halsted Press.

Hoskin, F. P. 1973. *The Functions of Cities.* Cambridge, Mass.: Schenkman.

Kain, J. F. 1970. "The Distribution and Movements of Jobs and Industry." In J. Q. Wilson, ed., *The Metropolitan Enigma.* Cambridge, Mass.: Harvard University Press.

Kasarda, J. D. 1972. "The Impact of Suburban Population Growth on Central City Service Functions." *American Journal of Sociology,* 77:1111–1124.

—— 1976. "The Changing Occupational Structure of the American Metropolis: Apropos the Urban Problem." In B. Schwartz, ed., *The Changing Face of the Suburbs,* pp. 113–136. Chicago: University of Chicago Press.

Kasarda, J. D. and G. Redfearn. 1975. "Differential Patterns of Urban and Suburban Growth in the United States." *Journal of Urban History* 2:43–66.

McKenzie, R. D. 1929. "Ecological Succession in the Puget Sound Region." *Publications of the American Sociological Society,* 23:60–80.

—— 1933. *The Metropolitan Community.* New York: McGraw-Hill.

Manners, G. 1974. "The Office in the Metropolis: An Opportunity for Shaping Metropolitan America." *Economic Geography,* 50:93–110.

Meyer, J. R., J. F. Kain, and M. Wohl. 1965. *The Urban Transportation Problem.* Cambridge, Mass.: Harvard University Press.

Mills, E. S. 1970. "Urban Density Functions." *Urban Studies,* 7:5–20.

Mueller, P. O. 1976. *The Outer City: Geographical Consequences of the Urbanization of the Suburbs.* Washington, D.C.: Association of American Geographers, Resource paper no. 75-2.

Mulvihill, D. J., M. M. Tumin, and L. A. Curtis. 1969. *Crimes of Violence.* Staff Report to the National Commission on the Causes and Prevention of Violence. Washington, D.C.: GPO.

Neenan, W. 1970. "The Suburban-Central City Exploitation Thesis: One City's Tale." *National Tax Journal*, 23:117–139.

Park, R. E. 1952. *Human Communities*. New York: Free Press.

Park, R. E. and E. W. Burgess. 1921. *Introduction to the Science of Sociology*. Chicago: University of Chicago Press.

Sjoberg, G. 1955. "The Pre-Industrial City." *American Journal of Sociology*, 60:438–445.

—— 1960. *The Pre-Industrial City, Past and Present*. New York: Free Press.

Tobin, G. A. 1976. "Suburbanization and the Development of Motor Transportation: Transportation and the Suburbanization Process." In B. Schwartz, ed., *The Changing Face of the Suburbs*, pp. 95–112. Chicago: University of Chicago Press.

Tucker, C. J. 1976. "Changing Patterns of Migration Between Metropolitan and Nonmetropolitan Areas in the United States: Recent Evidence." *Demography*, 13:435–444.

U.S. Bureau of the Census. 1960. *Historical Statistics of the United States, Colonial Times to 1957*. Washington, D.C.: GPO.

—— 1973. *Census of Governments, 1972*, vol. I: *Governmental Organization*. Washington, D.C.: GPO.

—— 1975a. *Mobility of the Population of the United States: March 1970 to March 1975*. Washington, D.C.: GPO.

—— 1975b. "Social and Economic Characteristics of the Metropolitan and Nonmetropolitan Population: 1970 to 1974." Current Population Reports, series P-23, no. 55. Washington, D.C.: GPO.

Ward, D. 1971. *Cities and Immigrants: A Geography of Change in Nineteenth-Century America*. New York: Oxford University Press.

Webber, M. M. 1963. "Order in Diversity: Community Without Propinquity." In L. Wingo, ed., *Cities and Space: The Future Use of Urban Land*, pp. 23–54. Baltimore: Johns Hopkins University Press.

Wilburn, Y. 1964. *The Withering Away of the City*. Bloomington: Indiana University Press.

Winsborough, H. H. 1963. "An Ecological Approach to the Theory of Suburbanization." *American Journal of Sociology*, 68:565–570.

Zimmer, B. G. 1975. "The Urban Centrifugal Drift." In A. H. Hawley and V. P. Rock, eds., *Metropolitan America in Contemporary Perspective*, pp. 23–92. New York: Halsted Press.

2
How Many More New Yorks?

TERRY NICHOLS CLARK

IS NEW YORK the "bellwether" city for America in its financial difficulties? If others follow New York's path, their futures will certainly be bleak. Many observers, especially those based in Manhattan, have suggested that other cities must be close behind. But, what is the evidence?

This was the first question my associates and I posed a few months ago.[1] To answer we used the Permanent Community Sample, fifty-one cities (municipalities) chosen as representative of the places of residence of the American urban population. About half are central cities and half suburbs, with populations as low as 50,000. We have monitored these sample cities for eight years, conducting interviews with local leaders through the staff of the National Opinion Research Center, and continually updating socioeconomic and fiscal data. For our work on fiscal strain in American cities, data for New York, Chicago, and Los Angeles were added.

There is no single thermometer to test for fiscal health. We therefore computed most measures used by municipal finance analysts, twenty-nine in all. Since many are slightly different versions of the same thing, we isolated four basic indicators, each quite distinct: (1) per-capita long-term debt;

(2) per-capita short-term debt; (3) per-capita expenditures for nine functions common to most cities (police, fire, highways, parks and recreation, sewerage, sanitation, financial administration, courts, and city buildings); and (4) the ratio of total revenue from local sources to sales value of all local taxable property. Ther four indicators were simply standardized and totaled for each city to form our Municipal Fiscal Strain Index (shown in column one of table 2.1). New York is indeed at the top, although Boston and San Francisco are not far behind.

One common argument is that New York is in fiscal difficulty because the city is forced to provide certain services, such as public education and welfare, which in other cities are the responsibility of school districts, special districts, or county or state governments. To deal with this issue, we created the County Area Fiscal Strain Index (shown in the second column of table 2.1). It includes four measures analogous to those for the Municipal Fiscal Strain Index, but is computed by totaling the debt or expenditure for all "overlapping" local governments serving the county (or counties) within which each municipality is located. This County Area Index thus shows the total debt or tax burden falling on residents and firms of the county area. New York again scores first on the County Area Index, but stands out much less than on the Municipal Index. The New York figures in both columns include the five boroughs.

Why Do Cities Differ in Fiscal Strain?

Many interpretations have been offered for New York's fiscal difficulties. Numerous statistical analyses are included in our technical report; these are mentioned here only to indicate that multivariate analysis, especially regression analysis, was used. These procedures permit us to isolate the amount of fiscal strain added, for example, by a 1 percent change in the tax base compared to a 1 percent change in population size, controlling for the effects of several other variables. The re-

Table 2.1.

	Municipal Fiscal Strain Index	County Area Fiscal Strain Index
New York	165.03	122.91
Boston	128.82	100.16
Newark, N.J.	105.91	97.79
San Francisco	102.97	95.25
Albany, N.Y.	102.88	115.99
Buffalo, N.Y.	89.00	71.59
Atlanta, Ga.	87.29	64.45
Cambridge, Mass.	81.44	40.08
Malden, Mass.	81.13	55.15
Seattle	79.34	59.09
Waterbury, Conn.	78.88	60.21
Jacksonville, Fla.	73.69	22.89
Utica, N.Y.	72.41	74.66
Los Angeles	68.27	46.05
Akron, O.	63.57	41.69
Memphis, Tenn.	60.28	40.48
Birmingham, Ala.	60.08	15.59
St. Louis, Mo.	58.76	54.76
Manchester, N.H.	58.20	42.63
Palo Alto, Cal.	55.67	42.49
Chicago	55.33	56.55
Pasadena, Cal.	54.47	44.26
St. Paul, Minn.	54.16	96.86
Minneapolis	51.35	63.95
Long Beach, Cal.	49.67	44.43
Pittsburgh	48.35	55.06
Milwaukee	45.38	58.46
Tampa, Fla.	44.27	49.80
Phoenix, Ariz.	42.38	30.30
Tyler, Texas	40.89	39.87
Charlotte, N.C.	39.95	33.65
South Bend, Ind.	39.24	35.47
Waco, Texas	38.67	18.24
Indianapolis	38.65	36.65
Fort Worth	38.65	38.23
Euclid, O.	36.64	41.54
Santa Monica, Cal.	35.39	39.24
Schenectady, N.Y.	32.68	40.35
Bloomington, Minn.	32.33	61.02
Irvington, N.J.	32.04	75.21
St. Petersburg, Fla.	32.03	16.69
Hamilton, O.	30.80	51.82
Hammond, Ind.	30.60	35.83
Berkeley, Cal.	29.81	52.25

	Municipal Fiscal Strain Index	County Area Fiscal Strain Index
Clifton, N.J.	27.85	26.83
San Jose, Cal.	25.95	56.56
Duluth, Minn.	25.32	55.05
Gary, Ind.	21.21	31.38
Waukegan, Ill.	20.70	28.05
Warren, Mich.	20.43	43.51
Salt Lake City	18.99	19.74
Amarillo, Texas	18.05	21.46
Fullerton, Cal.	13.25	35.90
Santa Ana, Cal.	10.53	39.73

Note: Both indexes, as described in the text, total the z scores for four separate indicators of fiscal strain. Five was then added to make all scores positive, and the result multiplied by ten. Consequently, if a city was precisely at the mean on all eight fiscal strain indicators, it would receive a score of fifty on both of the indexes.

The four indicators totaled to create the County Area Index were (1) per-capita overlapping long-term debt; (2) per-capita overlapping short-term debt (both for the municipality, school district, special district, and county governments); (3) overlapping revenues (for these county area governments plus the per-capita share of total state revenues); (4) tax effort (county area total revenues/municipal taxable property value).

The Municipal Index data were for 1973–1974, County Area data for 1971–1972. Both were the most recent comparable figures available in April 1976 from the U.S. Census (*Finances of Municipalities* 1973–1974 and the U.S. *Census of Governments,* 1972, vol. 4, no. 5). Some municipalities, school districts, and special districts are coterminous with a county, others are not. Measurement error is thus introduced into the County Area Fiscal Strain Index, which indicates the average level of fiscal strain for the entire county area.

sults come from comparing the fifty-one cities to one another; any single city may thus be an exception for certain findings. Data are taken from fiscal 1973–1974 or the closest years for which comparable data were available. A number of unexpected results emerged. Consider four:

Population size. Population size, despite the stereotype, has almost no relation to fiscal strain. Although New York and other large cities in table 2.1 do show more fiscal strain than the smaller cities, population size is a "spurious" explanation—size becomes insignificant when we take into account other variables associated with size, such as the percentage of poor residents.

Population growth (or decline). The percentage of population change from 1960 to 1974 was practically unrelated to fiscal strain.

Older cities. City age (years since population exceeded twenty thousand) and old housing (percentage of structures built prior to 1950) were also unrelated to fiscal strain.

Region. Cities in the Northeast and Midwest were not distinctly high in fiscal strain.

These four results initially surprised us as they directly contradict the common wisdom that large, declining, older cities of the Northeast and Midwest suffer most fiscal strain while the "Sunbelt" cities are fiscally sound. New York, Boston, Newark, and Albany are, in fact, under great fiscal strain, but Waukegan, Hammond, Schenectady, and Pittsburgh are fiscally sound. More important than these first four characteristics are others, which do make significant, independent contributions to fiscal strain when the above four (and others) are controlled.

The tax base. Cities with lower taxable property values suffer greater fiscal strain. This time the folk wisdom is sustained.

Poor residents. Cities with higher percentages of families with annual incomes below the federal government's definition of "low" ($3,721 in 1969) suffered greater fiscal strain. New York, however, is not unusual in having 11.5 percent of its residents classified as "low-income"—Chicago had 10.6 percent below the line, Memphis 15.7 percent, Birmingham 17.4 percent, and Newark 18.4 percent. We note in passing that New York also does not have an exceptionally high percentage of welfare recipients (12.4 percent compared to 11.1 percent in Chicago, 16.9 percent in Boston, and 14.4 percent in Newark—data for county areas in 1974).

Are all New Yorkers "poorer" because of a higher cost of living? Only a little. The Bureau of Labor Statistics provides an Intermediate Family Budget Index on which New York ranks 116, above Chicago (103) and San Francisco (106), but similar to Boston (117) and Newark (116).

The Irish Factor

A few years ago, it was discovered, almost by chance, that the percentage of city residents born in Ireland, or with one or more parents born in Ireland, was highly related to municipal spending. We initially thought it was spurious and contemplated dropping it out of the study after controlling for elements like having a strong Democratic Party or population size or city age. But although we introduced twenty-six such variables to the study and checked the same pattern in 1880, 1930, and 1968, it held strong.

Why? To construct a meaningful answer, we analyzed several surveys of the American population.[2] For example we classified the places of birth and names of all municipal employees in Albany by decade—from 1870 to 1970. The percentage of Irish dipped dramatically about 1900 when the Republicans came to power, but from 1920 to the present the figure rose continually to about 50 percent. Dan O'Connell has astutely led Albany's Democratic Party for the post 1920 period. Using another approach, a survey asked four questions of 3,095 Americans: if they had ever worked for a party or candidate in elections, attended political meetings, contributed money, or tried to persuade others about a candidate or party. The four items were combined in a campaigning index on which Irish Catholics scored 37, Slavic Catholics 15; most other groups were under 5.

Although they comprise only 4 percent of the American population, Irish Catholics have exerted an impact on municipal politics and finance that far transcends their numbers. It has been a style distinguished not by abstract ideology, but by a dense network of friendship and social relations. On several surveys, Irish Americans report they are unusually *sociable* ("like to do things with others"), *trusting* ("think most people can be trusted"), *localistic* ("prefer a local man"), *practicing Catholics* (over 90 percent attended weekly Mass and sent their children to parochial schools in the 1960s, compared to about a third of Italian-Americans), and *socially conservative* (in favor of compromise and moderate solutions). Together these five sets of beliefs comprise what we have called "the Irish ethic." Reinforced by such organizations as the Democratic Party and the Roman Catholic Church, it helps support a distinctive style of politics. Patronage is central. Most important, the emphasis on friendship and enduring social contacts (the Irish ethic) makes patronage politics legitimate. For example, when Mayor Daley was recently criticized by the press for awarding insurance contracts to his sons' firm, he replied, "What's wrong with a father helping his sons?" Imagine the same response from Mayor Lindsay! The important point here is that Mayor Daley was not being hypocritical, but essentially reflecting the Irish ethic. The ethical consistency of Richard Daley far transcends that imagined by many of his critics.

Personal networks, and rewards for party work and campaigning activities, have increased municipal payrolls for Irishmen and their political allies. The pattern is familiar in Chicago; more striking was to learn how important it was nationally. Indeed, although previous discussions of municipal finance have generally ignored the Irish, we found that the percentage of Irish residents in the municipality was often the most powerful single variable predicting fiscal strain. Certainly the Irish ethic is not unique to the Irish, but along with some knowledge of English and slightly earlier arrival in the U.S., it helped the Irish in urban politics. If Italian-Americans, blacks, and others are succeeding the Irish in many American cities, they often seek to follow similar patterns of governance.

The Leadership Factor

Chicago may be unique with its highly organized Democratic Party, but other cities still use related leadership and decision-making patterns. These significantly affect fiscal strain.

Strong mayors and weak businessmen. In interviews conducted with local leaders in each of the fifty-one cities, we asked about the importance of different actors for such decisions as mayoral elections, floating municipal bonds, and antipoverty and urban renewal programs. Two major actors were mayors and local businessmen. They were assigned scores for their importance in these decisions. Cities with moderately strong mayors and weak businessmen suffered greater fiscal strain.

Union contracts. About half the cities had signed collective-bargaining contracts with the American Federation of State, County, and Municipal Employees. Those that had scored higher on fiscal strain.

Numerous municipal employees. The (per-capita) number of municipal employees in each city working in the nine common functions discussed above was computed. It was adjusted for basic socioeconomic characteristics of the city (taxable property base, percentage poor, and so on). The result was a standardized score indicating the number of municipal employees above or below what one would expect in the city based on its socioeconomic characteristics. Albany scored highest (+2.58); San Jose and Santa Ana lowest (−1.2, −1.4); zero was average. This Index of Overstaffing also correlated positively, as expected, with the percentage of Irish residents and with fiscal strain.

Tax collection rates. We sought a measure of sound fiscal management that could be used across cities, and found that cities vary substantially in the percentage of levied taxes collected. Boston was lowest, collecting only 85 percent of all taxes levied, whereas many cities collect 99 percent or more. (New York collects 94 percent.[3])

These five dimensions of local leadership are generally interrelated; that is, cities with strong mayors also tend to have weak businessmen, union contracts, numerous municipal employees, and low tax collection rates. We thus combined the five dimensions in a single Index of Political Leadership. It was one of our strongest predictors of fiscal strain. The basic pattern looked like this:

$$\text{Numerous Irish Residents} \rightarrow \begin{array}{c}\text{High}\\\text{Index of}\\\text{Political}\\\text{Leadership}\end{array} \rightarrow \begin{array}{c}\text{High}\\\text{Capital}\\\text{Outlays}\end{array} \rightarrow \begin{array}{c}\text{Fiscal}\\\text{Strain}\end{array}$$

Capital Outlays

The distinction between municipal operating expenditures (salaries and the like) and capital outlays (normally for highways, public buildings, and so forth) is important. Cities can issue bonds to finance capital outlays, whereas operating expenditures must be funded from taxes and revenues for the same fiscal year (according to most state laws). In 1960, Chicago's capital outlays were $42 per capita; in 1974 they were still $42 per capita. By contrast, New York's capital outlays were $54 in 1960, but they jumped to $153 in 1973 and to $195 in 1974. The average for our fifty-one cities in 1974 was $60. Cities were often high on capital outlays if (as in the diagram) they had numerous Irish residents and a high score on the Index of Political Leadership. High capital outlays, in turn, lead to fiscal strain.

This is perhaps obvious—if you build new capital facilities and pay for them by borrowing, eventually interest payments on the debt can strain the budget. The story is familiar for New York, where the problem was compounded by supporting certain operating expenditures using the capital budget. What deserves emphasis is that in New York as elsewhere, one of the most important and direct causes of fiscal strain is high capital spending in earlier years. Supporting projects like the reconstruction of Yankee Stadium can cause more fiscal strain than supporting the poor.

Predicting Fiscal Strain

The most consistent message of these findings is that local leadership can make a substantial difference. Fiscal strain is greater on local officials in cities with weak tax bases and large numbers of poor residents. But some cities are fiscally healthy (like Pittsburgh, Schenectady, and St. Louis) even though they share many socioeconomic problems with Boston and New York. If the leadership characteristics we have isolated are crucial in explaining fiscal strain, and some cities are fiscally sound, one might conclude that at least some cities can solve their own problems without major assistance from higher levels of government. This is not to argue against more federal and state assistance, especially for programs like higher education, which affect the entire society as students migrate, or income transfer programs, which people can migrate from to avoid supporting.[4] But as far as the fiscal well-being of American cities is concerned, the evidence suggests that much can be done at the local level.

In many cities in the past, only the financial officials paid close attention to fiscal difficulties. The major elected officials are now focusing more attention on such matters with support from the press and local citizens. Comparisons with past fiscal performance for the individual city are useful; so are comparative rankings. Increasingly, officials will have to try to spot fiscal overburden before the situation becomes critical.

If this is to be done, fiscal reporting will have to be improved. Even many elected officials, not to mention municipal employees and citizens, have only a cloudy picture of their local finances. Current reporting of fringe benefits for municipal employees, pension provisions, and short-term debt is also poor (although improving). City workers might appreciate their jobs more if they knew just how much they received in fringe benefits and pensions. The municipal bond market could charge cities less interest if it were clear that their finances were sound.

The city tax burden must be kept competitive if fiscal strain is to be avoided. If local leaders do not compare their tax burdens to those elsewhere, citizens and firms do. Newer towns and suburbs in the Sunbelt are growing for many reasons, but one seems to be their low tax rates. Given free migration, if any city deviates too far from the others, it is likely to lose residents and firms. This has been happening to Boston, New York, and many cities in the Northeast and Midwest for some time—but not to all of them. From 1970 to 1974, Chicago's Cook County lost about 2 percent of its population, as did Los Angeles County, while New York's five boroughs lost 4 percent.[5] If the sunny California weather is more pleasant than wintry breezes off Lake Michigan, the taxes are still lower in Chicago. The average per-capita taxes and charges paid to all local and state governments for residents in the three county areas were approximately $765 in Chicago, $849 in Los Angeles, and $1,064 in New York. They were less in Jacksonville, Fla. ($536), and Fort Worth ($439) and Tyler ($474), Texas.

City officials must watch particularly closely the municipal payroll as well as capital expenditures. These are the two largest items in most city budgets. And, unlike welfare or Medicare, cities must rely primarily on local taxes and charges to support their employees. Capital expenditures can be eased through borrowing, but interest payments can obviously become burdens. Even if local officials are largely autonomous in payroll and capital expenditure decisions, some cities always seem to spend more, despite the wishes of leaders and citizens. What can be done?

Centralization and "Public-Goods"

Until recently, New York represented an extreme but not unique case of decentralized decision-making. "Decentralized" is here used to refer not to neighborhood participation, but to the involvement of numerous organizations and individuals in basic municipal decisions. The mayor of New York generally was only one of many participants in decisions. If LaGuardia built up a substantial following, Lindsay never succeeded. He, like many other actors in a decentralized context, had to provide a continual flow of benefits to piece together one fragile coalition after the next—which is expensive.

The situation was similar in turn-of-the-century Chicago. Construction firms and others complained that aldermen could not be "bought" for more than one vote at a time. A political organization gradually developed that coordinated the votes of aldermen. Today, unlike New York and other more decentralized cities, in Chicago both the mayor and the voters know that Richard Daley is responsible for major decisions. He can and does say no to demands for spending, because he is strong enough to say no. Few mayors are, and Chicago, as table 2.1 indicates, is fiscally sound.

If few Americans would welcome back political machines of the Tammany variety, they might nevertheless consider some of the advantages derived from giving mayors— or someone—enough legal authority to govern effectively.[6] This has happened by political if not literal fiscal default in New York. Creating the Municipal Assistance Corporation and Emergency Financial Control Board centralized power. They stand behind the mayor and help govern without having to respond to the demands of all interest groups in the city.

Goods provided by government may be classified along a continuum from "public goods" to "separable goods." Public goods, or, in this case, "bads" like air pollution or municipal bankruptcy, are shared by citizens throughout a city. By contrast, separable goods, like jobs or housing, are allocable to distinct individuals or interest groups. Thus, the comparison of Chicago and New York may be restated more abstractly: centralization encourages public goods, but decentralization generates separable goods. To achieve the public good of fiscal health, centralization helps. It is obviously not sufficient. But, unless enough authority is given to someone to confront the big issues, no one will. Instead, local officials usually become so caught up in responding to day-to-day demands that thinking beyond next week seems utopian. Yet it is hard for most local leaders to survive otherwise.

Centralization also helps to hold down costs because leaders can be less responsive to immediate demands. Over the last decade, some people have held that "democracy" is defined by immediate response to forceful citizen demands, especially from the poor. By now the short-sightedness of this view should be apparent: fiscal strain often follows.

Many American cities are declining; their economies are stagnant and their populations migrating. The New York fiscal crisis may have the salutary effect of frightening people enough to consider new modes of urban governance. To effect the sorts of dramatic changes that are taking place in New York, someone, most likely the mayor of a MAC-style committee, must be given more authority. There are many well-known legal alternatives: a longer term of office as well as broader veto, spending, and appointment powers. The civil service structures have been criticized by several commissions; they now largely tie the hands of chief executives. Centralization need not imply a larger budget or staff. Indeed, given the leveling of population, in the next decade mayors are likely to distinguish themselves by creatively doing more with less. But unless mayors have sufficient authority to implement such productivity improvements, they are unlikely to consider them seriously.

Notes

1. For more detail, see: Terry Nichols Clark, Irene Sharp Rubin, Lynne C. Pettler, and Erwin Zimmerman, "How Many New Yorks?—The New York Fiscal Crisis in Comparative Perspective," Research Report no. 72 of the Comparative Study of Community Decision-Making.

2. See Terry Nichols Clark, "The Irish Ethic and the Spirit of Patronage," Ethnicity, 2 (1975):305–359.

3. However, this ratio is affected by the tendency in some cities, like New York, knowingly to extend property tax levies against nontaxable property, which is then fictitiously shown as delinquent. The purpose is to permit a greater volume of seasonal borrowing in the form of tax anticipation notes.

4. There is a misconception that should be corrected—that is, most welfare costs have already been taken over by federal or state governments. Nationally, local governments pay only about 6 percent of public welfare from locally raised funds; New York City, because of its peculiar method of handling Medicaid, pays about 8 percent (1973–1974).

5. "Estimates of the Population of Metropolitan Areas, 1973 and 1974, and Components of Change since 1970," *Current Population Reports*, P-25, no. 618 (January 1976). Population data here and fiscal data below are for county areas.

6. Although we reported above that cities spent more if the mayor was stronger, "strong" was only relative to other cities. In virtually all major cities except Chicago, the mayor is relatively weak—at least by comparison with a president of a private firm. Mayors are thus much less able to choose a desirable level of spending and stick to it. See John P. Kotter and Paul R. Lawrence, *Mayors in Action* (New York: Wiley-Interscience, 1974), for documentation.

3

Toward a
Subcultural Theory
of Urbanism

CLAUDE S. FISCHER

THIS PAPER PRESENTS a theory designed to answer the question, What are the social effects of urbanism? There exists in sociology a very influential answer to that question, a theory detailed by Louis Wirth in his classic essay "Urbanism as a Way of Life" (1938). The major consequences are, he suggested, social disorganization and individual alienation. There also exists a significant challenge to Wirth's theory, identified with Herbert Gans's paper "Urbanism and Suburbanism as Ways of Life: A Re-Evaluation of Definitions" (1962b). The argument Gans and others make is that no particularly significant social effects can be attributed to urbanism. I shall argue that the facts, as best we know them, pose a difficult problem for both positions and thus call for a third alternative.

It should be understood that the question that concerns this paper is an analytical one. It involves tracing out the *independent* effects of population concentration: What cul-

Reprinted with permission from *American Journal of Sociology* (1975), vol. 80, no. 6, University of Chicago Press. Figure and text reference to figure were omitted because of space constraints.

tural and behavioral differences, if any, are generated just by residence in communities of differing levels of urbanization?

It is recognized, of course, that there are many differences between large and small communities in population composition—the ages, ethnicities, educational levels, and so on, of their residents—which would account at least in part for any cultural and behavioral differences (as Gans et al. argue). In addition, community characteristics other than urbanism, such as economic opportunities and political structure, will partly account for such differences. Nevertheless, the issue is whether urbanism is an additional meaningful causal factor.

It is also recognized that the cultural and behavioral phenomena to be examined are multidetermined. Among the causal variables, urbanism may not rank very high (compared with such factors as class, race, and sex). However, if urbanism does have an autonomous effect, even if it is not a primary cause of any specific phenomenon, such a finding would still be quite important for understanding the nature of urbanism. This theoretical issue—what the social effects of urbanism are—forms the analytical assignment of the present paper.

The theory I shall present is, briefly, that there are independent effects of urban size and density, including those that Wirth described as deviance and disorganization. The processes leading to these consequences are, however, quite different from those hypothesized by Wirth. The higher rates of "deviance and disorganization" in cities are not accounted for by such factors as alienation, anonymity, and impersonality, but instead by the congregation of numbers of persons, "critical masses," sufficient to maintain viable unconventional subcultures. It is the behavioral expressions of those subcultures that come to be called "deviant."

This paper is divided into five parts. In the first section, I present the empirical problem that challenges both Wirth's and Gans's positions and calls for a new formulation. The second is an exposition of a subcultural theory of urbanism, divided into four main propositions. The third illustrates the propositions with research conducted on the type of subculture that presents the greatest difficulty for the theory: ethnicity. The fourth section examines additional propositions that can be derived from the model. The final section discusses the implications of this subcultural theory of urbanism.

The Problem

The traditional sociological approach to urban styles of community and personality was founded in the work of Durkheim (1933), Simmel (1905), and Park (1916), and fully presented by Wirth (1938). The concentration of large and heterogeneous populations, Wirth posited, eventually leads to the weakening of interpersonal ties, primary social structures, and normative consensus. It does so largely for two reasons: the immediate psychological impact of the urban scene (Simmel 1905; compare Milgram 1970) and the complex structural differentiation generated by dynamic density. The ultimate consequences of these processes are individual alienation, societal anomie, and the prevalence of "disorganized," "nontraditional," and "deviant" behavior. (A detailed exegesis of this theory and a review of the relevant evidence is presented in Fischer 1972.)

However, the growing literature in urban ethnography brought this thesis into great doubt. Gans (1962a), Lewis (1952), Young and Willmott (1957), and others (see review in Gulick 1973) found a wealth of personal ties and thriving primary groups even in the innermost recesses of the large city. Consequently, they argued that "the variables of number, density and heterogeneity . . . are not crucial determinants of social life or personality" (Lewis 1965:497). This position, which might be termed "nonecological,"[1] asserts that there are few differences between urban and rural populations; those that do exist are attributable to differences in age, ethnicity, life cycle, or social class—not to any autonomous effect of ecological factors (Gans 1962b, 1967).

At this writing, the latter position seems to hold sway in sociology.[2] Although few critical tests of either theory have been conducted (Reiss 1959; Hauser 1965; Fischer 1972), those observations that have accumulated tend to support the non-ecological position. In particular, there is little evidence to confirm the hypothesis of urban alienation and anomie (Gulick 1973; Fischer 1972, 1973; Wellman et al. 1973).

There is, however, a serious flaw in the nonecological position. With regard to one realm of belief and behavior, urban residents do differ significantly from residents of nonurban places, and they differ to a degree insufficiently accounted for by the individual traits each group brings to its locale. They are more likely than rural residents to behave in ways that diverge from the central and/or traditional norms of their common society.

Cases in point: cities are disproportionately the locale of invention (Richardson 1973; Thompson 1965:49–50; Jacobs 1969; Turner 1941; Childe 1951; Ogburn and Duncan 1964; Bullough and Bullough 1971); crime, particularly with regard to property (Wolfgang 1970; Clinard 1963; Tobias 1972; Szabo 1960); and behaviors and attitudes that contravene standard morality—for example, illegitimacy, alcoholism, divorce, irreligiosity, political dissent, violence for social change, and the smoking of marijuana (Clinard 1963; Trice 1966; Argyle 1968; Blumenthal et al. 1972; Lipset 1963:264–267; A.I.P.O. 1972, report no. 82; Willitis et al. 1973; compare summary in Swedner 1960:30–45).[3] Some behaviors to which urbanites are prone are socially approved (such as artistic innovation), some severely disapproved (such as crime), and some unsanctioned (such as religious variation in the United States). What they have in common is that they diverge from the predominant norms of the society. I shall use the term "unconventional" to refer to these behaviors and beliefs.[4]

The association between urban residence and unconventionality is pervasive. It appears in many cultures, during various historical periods, and with regard to different specific norms. A nonecological explanation might account for the greater part of this relationship. The individual traits of urbanites (age, ethnicity, education, and so on) generate their high levels of unconventionality. Additionally, other divergent types migrate to cities, creating an association by self-selection.

This explanation will not suffice, however. The few studies that have sought to control for correlated personal traits have failed to account fully for the covariation between urbanism and unconventionality (Fischer 1975; Hoch 1972; Nelsen et al. 1971; Swedner 1960:esp. 30–45). Furthermore, the very pervasiveness and strength of the zero-order differences challenge the adequacy of an explanation based simply on compositional (age, education, and the like) differences between urban and rural populations. And the direction of self-selection itself calls for explanation. I am making no argument here that this residual covariation is of major practical importance (for social policy, that is), but only that it is of theoretical importance.

It is this state of our empirical knowledge that poses the problem: How can the greater unconventionality of urbanites be explained? Wirthian theory accounts for it—but by processes of alienation and anomie for which there is little substantiation. The approach termed here "nonecological" has been better supported by research—but it cannot account sufficiently for urban unconventionality. This paper is meant to resolve the problem by presenting a theory that reintroduces the variables of size and density, but in a manner quite distinct from Wirth's.

A Subcultural Theory

The model outlined in this section is based initially on a nonecological approach: simple ecological determinism (for example, the notion that crowding deranges people) is rejected, and the source of social action is sought in the small milieus of personal life. To quote Oscar Lewis (1965:497): "Social life is not a mass phenomenon. It occurs for the most part in small groups, within the family, within households, within neighborhoods, within the church, formal and informal groups . . ." (compare also Reiss 1955). Additions to the nonecological approach were suggested in part by social mobilization or communications theorists (Deutsch 1961; Sjoberg 1965a; Meier 1962), who stress the role of cities as locales for the origin and dissemination of modernizing ideas and in part by the urban "mosaic of social worlds" painted by the Chicago School (compare Short 1971; Park 1916). The elaboration of the model is an attempt to demonstrate that ecological factors, especially size, produce the urban "mosaic" and urban "unconventionality."

To commence with the definitions and assumptions undergirding the model, "urban" is defined solely in terms of population concentration—the greater the number of persons aggregated at a place of settlement the more urban the place. (Thus, the terms "urban" and "rural" are used solely as conveniences, not as references to a dichotomy.) A "subculture" is a set of modal beliefs, values, norms, and customs associated with a relatively distinct social subsystem (a set of interpersonal networks and institutions) existing within a larger social system and culture. (For ease of presentation, "subculture" will be used to refer to "subsystems" as well.)

"Unconventionality" was defined loosely earlier but requires further comment. The fact that the "unconventional" can be defined only in contrast to the "conventional" presents a difficulty. How does an observer determine the dominant standards of a society; how does he or she deal with internal variability and changes over time? These are not small problems; nor are they unique to this essay. Those who write on the topic of "deviance," Parsons and Merton included, confront the same issue. The common response is simultaneously to acknowledge that the concept of social norm is a vague one and yet to assert that behaviors at variance with those norms constitute a distinct category of social action. "Deviant behavior is behavior that violates the normative rules, understandings, or expectations of social systems" (A. K. Cohen 1968:148). Unconventional behavior is similar except that it incorporates also less socially significant (and unstigmatized) behavior, that in the realm of taste or style. When standards are in flux the "unconventional" is defined as that which is nontraditional.

The model that will be outlined is an abstracted one. That is, for clarity of presentation it assumes that all else is equal. Place of residence is assumed to be uncorrelated with such variables as wealth, age, education, and region, at least at time 1, the initial state of the processes. Of course, in any actual case, these factors, as well as other historical, cultural, and economic ones, will significantly alter the phenomenon that this theory, if it operated in a vacuum, would predict. This admission, however, does not invalidate the argument that urbanism *tends* to generate the effects described below, which can therefore be partly ascribed to the independent influence of urbanism.

Proposition 1

The more urban a place, the greater its subcultural variety.

In general, population concentration generates distinctive subcultures (Wirth's "heterogeneity," Park's "urban mosaic"), and it does so through at least two related, but independently sufficient, processes:

(a) Population size encourages structural differentiation through the familiar process of "dynamic density" (Durkheim 1933; Schnore 1958). As the forces of competition, comparative advantage, and associative selection produce distinguishable and internally elaborated subsystems, they thereby differentiate the cultures associated with those subsystems. The result is increased subcultural variation, particularly as evidenced among social class, occupational, life-cycle, and common-interest groups. This association between urbanization and differentiation has been commonly observed in both historical and cross-sectional studies, largely with regard to economic specialization, somewhat with regard to spatial differentiation, and only to a small extent with regard to other institutions (Hawley 1971; Gibbs and Martin 1962; Ogburn and Duncan 1964; Meade 1972; Betz 1972; Clemente and

Sturgis 1972; Crowley 1973).[5] The question of whether division of labor precedes or follows urbanization (Hawley 1971:328; Kemper 1972) is relevant but should not detain us. Clearly, the two reinforce each other. Furthermore, there is sufficient evidence on the microscopic level to assign some independent causality to size (compare literature on organizational size and differentiation). (As has often been noted, the process of differentiation, especially economic differentiation, requires relatively free exchange, movement, and interaction [Schnore 1958]. In rigidly segmented societies, it will be retarded. This point would apply to African and Asian cities often described as "large villages.")

The idea that these differentiated structural subsystems are accompanied by differentiated subcultures is consistent with systemic models of society. The hypothesis is that urban differentiation results in distinguishable subcultures tied to occupations, classes, stages in the life-cycle, and other common interests. Little systematic evidence in support is currently available, but the wealth of ethnographies on urban "social worlds" (from Gold Coast to slum, from "swinging singles" to criminal guilds) lends credence to the hypothesis. A specific example is Wilensky's survey of professionals in the Detroit area, which convinced him that "to say 'professional, technical, and kindred' captures more of social life [than do traditional class distinctions] but not much more. 'Lawyer' and 'engineer' move us closer to social reality, for these men develop quite different styles of life, rooted in diverse professional schools, tasks, work schedules, and organizational contexts" (1964:195). Other urban occupational subcultures have also been described: for example, longshoremen in Portland, Oregon, by Pilcher (1972) and printers in New York by Lipset et al. (1962).

(b) The second process by which urbanism generates subcultural variety involves migration. The larger a settlement, the larger its hinterland and the more it is a "central place" within its cultural region. In general, the larger a geographical area the greater the variety of groups within it. Given the general cityward direction of migration, the consequence is that a large settlement will draw migrants from a greater variety of subcultures than will a small one. This process, resulting from hierarchies of city sizes, manifests itself in, for example, the general association between community size and ethnic heterogeneity (for example, Schnore 1963; Hanna and Hanna 1971:109).

Proposition 2

The more urban a place, the more intense its subcultures.

By "intensity" I mean the antithesis of anomie and normlessness. It refers to the presence of, attachment to, and force of subcultural beliefs, values, norms, and customs. In place of the anomic city, it suggests a city of articulated value systems. Intensification comes about through at least two mutually reinforcing, though independently sufficient, processes.

(a) The first is based on the common notion of "critical mass." The larger a subculture's population, the greater its "institutional completeness" (Breton 1964).[6] That is, given basic market mechanisms, arrival at certain critical levels of size enables a social subsystem to create and support institutions that structure, envelop, protect, and foster its subculture. These institutions (such as dress styles, newspapers, associations) establish sources of authority and points of congregation and delimit social boundaries. In addition to the simple fact of the numbers themselves, they make possible and encourage the keeping of social ties within the group.

One illustration of this phenomenon is the criminal subcommunity. It has been common historically for large cities (to a greater extent than towns) to have distinguishable groups of professional criminals, with their own meeting places and quarters. The criminals are usually organized and have regular means of distributing stolen goods, finding protection, training apprentices, and enjoying each other's company (Tobias 1972; Lapidus 1966:153–163). Less dramatic but similar examples can be drawn from artistic subcommunities, student subcultures, "young singles," and other groups. Numbers bring the services and institutions necessary for a thriving "social world."

These are but examples; there is little yet in the way of systematic data on such subcultures. There is evidence that the larger a town, the more numerous and varied its institutions and services, both general and specialized, and the more likely the presence of any specific one (Keyes 1958; Ogburn and Duncan 1964; Thompson 1965; Abrahamson 1974). That the presence of specialized institutions should promote the internal ties, cohesion, and core values of a subculture is both reasonable and supported by some limited data on urban migrants (Breton 1964; Doughty 1970; Little 1965) and occupational groups (Lipset et al. 1962:170–208).

(b) The second process that promotes subcultural intensity involves intergroup relations. The greater the variety and sizes of subcultures in a place, the greater the contrast and conflict among them, and, consequently, the greater the subcultural intensity. On the group level, the competition and conflict that coresidence makes possible foster in-group cohesion (Simmel 1951; Coser 1956; Sherif 1956). On the individual level, contact with, or even simple observation of, strange others will lead, at least initially, to stronger affirmation of own-group standards. Clyde Kluckhohn (1960:78) has made a similar argument: "Another direct consequence of expansion of population arises from contact with divergent moral orders, with contrasting perspectives. . . . Reasons must be found to justify the existing moral order or it will be altered by negation, reshaping, or syncretism. . . . The moral order becomes for the first time a genuine problem. Ideas take their place as forces in history." Both psychological and group contact will strengthen subcultures. (This argument will be modified below.)

This sort of culture clash can be subtle and difficult to measure. Sharper instances, such as political and violent conflict, have been studied, and there is evidence that rates of such intergroup clashes are higher in larger communities (Tilly 1974; Coleman 1957; Scheuch 1969; Ennis 1962; Spilerman 1971; Morgan and Clark 1973; Danzger 1970). One can presume that these incidents reflect and/or increase in-group cohesion.

We do not as yet have solid evidence that confrontation with "odd" strangers in the subculturally heterogeneous city does lead to recoil and the embracing of own-group values. There are, however, ethnographic descriptions of this process in the literature on urban migrants. Their encounter with distinctively foreign behavior increases their self-conscious adherence to their own culture. (I expand on this point in the next section.)

In these two ways—institutional completeness due to "critical mass" and cultural opposition—subcultures are intensified by urbanism. This is, however, but one side of urban social change.

Proposition 3

The more urban a place, the more numerous the sources of diffusion and the greater the diffusion into a subculture.

Diffusion refers to the adoption by members of one subculture of beliefs or behaviors of another. This results from the variety (proposition 1) and strength (proposition 2) of the subcultures within the metropolitan area. The specific rates and directions of diffusion will vary according to the sizes of, relative intensities of, and dissimilarity between any two groups, as well as their degree of contact, their relative power and prestige, and the utility of the borrowed item.

The critical import of this proposition is that the urban process of subcultural intensification operates against another urban process, cultural diffusion. Regardless of conflict between or isolation of subcultures, some diffusion is highly probable when groups live in close proximity and functional interdependence. This does not imply that the two forces cancel each other out in any simple way. Instead, they occur simultaneously so that one finds both intensified and diffused elements in a subculture. For instance, one can observe in many American metropolitan areas the uneasy relationship between working-class youth ("hardhat") groups and quasi-student youth ("counterculture") groups. The former seem both to react against the latter, as on political issues, and to adopt life-style elements from them, as in hair and dress styles.

In any event, the counterplay of intensification and diffusion suggests some interesting hypotheses, which will be discussed below. Here I will point out only that there is probably a temporal dynamic involved, such that the intensification process precedes the leveling effect of diffusion.

One consequence of diffusion is the mixture and recombination of cultural elements into social innovations. This effect introduces the final proposition of the theory.

Proposition 4

The more urban a place, the higher the rates of unconventionality.

This is, of course, the empirical generalization that was presented as posing the theoretical problem. How do the three previous propositions explain this association?

(a) Proposition 4 follows, first, from the subcultural variety of urban places (proposition 1). The more variable and distinct subcultures there are, the more behavior there is that deviates from general norms.[7] Ogburn and Duncan (1964:70) stated it this way: "The larger the city the more likely it is to include within its population extreme deviations from the normal or average. . . . The tendency of phenomena to occur in clusters . . . adds to the likelihood that large cities will be the locus of the unusual." But if variety were the only factor, the nonecological model would suffice: the group membership characteristics of residents would explain the correlation of urbanism and unconventionality. There are two more processes, however:

(b) The present theory posits, second, that the effect of subcultural intensification (proposition 2) increases the urban-rural differential in deviance above that accounted for by a model based solely on individual characteristics and ignoring the ecological factor of size. Instead, the aggregation of numbers does have an effect. (To quote Simmel: "The strange thing is that the *absolute* numbers of the total group and of its prominent elements so remarkably determine the relations within the group—in spite of the fact that their numerical ratio remains the same" [1950:98].) The size and distinctiveness of a group make behavior unique to it more likely to occur. For example, a small town may have a few delinquent youths, but only in a large city will there be sufficient numbers (a critical mass) sufficiently distinctive to establish a viable delinquent subculture. The same holds true for political dissidents, splinter religious sects, and criminals. Cities provide the critical mass necessary for a viable subculture and the clashes that accentuate that culture. With size comes "community"—even if it is a community of thieves, counterculture experimenters, avant-garde intellectuals, or other unconventional persons.

There are studies, particularly in the realm of criminal deviance, that suggest that the existence of cohesive deviant groups is important in encouraging individual deviant behavior (Miller 1958; Becker 1963; Wolfgang and Ferracuti 1967).[8] Certainly, harder data would be useful (Wilson 1971), but little has been done to estimate systematically the effects of "grouping" across various realms of action.

(c) Third, rates of unconventionality will be increased in larger communities by the process of diffusion into the mainstream culture of behaviors and beliefs from the periphery (proposition 3). The larger the town, the more likely it is to contain, in meaningful numbers and unity, drug addicts, radicals, intellectuals, "swingers," health-food faddists, or whatever; and the more likely they are to influence (as well as offend) the conventional center of society. In most communities, large and small, the influence of "Middle-American" culture is pervasive and weighty. It is, however, in the larger communities that counterinfluence from unconventional subcultures occurs. This diffusion, too, will boost rates of urban unconventionality above those accounted for by the nonecological model.

More anecdotes than systematic research can be cited at this time in support of such "climate-of-opinion" effects; for example, the spread in urban areas of language from the drug subculture or dress styles from the black (Superfly) under-world and the homosexual communities. Some data can also be pointed to; for example, those concerning the influence of community educational levels on individual racial attitudes (Schuman and Gruenberg 1970).[9]

It is these three processes that explain the association of urbanism and unconventionality. They account for it more fully than does the approach I have labeled "nonecological." And unlike Wirthian theory, this explanation does not as-sume an association between urbanism and anomie for which there is little empirical support.

The Special Case of Ethnicity

The theory I have presented is that urban unconventionality is accounted for by the strengthening of subcultures that en-courage or tolerate behaviors that the wider society finds to be deviant or unusual. The references have largely been to groups that emerge or become defined in an urban setting because of the numbers provided there—intellectuals, crimi-nals, "life-stylers," and the like. This section of the paper will be particularly concerned with a different type: the ethnic group.[10] This group forms a distinctive subculture in both rural and urban settings (though the meaning and nature of ethnicity may vary somewhat; see Epstein 1967). Also, unlike the others, it rests on a "primordial" basis of association: de-scent. While recognizing these special characteristics of eth-nicity, I will attempt here to assess the applicability of the propositions outlined above to ethnic subcultures, for two reasons. First, there have been relatively few studies of sub-cultures based on such variables as life-style and occupation, and almost none that incorporate intercommunity compari-sons, but there is a wealth of ethnic studies, including some comparative ones. Therefore, if one wishes to examine the plausibility of the arguments advanced above, one is com-pelled to turn to the ethnicity literature. Second, for certain of the propositions described above, ethnic subcultures provide the extreme test case. If one can demonstrate that ethnic subcultures are intensified by urbanism, in spite of the fact that they are the most threatened by the generation in cities of alternative bases of association, then the arguments about the intensification of those alternative subcultures are buttressed. These two points explain the consideration here and below of ethnic groups. The reader should understand that this discussion implies neither that the theory is about ethnicity nor that evidence about ethnic groups is necessary to establish the validity of the theory.

The first and third propositions do not require much discussion. Urbanism and ethnic minority concentration seem to be associated in most societies (see, for example, Hanna and Hanna 1971:109), though there are of course notable exceptions (such as, until recently, American blacks). The cultural diffusion of urban life is a commonplace. Virtually all historical and anthropological descriptions of urban ethnicity note the adoption of language, styles of behavior, and other cultural elements by ethnic groups from one another, and especially from the most powerful group in the urban setting. Indeed, this assimilationist understanding of urban ethnicity is so pervasive that when the second proposition is applied to ethnic groups it seems counterintuitive.

With regard to proposition 2, it was argued that the intensification of subcultures occurred through two processes: institutional completeness due to critical mass, and culture clash. There are a good number of descriptions of the first. To the extent that numbers permit, urban migrants tend to establish institutions of all sorts, many of which never existed in the rural village—sports clubs, mutual aid associations, festival committees, newspapers, political organizations (see Doughty 1970; Handlin 1959, 1969; Little 1965; Bascom 1963; Hanna and Hanna 1971, among others). Breton's (1964) study of immigrants in Montreal revealed that those groups that had such institutions were best able to keep their members' social ties internal. Whether such organizations existed was partly a function of group size. These ethnic institutions also preserve elements of the traditional culture and selectively introduce new elements from the urban environment (Little 1973). For instance, leaders of associations will instruct newcomers simultaneously on etiquette appropriate for job finding and on the need for maintaining ties with the home village (for example Bruner 1961).

Suttles (1968) provides an example of the relationship of size to institutions of cultural continuity in his study of the Addams area of Chicago. Of the four ethnic groups inhabiting the neighborhood, the Puerto Ricans were the only ones threatened with an erosion of their culture. This Suttles attributes to the lack of institutions, particularly an ethnic church, which he in turn attributes to the small number of Puerto Ricans (see also Kornblum 1974).

The second process, cultural opposition, was explained in part by encounters between members of different subcultures which lead them to affirm even more strongly their own groups' world views. Descriptions of this process are common in the literature on African migrants. It is a main contributor to what has been called "retribalization" or "supertribalization"—the elevation to conscious awareness of, and increased attachment to, tribal identity (compare Epstein 1967; Hanna and Hanna 1971:ch. 4).[11] Similar observations have been made about other migrants (for example Rowe 1973), including those to American cities (Nelli 1970; Handlin 1969; Suttles 1968). Some quantitative evidence is provided by a survey of Ukrainians living in two communities in Canada. Those who lived in the larger, more heterogeneous city, instead of the small homogeneous town, were the most resistant to assimilation (Borhek 1970).[12]

Finally, there is evidence to support the proposition that, by these processes, urbanism increases (or at least maintains) the cohesion and identity even of ethnic subcultures—in spite of all the disorganizing aspects of urbanization, such as migration, economic change, and alternative subcultures.

I have already referred to the evidence of tribalism among new urbanites in Africa and to Borhek's (1970) study of Ukrainian consciousness in Canada. Doughty (1970) has described a wealth of organizations and activities in Lima, Peru, which sustain Andean village identification and culture. Bruner's studies (1961, 1963) of a Christian ethnic group, the Toba Batak, residing in the Moslem city of Medan, Indonesia, indicate that ties there to traditional kinship norms and values were at least as strong as, if not stronger than, those in the village home of the community. Lewis' descriptions (1952, 1965) of migrants to Mexico City seem quite similar. Finally, Handlin's histories (1959, 1969) of immigrants to American cities indicate not only the plethora of culture-maintaining mechanisms that arose there, but also the strengthening of old institutions, such as the church, which resulted from culture clash.

These illustrations are presented, not to deny that assimilational pressures operate on ethnic groups in cities—one such pressure being the emergence of subcultures that accompanies urbanism—but to bolster the argument that the processes of intensification do occur, even in the most difficult instance—that of ethnic groups. In all probability, the extent of intensification is limited by time and other factors (such as the duration of in-migration, attributes of the ethnic culture), so that it is often transient, succumbing frequently to the intensification of competing subcultures. Nevertheless, it does occur.

The fourth proposition, relating urbanism to unconventionality, is exhibited in ethnic groups in the following ways. The greater ethnic variety of cities means that they will exhibit greater amounts of unconventionality based on ethnicity (process 4a). For example, simply because of this population distribution, cities will tend to have more dissident and unusual forms of religious behavior. The greater "intensity" of ethnic groups, which tends to be associated with urbanism (especially because of group size), means that minority group members will be more able and willing to maintain their unconventional behaviors and beliefs (process 4b). Also, the diffusion of cultural elements from minority to majority groups will act to increase rates of urban unconventionality (process 4c). Usually, the diffusion will operate from majority to minority subcultures, but there are instances of the reverse. For example, black ghetto culture clearly influences middle-class white culture in certain realms.

This discussion of ethnic groups is not intended to prove my theory, support for which will depend on other sources. Instead, it represents an effort to illustrate the theory with data on a type of subculture on which much research has been done and which forms the most difficult test case.

Further Derivations

The four propositions that constitute this subcultural theory of urbanism seem to be consistent with currently available data, limited as they are. Yet any plausible ex-post-facto theory will incorporate the data it was created to explain. The critical test is whether the theory suggests further, novel hypotheses that are also borne out. I turn now to a few of these.

One of the intriguing processes in the model is the counterplay of subcultural intensification and increased diffusion across subcultures, both resulting from urbanism. It was argued earlier that this process did not mean mutual negation, but, instead, selective changes.[13] Three predictions about these changes can be made.

The first requires an additional concept—"cultural centrality." I shall assume that cultural items (customs, values, artifacts, and so on) can be scaled on a continuum ranging from a central core that is fundamental to the subculture and firmly defended (for example, *Weltanschauung*, family relations) to relatively peripheral and unimportant items (such as dress style). The first of two related hypotheses that follow from the present theory is that peripheral cultural items will be most easily and earliest modified by diffusion; central items will be bolstered by the processes of intensification. Put another way:

Proposition 5a
For a given subculture, diffusion effects of urbanism should be greatest with regard to peripheral items and least with regard to central items.[14]

There are some data, drawn again from the ethnicity literature, to illustrate the point. In their review of the urban
African literature, Hanna and Hanna (1971) make a distinction between bicycles and beliefs (p. 135), by which they refer to the common observation that tribal members residing
in the city differ from their kin in the hinterland in terms of
consumer habits and material goods (peripheral items), but
not in terms of basic values (central items). Bruner's (1973)
study of the Batak in Indonesia is particularly illustrative of
this distinction. In the very pluralistic city of Medan, the Batak subculture is quite like the village version. In Bandung, a
city in which their members are fewer and there is a very
large majority subculture (the Sundanese), the Batak changed.
They dropped far more of their customs in favor of Sundanese ones, particularly regarding public behavior. Yet, even
in Bandung, the Batak form a distinguishable and self-conscious group.

Proposition 5b

One can also derive a prediction of time lag: *as urbanism
increases over time, increases in subcultural intensity pre-
cede the diffusion into the subculture of outside elements.*
This lag can best be seen when those forces that energize the
processes of the model—growth of a subculture due to city
growth or ethnic in-migration—cease. A simple example is
the history of American ethnic groups that are facing (though
resisting) assimilation now, fifty years after the great waves
of migration ended.

Proposition 6

The model states that the forms urban unconventionality
takes are a function of specific societal norms and specific
emergent urban subcultures. The main implication is that
there is no universal direction to urban unconventionality.
In contrast to Wirth's theory, there is no a priori reason why
cities should deviate in such directions as rationalism, secularism, and universalism. Cities need only differ from the
modal standards.[15]

There is some illustrative support for this prediction of "content-free" differences. In pre World War II Japan, divorce rates tended to be lower in the more urban places (Kawashima and Steiner 1960; compare comments in Goode 1963:360–365). The former's explanation suggests that urban anomie had little to do with this phenomenon. High divorce rates were traditional in Japan, but cities deviated from such traditions (pp. 238–239). Tiryakian (1972) has recently reported a French survey that revealed that belief in astrology was greater in urban than in rural areas (p. 495; it was also greater among middle than among lower classes). My contention is that secularism and rationality have little to do with this correlation: the explanation is that cities are the places where nonconventional ideas flourish.

Proposition 7

Cultural differences between urban and rural persons are persistent.

Although it is often claimed that differences between city and country are disappearing, my theory implies that, at least with respect to the conventional-unconventional, traditional-nontraditional dimension, such differences will persist. (It is of course acknowledged that there will be many specific exceptions; I refer only to general trends.) Social changes, the theory suggests, usually begin in the unconventionality of a few and then spread to the wider society. The importance of size for the support of innovative subcultures means that cities will always have an advantage in this regard. Even as rural areas adopt and make generally normative a new value, ones discrepant with it are arising in the cities. Thus, there is a lag in social change as successive "waves" diffuse from the urban center to the rural periphery.[16] (The degree of lag is, however, quite variable.)

Friedl (1964) has coined the term "lagging emulation" for this process and has described a pattern among Greek villagers of adopting urban elite styles and views just as those standards are being supplanted in the city. Recent research indicates that urban-rural differences even in the United

States, presumably the most "massified" society, have not been erased (Willitis et al. 1973; Glenn and Alston 1967; Fischer 1975; Glenn and Simmons 1967). In sum, it is in the nature of urbanism constantly to foster innovation and change.

Implications

I am quite aware of the clarifications and qualifications this theory requires. In this section, however, I shall presume that the propositions intrinsic to and those logically deducible from the subcultural model are empirically valid. Certain points then follow.

Primarily, the "unconventionality" of urban life, the problem that initiated the search for a theory, is accounted for.

The model does not rely on the Wirthian mechanisms to provide the explanation. There is no proposition stating that urbanism creates alienation, isolation, impersonality, superficiality, stress, strain, anxiety, or dehumanization. While such hypotheses remain plausible and worthy of investigation, this theory renders them unnecessary for explaining the "disorganization" Wirth wished to account for.

Yet the theory does rely on ecology. Population density, heterogeneity, and especially size *are* determinants of social life. The nonecological model is not sufficient.

The subcultural model does not, however, imply that such ecological factors have large, practical, or policy-relevant effects. By far the more important influences on behavior are the nonecological ones. The real implication is theoretical; a full understanding of life in cities requires incorporation of ecological factors, subcultural development, and diffusion in a dynamic model.

This theory does raise an important question with regard to a community's "moral order." Implicit in the analysis presented here is the contention that the large city is integrated neither by virtue of its citizens' sharing a common "social world" nor by the formal instruments of an anomic "mass society." How, then, is it integrated? To some extent, it is not; that is, value consensus is less likely to exist in larger than in smaller communities. Rather than unanimity, there is "multinimity" (Meadows 1973). The integration that does exist is, I will suggest without elaborating, based on exchange, negotiation, and conflict among the various subcultures of the city. This process does not mean, however, that individuals are psychically fractured in some sort of miniature replication of their city and thus alienated or disordered in some manner. Instead, they, like their rural fellows, live within ongoing, psychically supportive and restraining subcultures. In the city, those subcultures are more often unconventional.

A final comment: in popular evaluations of urban life, much effort has been expended to explain the "evil" of cities—the destructive or disturbing unconventionality. Urbanism per se has been blamed, or causes have been discovered in population composition, temporary social change, and so on. The theory presented here explains the "evil" and the "good" of cities simultaneously.[17] Criminal unconventionality and innovative (such as artistic) unconventionality are both nourished by vibrant subcultures. Less pleasing, perhaps, is the conclusion that it may be difficult to achieve the latter without the former, for they both result from the same dynamics (compare Cook 1963).

Notes

1. Although Sjoberg (1965b) refers to this school as "nonmaterialist," Herbert Gans has pointed out (in personal communication) that he and other "nonmaterialists" do recognize the importance of material factors such as income, but doubt the importance of ecological variables. Hence, "nonecological" seems most appropriate.

2. There are, of course, other theories of urbanism (see Sjoberg 1965b; Fischer 1972), but the Wirthian/nonecological polarity is a central one in urban sociology.

3. There are reversals (e.g., illegitimacy in Scandinavia, criminal violence in many nations), but this is the pervasive pattern.

4. In an earlier version of this paper, the term "deviance" was used to label this phenomenon. The connotations of that word were, however, so

salient that they hindered understanding of the specific meaning intended. Near-synonyms for "unconventional" which I also considered include unusual, divergent, idiosyncratic, nonglobally normative. The difficulties in employing this definition of "unconventional" are evident: contradictions between expressed norms and statistically normative behavior; situations in which a plurality of norms appears to exist; periods in which a previous minority viewpoint wins majority acceptance; problems of defining a society's normative center; the criteria for the minimum amount of divergence that can be called unconventional, and so on. Yet, while these distinctions will require clarification in any research, a great amount of behavior exists which can clearly be categorized as unconventional and the urban nature of which calls for explanation.

5. Indian history provides an example: "The distinguishing mark of a town or city in the ancient texts was that *only* there did one find all the castes resident. It was in the city alone that the more specialized ritual castes, the learned Brahmins and astrologers, as well as the artisans producing luxury goods, could be maintained" (Rowe 1973:213).

6. Implicit is the proposition that urbanism increases group sizes and thereby leads to the achievement of critical masses. It is because the size of specific subgroups mediates the effect of urbanization that specialized subcultures are occasionally found in nonurban areas (e.g., the college town).

7. This statement is not a tautology but an empirical generalization. Membership in a distinguishable subgroup does not mean, ipso facto, unconventionality. Being Swedish-American or being a pipefitter need not necessarily imply unconventional behavior. But the greater the number of such distinguishable subcultures, the greater the likelihood of unconventionality.

8. Here I do not intend to evoke the debate between theses of lower-class cultures and lower-class "value stretch" or to raise the role of societal definition in creating "deviance." My point is simple: given a distinctive set of values or behavior patterns, group cohesion (itself partly a function of numbers) promotes conformity to those patterns instead of to outside alternatives.

9. Recently a debate has arisen on the importance of contextual effects (see Hauser 1970, 1974; Farkas 1974). The present model clearly rides on the assumption that they exist and are meaningful. It also suggests a distinction between two types of contextual effects. The first is influence resulting from structural characteristics of one's own subculture. For example, the number of nonconformists will affect the likelihood of a given nonconformist expressing his feelings (Lipset et al. 1962:186–194; Asch 1958). The second is the contextual effect of conflict with or diffusion from other groups in the environment (e.g., the dissemination of racial attitudes from the educated elite [Schuman and Gruenberg 1970]). The existence of both types is assumed by the model.

10. By ethnic group I mean a culturally distinct group, membership in which is determined by descent. The fineness with which one determines cultural distinctiveness is, as with other subcultures, dependent on the specific analytical problem.

11. There exists a seemingly contrary perspective on urban ethnicity that stresses its fabricated character (as opposed to its primordial nature). According to this influential viewpoint, ethnic lines, identity, and even culture derive from political and economic structures and may even be imposed by elites (as in divide-and-conquer colonial rule). Cohen (1969), for example, has documented a revival of Moslem orthodoxy among Hasau traders in Yoruba cities of Nigeria. He contends that it was a political stratagem used to maintain economic control over trade and that some of the "tradition" was invented for that purpose. This argument seems to challenge the present one as an explanation for the association of urbanism and ethnicity. My analysis, however, is more supplement than substitute. While it is no doubt true that politicoeconomic forces can stimulate ethnic divisions (and perpetuate them), this fact does not negate the possible independent influence of urbanism on "intrinsic" ethnic culture. Indeed, it is likely that the two processes are interdependent, "constructed ethnicity" being more likely to occur when prior cultural distinctions exist and more likely to occur in urban contexts where there are confrontations between sizable ethnic groups.

12. Bruner (1973) describes an example of culture clash in the confrontation of the immigrant Batak and the dominant Sundanese in Bandung, Java:

"The Sundanese and the Batak each approach the initial interaction guided by their own customs and emotional set, and at first they judge the other by their own standards. What the Sundanese define as being crude the Batak define as being honest, straightforward, and strong. What the Sundanese regard as refined behavior the Batak regard as being evasive, insincere, and feminine. Each group feels morally superior to the other and at least initially the behavior of each tends to validate these stereotypic evaluations. Each group in doing what it thinks is right and proper behaves in ways that the other feels are morally deficient" (p. 256).

13. A similar argument is made by an anthropologist student of ethnic groups:

"It is clear that [ethnic] boundaries persist despite a flow of personnel across them. In other words, categorical ethnic distinctions do not depend on the absence of mobility, contact and information, but do entail social processes of exclusion and incorporation whereby discrete categories are maintained despite changing participation and membership in the course of individual life histories. . . . Ethnic distinctions do not depend on the absence of social interaction and acceptance, but are quite to the contrary often the very foundations on which embracing social systems are built" (Barth 1969:9–10).

14. The terms "central" and "peripheral" are borrowed in this instance from Rokeach's (1967) parallel formulation of the structure of psychological attitudes.

15. Gerald Suttles has suggested (in personal communication) that those subcultures generated by cities (such as ones based on art, literature) virtually require a libertarian atmosphere. Thus, urban-rural differences should tend to be in that direction. It is plausible to argue that innovative subcultures would collectively have an interest in maintaining an atmosphere tolerant of innovation. "Libertarian" is not necessarily liberal, however, nor are the beneficiaries of civil liberties necessarily modern, secular, rational, and so on, or themselves libertarian. I suspect, therefore, that social changes in the direction of the sacred, the nonscientific, and the repressive would also tend to be initiated in the city.

16. Ogburn and Duncan (1964) have described a similar process in the form of different diffusion curves for metropolitan, urban, and rural places with reference to radio, television, and hospital births. The smaller places have parallel "learning" curves (elongated Ss) to those of larger communities, but with a few years' lag. The argument I am presenting here is that, with regard to behavioral patterns, the peak of the S is not an absorbing state. Instead, adherence to a particular norm begins to decline in favor of a newer, urban-bred one; e.g., one can view the movement for natural childbirth as an innovation following a delayed version of the same diffusion pattern as that for anesthetized birth.

17. This point was generously contributed by an anonymous member of the ASA audience.

References

Abrahamson, M. 1974. "The Social Dimensions of Urbanism." *Social Forces* (March), 52:376–384.

A.I.P.O. (American Institute of Public Opinion). 1972. Gallup Opinion Index. Princeton, N.J.: American Institute of Public Opinion.

Argyle, M. 1968. "Religious Observance." In D. L. Sills, ed., *International Encyclopedia of the Social Sciences*. New York: Macmillan.

Asch, S. 1958. "Effects of Group Pressure Upon the Modification and Distortion of Judgments." In E. E. Maccoby et al., eds., *Readings in Social Psychology*, 3rd ed., pp. 174–183. New York: Holt, Rinehart & Winston.

Barth, F. 1969. "Introduction." In F. Barth, ed., *Ethnic Groups and Boundaries*, pp. 4–38. Boston: Little, Brown.

Bascom, A. (1963) 1968. "The Urban African and His World." In S. Fava, ed., *Urbanism in World Perspective*, pp. 81–92. New York: Crowell.

Becker, H. S. 1963. *The Outsiders*. New York: Free Press.

Betz, D. M. 1972. "The City as a System Generating Income Equality." *Social Forces* (December), 51:192–198.

Blumenthal, M. D., R. L. Kahn, F. M. Andrews, and K. B. Head. 1972. *Justifying Violence: Attitudes of American Men.* Ann Arbor, Mich.: Institute for Social Research.

Borhek, J. T. 1970. "Ethnic-Group Cohesion." *American Journal of Sociology* (July), 76:33–46.

Breton, R. 1964. "Institutional Completeness of Ethnic Communities and the Personal Relations of Immigrants." *American Journal of Sociology* (September), 70:193–205.

Bruner, E. M. 1961. "Urbanization and Ethnic Identity in North Sumatra." *American Anthropologist*, 63:508–521.

—— (1963) 1970. "Medan: The Role of Kinship in an Indonesian City." In W. Magnin, ed., *Peasants in Cities*, pp. 122–134. Boston: Houghton-Mifflin.

—— 1973. "The Expression of Ethnicity in Indonesia." In A. Cohen, ed., *Urban Ethnicity.* London: Tavistock.

Bullough, B. and V. Bullough. 1971. "Intellectual Achievers: A Study of Eighteenth-Century Scotland." *American Journal of Sociology* (May), 76:1048–1064.

Childe, V. G. 1951. *Man Makes Himself.* New York: Mentor.

Clemente, F. and R. B. Sturgis. 1972. "The Division of Labor in America: An Ecological Analysis." *Social Forces* (December), 31:176–181.

Clinard, M. B. (1963) 1964. "Deviant Behavior: Urban-Rural Contrasts." In C. E. Elias, Jr., J. Gelles, and S. Riemer, eds., *Metropolis: Values in Conflict*, pp. 237–244. Belmont, Calif.: Wadsworth.

Cohen, A. 1969. *Custom and Politics in Urban Africa.* Berkeley: University of California Press.

Cohen, A. K. 1968. "Deviant Behavior." In D. L. Sills, ed., *International Encyclopedia of Social Sciences*, vol. 4, pp. 148–155. New York: Macmillan.

Coleman, J. S. 1957. *Community Conflict.* New York: Free Press.

Cook, D. A. 1963. "Cultural Innovation and Disaster in the American City." In L. Duhl, ed., *The Urban Condition*, pp. 87–96. New York: Simon & Schuster.

Coser, L. 1956. *The Functions of Social Conflict.* New York: Free Press.

Crowley, R. W. 1973. "Reflections and Further Evidence on Population Size and Industrial Diversification." *Urban Studies*, 10:91–94.

Danzger, M. H. 1970. "Critical Mass and Historical Process as Factors in Community Conflict." Paper presented to the American Sociological Association, Washington, D.C., September.

Deutsch, K. 1961. "Social Mobilization and Political Development." *American Political Science Review* (December), 55:493–515.

Doughty, P. L. 1970. "Behind the Back of the City: 'Provincial' Life in Lima,

Peru." In W. Magnin, ed., *Peasants in Cities*, pp. 30–46. Boston: Houghton-Mifflin.

Durkheim, E. 1933. *The Division of Labor in Society*. Glencoe, Ill.: Free Press.

Ennis, P. H. 1962. "The Contextual Dimension in Voting." In W. M. McPhee and W. A. Glaser, eds., *Public Opinions and Congressional Elections*, pp. 180–211. New York: Free Press.

Epstein, A. L. 1967. "Urbanization and Social Change in Africa." *Current Anthropology*, 8(4):275–296.

Farkas, G. 1974. "Specification, Residuals and Contextual Effects." *Sociological Methods and Research* (February), 2:333–365.

Fischer, C. S. 1972. " 'Urbanism as a Way of Life': A Review and an Agenda." *Sociological Methods and Research* (November), 1:187–242.

—— 1973. "On Urban Alienations and Anomie: Powerlessness and Social Isolation." *American Sociological Review* (June), 38:311–326.

—— 1975. "The Effect of Urban Life on Traditional Values." *Social Forces* (March), 53:420–432.

Friedl, E. 1964. "Lagging Emulation in Post-Peasant Society." *American Anthropologist*, 66:569–586.

Gans, H. J. 1962a. *The Urban Villagers*. New York: Free Press.

—— 1962b. "Urbanism and Suburbanism as Ways of Life: A Re-Evaluation of Definitions." In A. M. Rose, ed., *Human Behavior and Social Processes*, pp. 625–648. Boston: Houghton-Mifflin.

—— 1967. *The Levittowners*. New York: Vintage.

Gibbs, J. P. and W. T. Martin. 1962. "Urbanization, Technology, and the Division of Labor: International Patterns." *American Sociological Review* (October), 27:667–677.

Glenn, N. D. and J. Alston. 1967. "Rural-Urban Differences in Reported Attitudes and Behavior." *Southwestern Social Sciences Quarterly* (March), 47:381–400.

Glenn, N. D. and J. L. Simmons. 1967. "Are Regional Cultural Differences Diminishing?" *Public Opinion Quarterly* (Summer), 30:176–193.

Goode, W. J. 1963. *World Revolution and Family Patterns*. New York: Free Press.

Gulick, J. 1973. "Urban Anthropology." In J. J. Honigman, ed., *Handbook of Social and Cultural Anthropology*, pp. 979–1029. Chicago: Rand-McNally.

Handlin, O. 1959. *The Uprooted*. New York: Grosset & Dunlop.

—— 1969. *Boston's Immigrants*, rev. and enlarged ed. New York: Atheneum.

Hanna, W. J. and J. L. Hanna. 1971. *Urban Dynamics in Black Africa*. Chicago: Aldine-Atherton.

Hauser, P. H. 1965. "Urbanization: An Overview." In P. H. Hauser and L. F. Schnore, eds., *The Study of Urbanization*, pp. 1–48. New York: Wiley.

Hauser, R. M. 1970. "Context and Consex: A Cautionary Tale." *American Journal of Sociology* (January), 75:645–664.

—— 1974. "Contextual Effects Revisited." *Sociological Methods and Research* (February), 2:365–375.

Hawley, A. 1971. *The Urban Society*. New York: Ronald.

Hoch, I. 1972. "Income and City Size." *Urban Studies* (October), 9:299–328.

Jacobs, J. 1969. *The Economy of Cities*. New York: Random House.

Kawashima, T. and K. Steiner. 1960. "Modernization and Divorce Rates in Japan." *Economic Development and Cultural Change* (October), 9:213–239.

Kemper, T. D. 1972. "The Division of Labor: A Post-Durkheimian View." *American Sociological Review* (December), 37:739–753.

Keyes, F. 1958. "The Correlation of Social Phenomena with Community Size." *Social Forces* (May), 36:311–315.

Kluckhohn, C. (1960) 1973. "The Moral Order in the Expanding Society." In G. Germani, ed., *Modernization, Urbanization, and the Urban Crisis*, pp. 72–86. Boston: Little, Brown.

Kornblum, W. 1974. *Blue Collar Community*. Chicago: University of Chicago Press.

Lapidus, I. M. 1966. *Muslim Cities in the Later Middle Ages*. Cambridge, Mass.: Harvard University Press.

Lewis, O. 1952. "Urbanization Without Breakdown." *Scientific Monthly* (July), 75:31–41.

—— 1965. "Further Observation on the Folk-Urban Continuum and Urbanization with Special Reference to Mexico City." In P. H. Hauser and L. Schnore, eds., *The Study of Urbanization*, pp. 491–503. New York: Wiley.

Lipset, S. M. 1963. *Political Man*. Garden City, N.Y.: Doubleday.

Lipset, S. M., M. Trow, and J. Coleman. 1962. *Union Democracy*. Garden City, N.Y.: Doubleday.

Little, K. (1965) 1968. "The Migrant and the Urban Community." In S. Fava, ed., *Urbanism in World Perspective*, pp. 312–321. New York: Crowell.

—— 1973. "Urbanization and Regional Associations: Their Paradoxical Function." In A. Southall, ed., *Urban Anthropology*, pp. 407–424. New York: Oxford University Press.

Meade, A. 1972. "The Distribution of Segregation in Atlanta." *Social Forces* (December), 51:182–191.

Meadows, P. 1973. "The Idea of Community in the City." In M. I. Urofsky, ed., *Perspectives on Urban America*, pp. 1–22. Garden City, N.Y.: Doubleday.

Meier, R. L. 1962. *A Communication Theory of Urban Growth*. Cambridge, Mass.: M.I.T. Press.

Milgram, S. 1970. "The Experience of Living in Cities." *Science* (March), 167:1461–1468.

Miller, W. B. 1958. "Lower-Class Culture as a Generating Milieu of Gang Delinquency." *Journal of Social Issues,* 14(3):5–19.

Morgan, W. R. and T. N. Clark. 1973. "The Causes of Racial Disorder." *American Sociological Review* (October), 38:611–624.

Nelli, H. S. 1970. *The Italians in Chicago 1880–1930.* New York: Oxford University Press.

Nelsen, H. M., R. L. Yokley, and T. W. Madron. 1971. "Rural-Urban Differences in Religiosity." *Rural Sociology* (September), 36:389–396.

Ogburn, W. F. and O. D. Duncan. 1964. "City Size as a Sociological Variable." In E. W. Burgess and D. J. Bogue, eds., *Urban Sociology,* pp. 58–76. Chicago: University of Chicago Press.

Park, R. (1916) 1969. "The City: Suggestions for Investigation of Human Behavior in the Urban Environment." In R. Sennett, ed., *Classic Essays on the Culture of Cities,* pp. 91–130. New York: Appleton-Century-Crofts.

Pilcher, W. W. 1972. *The Portland Longshoremen.* New York: Holt, Rinehart & Winston.

Reiss, A. J., Jr. 1955. "An Analysis of Urban Phenomena." In R. M. Fisher, ed., *The Metropolis in Modern Life,* pp. 41–51. Garden City, N.Y.: Doubleday.

—— 1959. "The Sociological Study of Communities." *Rural Sociology* (June), 24:118–130.

Richardson, H. W. 1973. *The Economics of City Size.* London: Saxon.

Rokeach, M. 1967. "The Organization and Modification of Beliefs." In E. P. Hollander and R. G. Hunt, eds., *Current Perspectives in Social Psychology,* 2d ed., pp. 374–383. New York: Oxford University Press.

Rowe, W. L. 1973. "Caste, Kinship, and Association in Urban India." In A. Southall, ed., *Urban Anthropology,* pp. 211–250. New York: Oxford University Press.

Scheuch, E. K. 1969. "Social Context and Individual Behavior." In M. Dogan and S. Rokkan, eds., *Quantitative Ecological Analysis in the Social Sciences,* pp. 133–155. Cambridge, Mass.: M.I.T. Press.

Schnore, L. F. 1958. "Social Morphology and Human Ecology." *American Journal of Sociology* (May), 63:620–634.

—— 1963. "Some Correlates of Urban Size: A Replication." *American Journal of Sociology* (September), 69:185–193.

Schuman, A. and B. Gruenberg. 1970. "The Impact of City on Racial Attitudes." *American Journal of Sociology* (September), 76:213–262.

Sherif, M. 1956. "Experiments in Group Conflicts." *Scientific American* (November), pp. 1–6.

Short, J. F., Jr. 1971. "Introduction." In *The Social Fabric of the Metropolis,* pp. xi–xlvi. Chicago: University of Chicago Press.

Simmel, G. (1905) 1957. "The Metropolis and Mental Life." In P. K. Hatt and A. J. Reiss, Jr., eds., *Cities and Society*, pp. 635–646. New York: Free Press.

—— 1950. "On the Significance of Numbers for Social Life." In K. H. Wolff, trans., *The Sociology of Georg Simmel*. Glencoe, Ill.: Free Press.

—— 1951. *Conflict*. Glencoe, Ill.: Free Press.

Sjoberg, G. 1965a. "Cities in Developing and in Industrialized Societies: A Cross-Cultural Analysis." In P. H. Hauser and L. F. Schnore, eds., *The Study of Urbanization*, pp. 312–363. New York: Wiley.

—— 1965b. "Theory and Research in Urban Sociology." In P. H. Hauser and L. F. Schnore, eds., *The Study of Urbanization*, pp. 157–190. New York: Wiley.

Spilerman, S. 1971. "The Causes of Racial Disturbances: Tests of an Explanation." *American Sociological Review* (June), 36:427–442.

Suttles, G. D. 1968. *The Social Order of the Slum*. Chicago: University of Chicago Press.

Swedner, H. 1960. *Ecological Differentiation of Habits and Attitudes*. Lund: Gleerup.

Szabo, D. 1960. *Crimes et villes*. Paris: Cujas.

Thompson, W. R. 1965. *A Preface to Urban Economics*. Baltimore: Johns Hopkins University Press.

Tilly, C. 1974. "The Chaos of the Living City." In C. Tilly, ed., *The Urban World*, pp. 86–107. Boston: Little, Brown.

Tiryakian, E. A. 1972. "Toward the Sociology of Esoteric Culture." *American Journal of Sociology* (November), 78:491–512.

Tobias, J. J. 1972. *Urban Crime in Victorian England*. New York: Schocken.

Trice, H. M. 1966. *Alcoholism in America*. New York: McGraw-Hill.

Turner, R. E. 1941. "The Industrial City: Center of Cultural Change." In C. F. Ware, ed., *The Cultural Approach to History*, pp. 228–242. New York: Columbia University Press.

Wellman, B., P. Craven, M. Whitaker, H. Stevens, A. Shorrer, S. Dutoit, and H. Bakker. 1973. "Community Ties and Support Systems: From Intimacy to Support." in L. S. Bourne, R. D. MacKinnon, and J. W. Simmons, eds., *The Form of Cities in Central Canada*, pp. 152–167. Toronto: University of Toronto Press.

Wilensky, H. L. 1964. "Mass Society and Mass Culture: Interdependence or Independence." *American Sociological Review* (April), 29:173–197.

Willitis, F. K., R. C. Bealer, and D. M. Crider. 1973. "Leveling of Attitudes in Mass Society: Rurality and Traditional Morality in America." *Rural Sociology* (Spring), 38:36–45.

Wilson, R. A. 1971. "Anomie in the Ghetto: A Study of Neighborhood Type, Race, and Anomie." *American Journal of Sociology* (July), 77:66–88.

Wirth, L. 1938. "Urbanism as a Way of Life." *American Journal of Sociology* (July), 44:3–24.

Wolfgang, M. E. 1970. "Urban Crime." In J. Q. Wilson, ed., *The Metropolitan Enigma*, pp. 270–311. Garden City, N.Y.: Doubleday.

Wolfgang, M. E. and F. Ferracuti. 1967. *The Subculture of Violence.* London: Tavistock.
Young, M. and P. Willmott. 1957. *Family and Kinship in East London.* Baltimore: Penguin.

PART TWO

Neighborhood Revitalization in the Inner City

EDITOR'S NOTE:

GALE ANALYZES RESIDENT surveys in neighborhoods that have experienced improvements. A profile of the "revitalizer's" characteristics emerges: white, young, childless, and professional. These are mostly city residents seeking low-cost housing and accessibility to the downtown. The several stages leading up to the development of new neighborhood stability are also outlined. Sumka considers the highly controversial subject of "displacing" low-income and minority residents through the revitalization process. He finds the case for widespread displacement weak though he considers the need for future monitoring of this phenomenon as essential.

4
Middle-Class Resettlement in Older Urban Neighborhoods: The Evidence and the Implications

DENNIS E. GALE

IN RECENT YEARS, a small but growing number of middle-class households have moved into declining, older central-city neighborhoods in the United States. Although a few of these areas were the sites of Urban Renewal programs, most have undergone renovation and restoration through private investment activity. The significance of this movement, termed "neighborhood resettlement" here, lies in its stark contrast to the urban-to-suburban migration patterns that have predominated in metropolitan areas at least since the 1950s. Indeed, an elaborate body of residential location theory has developed since the 1920s, much of which assumes that households "filter up" through the housing supply as their family size and economic status grow. Housing and neighborhoods, on the other hand, filter downward as increasing

Reprinted with permission from *Journal of the American Planning Association* (July 1979), vol. 45. Tables and text references to tables, omitted because of space constraints, are available from the author.

age renders both architectural styles and technological features obsolete (Lowry 1960) and these areas became econom-
ical for progressively lower income groups (Grigsby 1963).
One common result in older urban residential areas is invasion and succession, whereby households of lower socioeconomic status displace those of higher status (Duncan and
Duncan 1957). Conversely, there is evidence that in the 1970s
significant numbers of young households have filtered downward to an older housing stock and consequently, their
neighborhoods have filtered upward through a myriad of individual rehabilitations. In effect, a reverse invasion and
succession process is replacing households of lower socioeconomic circumstances with those of higher circumstances. To
be sure, such patterns are not unprecedented. Theories such
as Firey (1947), Hoover and Vernon (1959), and Birch (1971)
have identified isolated urban locations where deviations from
these norms have occurred. Research on the 1960–1970 period has shown that a few older urban neighborhoods near
central business districts experienced increases in median
family income (Lipton 1977). Many of these, however, appear
to have resulted from redevelopment (such as urban renewal)
rather than from private market investment in rehabilitation
of the existing housing stock. But growing evidence suggests
that in the 1970s the incidence of middle-class inmigration
to these types of areas has increased rather substantially.

In a survey of public officials and real estate officials in
143 cities, Black found that 48 percent of communities over
fifty thousand population had some degree of private market,
nonsubsidized housing renovation underway in older deteriorated neighborhoods (1975). Another survey, of public officials and local citizen organizations in the thirty largest U.S.
cities, discovered that resettlement was occurring in almost
all of them. Fifty-three such neighborhoods were found (Clay
1978). In a study of forty-four cities, substantial private market rehabilitation was identified in almost 75 percent (National Urban Coalition, 1978). Sixty-five resettlement neighborhoods were located.

One important key to understanding the reasons for this

apparent departure from classical precepts of residential location theory is the development of broad-based data from opinion surveys of resettlement households. Unfortunately, such comprehensive statistics do not yet exist. Nevertheless, a number of individual, separately conducted surveys have been performed recently in American resettlement neighborhoods and together their results provide some important indications as to the identity of the resettlers, their geographic origins, and the reasons for their residential location choice. These studies were conducted in Atlanta (McWilliams 1975), Boston and Cambridge (Pattison 1977), New Orleans (Ragas and Miestchovich 1977), New York (New York Landmarks Conservancy 1977), St. Paul (Urban Land Institute 1976), and Washington, D.C. (Gale 1977a, 1976).

Other evidence indicates that negative externalities occur in the form of the displacement of many low- and moderate-income households by the renovation process. Together these data form a preliminary composite description of the extent and character of neighborhood resettlement. Although the condition of this evidence does not permit more sophisticated analyses, the sheer paucity of published quantitative studies and the critical nature of the subject itself warrant the present preliminary investigation.

Demographic Characteristics of Resettlers

Data sources are sufficient to permit observations on six demographic characteristics of resettler households: household size, racial composition, annual income, and the age, education, and occupation of the household head.

Household size. With comparatively few exceptions, resettler households tend to be small. At least one-half (48 percent) in one Boston neighborhood and as many as 97 percent in an Atlanta area are composed of one or two persons. Nationwide, about one-half of all households are composed of one or two persons (U.S. Bureau of the Census, 1977a). At least 60 percent in each neighborhood have no children present. Household size in the New York neighborhood tended to be larger, though this may be attributable to the fact that it underwent resettlement several years ago.

Racial composition. With pitifully few exceptions, the resettler households were composed of whites. In a few cases, mixed households (one black and one white) appeared. In three cities white households composed between 94 and 97 percent of all resettler households. One Washington neighborhood showed a black resettler proportion of 14 percent, though blacks make up 75 percent of the city's population. By contrast, the mean proportions of whites and blacks in metropolitan central cities in the United States in 1970 were 75 and 23 percent respectively (Advisory Commission on Intergovernmental Relations, 1977).

Annual income. Neighborhoods in only four cities provided data on household income and it is not apparent whether gross or net income figures were presented. Nonetheless, the evidence confirms suspicions that resettler households generally are comfortably middle income. More than one-half (56 percent) in the Atlanta neighborhood and 88 percent in the New York area had incomes of $15,000 or more. Almost one-half (46 percent) in New Orleans reported incomes of $20,000 or more while 73 percent and 90 percent in two Washington neighborhoods had such incomes. These figures compare closely to the 49.4 percent of families nationally earning $15,000 or more in 1975, when the median family income was almost $14,900 (U.S. Bureau of the Census, 1977a).

Age. Clearly, the largest group of household heads in resettlement families tends to range in age from the mid twenties to the mid thirties. No city reported less than 40 percent in this age group. Nationally, only 20 percent of household heads fell in this range in 1976 (U.S. Bureau of the Census, 1977a). Those resettlers in the age 35 to 44 interval represent the next largest group; at least 20 percent fell in this range while nationally 16 percent did so.

Education. No other indicators are as impressive as those on the level of education achieved by resettler household heads. Most had completed at least a four-year college degree program in Atlanta (62 percent), New York (79 percent), St. Paul (80 percent), and Washington (97/86 percent). By comparison, only 14.7 percent of the U.S. population age twenty-five and older held a four-year college degree in 1976 (U.S. Bureau of the Census, 1977b). In highly competitive employment markets such as New York and Washington, where specialized graduate education is often required, 61 percent and 87 percent had achieved graduate degrees. But, even in Atlanta, a rapidly growing regional center, fully one-fourth (24 percent) of resettlers hold graduate degrees.

Occupation. Closely correlated to education is the head-of-household's occupation. More than one-half of household heads in resettlement neighborhoods in Atlanta, New York, St. Paul, Boston, and Cambridge, Massachusetts, were classified as professionals. Managerial and administrative occupations were much less in evidence in most neighborhoods, though in St. Paul 27 percent were found to fall in this category. Clerical, sales, and blue-collar employees constituted as much as 35 percent of the remaining portion. As a rough basis of comparison, 15.2 percent of U.S.-employed persons were classified as professional or technical workers in 1976 and 10.6 percent were in managerial and administrative positions (U.S. Bureau of the Census, 1977b).

Collectively, these data lend considerable weight to popular characterizations of resettlers. The most typical such household is childless and composed of one or two white adults in their late twenties or thirties. College educated, often possessing graduate education, the household head is most likely a professional or (less commonly) a manager. The annual household income varies among metropolitan areas but is likely to range between $15,000 and $30,000, with several resettlers earning more than $40,000. Doubtless, many of those earning higher incomes are composed of two workers. For the most part, the above evidence seems to be supported by more descriptive accounts of resettlement in several American cities.

Geographic Origins of Resettlers

One of the most misunderstood notions about the inner-city neighborhood resettlement phenomenon is the origin of its participants. Where are the resettlers moving from? The answer is important for obvious reasons. To the extent that the reinvestment process continues and grows, it could have a substantial effect on the future viability of central cities. The list of benefits that municipal governments derive from this process—improved housing stock, lower demands for social services, higher real estate taxes and other revenues, more affluent consumer participation in the central-city economy—are considerable.

If the resettlers were migrating in from the surrounding suburbs in sufficient numbers, they would help to offset the well-documented suburban movement of city dwellers, the bane of large-city governments for many years. In order for public officials to stimulate private market investment in older urban neighborhoods, it is important for them to understand from whence the current resettlers—and therefore, potential future resettlers—are coming.

Unfortunately, a popular wisdom has developed that refers to resettlement as the "Back-to-the-City Movement." Thus many observers have assumed, with little or no evidence, that most resettlers are dissatisfied former suburbanites.

> What is beginning to happen now in America is a flow-back of people from suburbs to inner cities. They rehabilitate old housing because it's cheaper than building new homes. Older people flow back because their children, products of the post-war baby boom, are now grown and departed. Young couples do it because they can't afford the suburbs and because they prefer the lifestyle of the cities. It's not a universal pattern and no one yet knows how far it will go. But it's on its way. (Eric Sevareid, CBS Evening News, July 8, 1977)

To the contrary, evidence indicates that a relatively small minority of households moved into resettlement neighborhoods from the city's encircling suburbs. Less than 20 percent of resettlers surveyed in Atlanta, Boston, Cambridge, and

Washington said that they had done so. In fact, more appear to have located in some cities from outside the metropolitan area altogether (that is, from communities in older parts of the United States). The data indicate that more than one-half (and in some cases as many as 90 percent) already were seasoned urbanites, having moved to the renovating area from somewhere within the city's municipal boundaries. Evidence on the previous housing type and tenure of resettling homebuyers is limited to studies of two Washington, D.C., neighborhoods. About one-half of the resettlers had moved to their current location from an apartment and two-thirds had been renters in their previous location.

If these figures are even roughly representative of resettlers in other cities, they suggest that most are first-home buyers. It is likely that they migrated to the city to attend college or graduate school or to take employment there. After working a few years, they accumulated enough capital to make a down payment on a house and were encouraged to do so by their rising incomes and favorable federal tax policies.

Not only do few resettlers appear to be exsuburbanites, there is evidence that most consciously embraced inner-city living and/or rejected a suburban location when looking for a house to purchase. In other words, few appear to have "settled" for an inner-city dwelling as a second-best alternative to a suburban home. On the contrary, other observers suggest that the life-style associated with suburban residence and/or the presumed ideology of its inhabitants is at odds with those of most resettlers.

There is a very conscious rejection of suburbia, or rather a conscious rejection of the somewhat stereotyped "image" of suburbia . . . by residents in the area, and a correspondingly positive assertion of the values of "urban living." . . . From this perspective suburbia is seen as a retreat from the reality of major social problems facing American society; and residents who . . . move from the area are defined by others and to a degree, themselves, as "selling out"—not simply a house—but an ideology and a movement. (Hunter 1975)

Resettlers in Boston contrasted themselves to suburbanites as "more interesting" and "intellectual" and less concerned with traditional status symbols such as membership in a country club: "there are very often feelings of superiority toward his or her suburban counterparts. In this sense, at least for the duration of their time in the core city, young professionals identify themselves as part of an elite within the middle-class elite" (Parkman Center for Urban Affairs, 1977:2).

Statistics from a survey of resettlers in an Atlanta neighborhood indicate that over two-thirds (69 percent) preferred a central-city, rather than a suburban, residential setting. More than one-third looked only in the study neighborhood for a home. More than one-half of the remainder (51 percent) looked only in city neighborhoods, mostly renovation areas (McWilliams 1975).

The strongly urban-oriented predilections of resettlers, at least in transitional neighborhoods, contrast sharply with their earlier experiences, if the results of the Washington surveys are representative of most resettlers nationwide (Gale 1977a, 1976). Slightly less than two-thirds (64 percent and 61 percent) in two such neighborhoods reported that they had spent all or most of their childhood years in a suburban, small-town, or rural setting. In addition, at least three-fourths (77 percent and 88 percent) spent those years living in a single-family detached house, the style most associated with suburban and suburbanlike living. This latter finding is significant because most Washington resettlers (indeed, it appears, most resettlers nationwide) live in row houses located in higher-density areas, a dwelling type more commonly linked to inner-city living. Hence, their current locational choice, although a continuation of their adult urban locational preference, represents a decided departure from their childhood experiences.

Why Did They Move to the Neighborhood?

No factor related to the resettlement phenomenon so intrigues some researchers and public officials as the explanation of why it is happening at all. Although the varied sources of the data discussed here permit only loose comparisons, it is clear that four conditions most appealed to the respondents: an acceptable housing price, the investment potential of the property, accessibility to place of employment, and the architectural/historical character of the house and/or neighborhood. Of these four, the last showed the most consistently high ratings. From 72 to 85 percent of the respondents in Atlanta, New Orleans, and New York rated architectural/historical character highly, and those in Washington valued it only slightly less so than their property's investment potential.

Generally, economic variables related to the price and the investment potential of the house and to the employment accessibility variable appear to be of approximately equal importance overall. Although individual resettlers vary in the relative weight they ascribe to each characteristic, there are few who are likely not to cite one or more as critical in their locational choice. From 42 to 70 percent of resettlers in three cities rated an acceptable housing price as among their highest concerns in locational choice; in Washington, it was comparably rated. Although data are sparse, the resettler's concern over the investment potential of his property was an even more compelling consideration than its price. Because most resettlers are purchasing their first home, it is likely that they do so with an especially critical eye to the promise of a substantial, relatively rapid, capital gain in the future.

Easy access to place of employment was a salient matter also, ranging from 39 to 70 percent in the proportion of resettlers who rated it highly in three renovation neighborhoods. Again, in Washington, results were comparable.

Washington, D.C.: A Case Study

The preceding analysis, based on findings from studies of several reinvestment neighborhoods in the United States, is an attempt to characterize demographic and attitudinal traits of resettler households. The absence of standardized survey research among a representative sampling of such neighborhoods and households renders this exercise necessary. Nevertheless, though necessary, it is not sufficient. Each study was conducted independently and therefore, the bases of comparison are limited to the topics discussed thus far. A second examination, an in-depth analysis of resettlers in the area of Washington, D.C., will yield further insights into their motivations and behavior. Of course, we cannot generalize nationwide on the basis of either approach; but together, the two investigations will provide a more comprehensive impression of the nature and character of neighborhood resettlement than the author has been able to discover anywhere in the literature.

Graduate students studying urban and regional planning conducted household surveys under the author's direction in the Mount Pleasant and Capitol Hill sections of Washington (Gale 1976, 1977a). Both neighborhoods have been experiencing resettlement and reinvestment, though the process has been underway longer on Capitol Hill. Both are composed predominantly of masonry row dwellings built in the late nineteenth and early twentieth centuries and have significant populations of black, low- and moderate-income households. The close proximity of the Capitol Hill neighborhood to employment centers such as the U.S. Congress, Library of Congress, Supreme Court, Executive Branch agencies, and ancillary private organizations has made it a popular residential setting for those who work nearby. The Mount Pleasant area, located about two miles north of the White House, has a more varied work force among its resettler residents. The Capitol Hill neighborhood has no commonly accepted boundaries and thus has spread to the northeast, east, and southeast in a fan-shaped pattern for at least one mile. Mount Pleasant, on the other hand, is tightly defined by an abutting linear park on the north and west and by wide, busily traveled streets on the east and south. It is about one-quarter mile in its horizontal and vertical axes.

New homebuyers in these areas were randomly sampled

and face-to-face interviews were completed. Generally, Washington resettler households tend to be composed of white, childless singles and couples in their late twenties or thirties. Income and educational levels are somewhat higher than among resettlers in other cities but this is due to the overwhelmingly professional, managerial, and clerical nature of the employment market in the nation's capital. At least two-thirds of resettlers in each neighborhood had moved to their current location from within the city of Washington while 54 percent of Washington movers overall had done so (Grier and Grier 1978). The proportion of resettlers moving in from outside the District of Columbia ranged from about one-fifth (Capitol Hill) to one-third (Mount Pleasant), though 15 percent and 18 percent, respectively, moved in from the city's suburbs.

The most consistently highly rated reasons for choosing to locate in Mount Pleasant and Capitol Hill were the investment potential of the house purchased, the relatively affordable price, accessibility to place of employment, and the architectural/historical character of the house and/or neighborhood. Lesser, though not insignificant, concern was shown for the social and cultural attractions of city living. The desire to live near friends who had preceded them into the resettlement area or to live in an integrated neighborhood were rarely cited reasons for the move.

Both neighborhood surveys sought insights on the reactions of resettlers to their new home and neighborhood. When asked to scale their sentiments about their dwelling unit and lot 71 percent of those in Capitol Hill rated their properties "most favorable" and 29 percent "favorable"; conversely, the Mount Pleasant sample rated theirs 37 percent "highly favorable" and 58 percent "favorable." Only negligible proportions showed neutral or unfavorable feelings. This divergence in enthusiasm was evident also in the mover's reaction to the *neighborhood*. Forty-seven percent of those on Capitol Hill were highly favorable and 50 percent were favorable. The corresponding figures for Mount Pleasantites were 23 and 61 percent respectively. Clearly, the Mount Pleasant resettlers showed less extreme feelings for their living conditions than those shown for Capitol Hill.

Similarly, when queried about the length of time they expected to remain at their current address, 29 percent of Capitol Hill movers and 14 percent of their Mount Pleasant counterparts said "10 years or longer." Thirty-four percent of the latter expected to remain less than 10 years. Indeed, the proportion of Capitol Hill respondents who had lived in that neighborhood prior to their current home purchase was three times as large as that of Mount Pleasantites who had lived previously in Mount Pleasant (52 percent versus 16 percent). Finally, when queried as to the length of time each group had lived in its current neighborhood (both current and previous residences) 57 percent of Capitol Hill and 86 percent of Mount Pleasant residents said "less than four years." Almost five times as large a proportion of the first group had lived on Capitol Hill as had the proportion for Mount Pleasant (24 percent versus 5 percent).

Another indicator of differences in level of commitment to each neighborhood was a question on future moving intentions. Forty-five percent of the Capitol Hill and 28 percent of the Mount Pleasant respondents would choose another dwelling in the same neighborhood if they decided to leave their current address. Nineteen percent of Capitol Hill and 32 percent of Mount Pleasant resettlers would move to a different neighborhood. Only five percent of each group would move to the suburbs, and the remainders were undecided or gave no response.

The differences in level of expressed enthusiasm between the two neighborhood resettler groups may be explained by the fact that Capitol Hill has been undergoing reinvestment for a considerably longer time than Mount Pleasant. To that extent, it is a more "mature" resettlement neighborhood. Therefore, those who choose to live there may be less interested in their homes as a stepping-stone to a more expensive dwelling in a more affluent area. Instead, they may have purchased homes on Capitol Hill with a commitment to remain several years. For them, living in that neighborhood appears to be an end in itself, not merely a way-station on the route to a better house and location. This could indicate that the Capitol Hill neighborhood has reached a more advanced level in the filtering-up process.

The significance of these data is their suggestion that reinvestment neighborhoods may experience gradual changes in the types of households that locate there. The reasons that they locate there, their reactions to the neighborhood and its residents, their participation and activity in citizen groups, and their willingness to exert time on behalf of efforts to improve neighborhood conditions and services may depend on the stage that the reinvestment neighborhood has reached demographically. This factor, in turn, would help to determine physical, economic, political, and social dynamics (Gale 1978b).

Further evidence to support a stage theory about the resettlement process appears in a closer analysis of the Capitol Hill area. Even within a single reinvestment neighborhood, varying phases can be identified. The study area is composed of two census tracts. The westernmost tract first experienced significant middle-class reinvestment in the late 1960s. This section is closest to the federal employment centers cited earlier. Because the reinvestment process is nearly complete and a large majority of the structures have been rehabilitated, it will be referred to here as the mature section. The other census tract, further to the east, has undergone reinvestment only since the early 1970s. It contains a substantial number of yet unrenovated buildings and its population is more varied both racially and socioeconomically than the mature section's. This tract is identified here as the transitional section. Although these census tract subsamples are too small to give statistically reliable distinctions, the consistency of their differences yields plausible support for the stage theory notion.

Generally speaking, among new homebuyers in the transitional section there were more single males, more childless households, more heads of households under age thirty-five, and more households that had been on Capitol Hill for less than three years. In addition, fewer respondents in the transitional section had "highly favorable" sentiments about their own property or their neighborhood. Too, fewer had moved to their current location from Washington's suburbs and more from other parts of Capitol Hill. However, about equal proportions of each group had been renters (two-thirds) just prior to purchasing their current dwelling. Finally, the transitional section respondents attached more importance to the sales price of their dwelling in making their locational choice; more felt that it was less costly than other altnernatives. For those in the mature section, sales price (even though generally higher) was less significant.

When asked how long they expected to live at their current address, resettlers in the transitional section clearly were less committed than those in the mature section to long-term residency. The latter group showed much less indecision about this matter and far more willingness to remain as much as ten years. Similarly, if transitional section respondents were to move in the future, they were less interested in remaining on Capitol Hill and more interested in moving to another area in the city than those in the mature section.

The comparisons between Mount Pleasant and Capitol Hill and those within Capitol Hill itself suggest several tentative conclusions about the phases through which a resettlement neighborhood is likely to progress. In the earliest stage resettlers tend to be younger, single males purchasing their first dwelling. Prior to this, they are likely to have been renters and to have lived in the central city, though not usually in the resettlement neighborhood itself. Rarely have they moved in from the suburbs.

They place great importance on the affordability of their house's purchase price and on its potential for future appreciaton in value. Being male, childless, and relatively young, they are able to take greater risks than other household types. Hence, they buy in deteriorated, predominately moderate- and lower-income areas where crime rates and "aggravations" are higher than city-wide averages. In exchange, they receive high accessibility to various goods and services, quaint architectural and historical surroundings, and ultimately sharp financial gains. These households, the most typical in stage one of the resettlement process, are characterized most fully by their willingness to accept a substantial degree of risk (Clay 1978; Pattison 1977). In effect, most have "less to lose" than those resettlers who characterize stage two.

On the other hand, stage two households seem less willing to take these risks. More single and married women are likely to appear, and households with children are more common. Heads of households tend to be somewhat older and more are former suburban families. By the time these families arrive, significant physical and demographic changes have occurred and the resettlement neighborhood reveals a strong middle-class influence. Consequently, they show greater enthusiasm for the area and more commitment to its future livability. They could afford to purchase a home in several parts of the metropolitan area and, therefore, their house's price is not as important a locational constraint as is the price for stage one resettlers.

Stage one resettlers are less committed to long-term residency in their current dwelling and show more indecision about the length of their stay than those in later stages. Also, fewer are likely to move to another dwelling in the same neighborhood in the future. They show more interest in relocating to another neighborhood in the city.

Thus far, the demographic characteristics of resettlers and their attitudes toward their neighborhood have been discussed. But what about their reactions to specific conditions in their new location?

Respondents in both Capitol Hill and Mount Pleasant identified several disagreeable conditions which they had experienced in their neighborhoods. Inadequate public schools and public play space, and insufficient curbside parking space for automobiles were cited by some. Others mentioned excessive traffic in the neighborhood, high property taxes, and poor trash collection. However, "excessive crime problems" was the most commonly identified drawback in both neighborhoods. Similarly, when asked if any condition could cause them to move out of the neighborhood in the future, they mentioned excessive crime activities most frequently. More than half the respondents said that a member of their household had been the victim of at least one crime incident or threatening gesture occurring in the neighborhood. Several related two or more incidents. Most of these involved burglary or vandalism to property. Very few circumstances leading to assaults on the person occurred. Incidents involving harsh words, harassment, or threatening gestures were not unusual, however. Most of these resulted between white resettlers and younger black residents. Most of the latter appeared to be passers-through in the neighborhood and not residents.

However, when interviewed on interracial behavior in the Capitol Hill neighborhood, 92 percent of the respondents said that conflict seldom occurred or happened only occasionally. Almost one-half (48 percent) of Capitol Hill interviewees said that they hoped that the neighborhood would stabilize in a racial composition that was 50 percent white and 50 percent black. About one-fourth hoped for a predominantly white population, with a minority of blacks. Almost none wanted an all-white, all-black, or largely black residency. Not insignificantly, one-fifth gave no response, suggesting perhaps the sensitive nature of this subject.

Implications for Theory

These data, though limited geographically, are important for the light they shed on the complex of factors that enter into the resettler's locational decision. Unfortunately, the few published attempts at this subject have been confined to arguments based largely on economic assumptions. For example, one observer claims that rapidly rising suburban prices for new homes, due to inflation in labor, materials, and financing costs, and to restrictive growth controls, have "forced many homebuyers with limited economic means to stay in cities" (James 1978). As the evidence previously cited indicates, though, most resettlers eschew suburban living, not for economic reasons, but due to matters of taste related to their life-styles. And, because few have children, most such households are not compelled to leave the cities to seek better public education. The absence of children and the high incidence of two-worker households increase family per-capita income and, if anything, render many suburban housing opportunities quite affordable. Clearly, most resettlers' urban locational choices are their first preferences and not a "second-best" alternative to suburban living.

Another researcher presents an interesting theoretical "model" to explain resettler behavior and concludes that two variables predominate: the number of household workers and household size (Yezer 1977). He argues that in many resettler households both husband and wife are employed. Hence, commuting costs are considerably higher. Therefore, it becomes economically rational to minimize commuting costs by living close to the central business district employment center. This argument, though plausible, ignores the fact that with two breadwinners, household income also rises. It is likely that this condition will overcome most increases in commuting costs and hence, two-worker resettler households will have great flexibility of locational choice within the metropolitan area.

The second variable, household size, is somewhat more helpful in contributing to an explanation of the resettler's locational choice. It is claimed that because most such households are childless and therefore need less dwelling and yard space, they act rationally in choosing the generally smaller properties available in older urban neighborhoods. Of course, it could be argued that many inner-city homes are, in fact, quite spacious when compared to new suburban dwellings. Built in the nineteenth century when larger numbers of children and extended families were de rigueur, many of these properties compete quite well with all but the most affluent suburban subdivision homes. It is true, however, that inner-city yard space is not likely to be as large. This argument aside, it is apparent that young singles and couples without children do have the option of reducing housing costs by purchasing less space. Therefore, the resettler's locational preference is economically rational (Gale 1977a).

Residential location models based on economic rationale provide a critically important theoretical framework for understanding metropolitan development patterns. Most such constructs, however, have assumed that it is economically rational behavior for younger middle-income households to move outward from the central business district to progressively more affluent neighborhoods as they pass through a conventional life-cycle (Hoover and Vernon 1959). In doing so, they make a choice to trade off greater commuting distance (that is, time and expense) for more living space, as well as a better "package" of public services. Generally, the models presuppose that these households will aspire to new housing and neighborhoods, leaving behind older areas as soon as economic circumstances permit (Birch 1971). Yet, as Firey demonstrated in the 1940s, many locational choices ignore these attractions (1947). Instead, they place an economic value on the cultural, historical, or architectural character of an area, as well as accessibility to the central business district. Consequently, small, centralized enclaves of older, well-maintained housing such as Boston's Beacon Hill or New York City's Grammercy Park have survived the "normal" deterioration process that accompanies architectural and technological obsolescence. The neighborhood resettlement phenomenon of the 1970s demonstrates a significant growth in this ethic. It is expressed in rising sales prices in neighborhoods where property values previously remained stagnant or declined. To the extent that this reinvestment process continues to burgeon, it will require planners and model-builders to reinterpret the filtering-up process, so as to include alternative economic choices based on architectural, historical, cultural, and accessibility values. The use of opinion survey data in conjunction with studies of economic indicators such as property value trends (Meadows and Call 1978) should help to explain the resettlement phenomenon and give insights into its future.

The Displacement Dilemma

Neighborhood resettlement gives prima facie evidence of providing myriad benefits to local governments at very little cost. Improvement of the housing stock, increased real estate taxes and other revenues, reduced demand for social welfare services, lower serious crime rates, diminished neighborhood population densities, higher homeownership rates, and reduced enrollment pressures on neighborhood schools are all probable outcomes of middle-class reinvestment in many older urban neighborhoods. Yet, it is apparent from mass media accounts and protests by neighborhood organizations that the rate at which disadvantaged households are being involuntarily displaced has increased significantly in recent years.

Typically, dislocation results when rapid reinvestment in formerly declining neighborhoods stimulates inflation in property values, causing rents and property taxes to rise and evictions for renovation to increase. Because most neighborhood resettlement is the result of private market investment activities and not a publicly controlled program such as urban renewal, the displacement impact is considerably more difficult to evaluate than it was when relocation programs were available to monitor and subsidize the process. The Uniform Relocation Assistance Act of 1970 does not provide for those uprooted by private rehabilitation efforts. Hence, the few dislocation relief programs that exist have been developed by local governments (Gale 1978 a, b).

Evidence on the magnitude and dimensions of displacement, especially by private market forces, is not yet in very precise form. One survey of realtors, public officials, and civic leaders in the thirty largest cities has concluded that significant dislocation was occurring in 82 percent of the neighborhoods undergoing middle-class renovation (Clay 1978). An analysis of R. L. Polk Company data and other sources estimated that in no community were more than one to two hundred households being displaced annually by private market forces except for a few cities such as Washington, D.C., and San Francisco (Grier and Grier 1978). The U.S. Department of Housing and Urban Development studied unpublished tabulations of the 1974–1976 Annual Housing Surveys and estimated that the annual number of metropolitan households displaced by public and private actions ranged from 364,000 to 373,000. These households constituted slightly less than four percent of the total population of movers in each year. The highest proportion of those displaced among all movers occurred in the northeastern region of the United States (4.3 percent) and the lowest, in the West (3.8 percent). Unfortunately, these data do not include moves due to rental increases, a major impetus in many household displacements (Cousar 1978).

The racial implications of resettlement were examined in a survey of local observers in forty-four cities by the National Urban Coalition (1978). About one-half of neighborhoods undergoing renovation were thought to have lost minority group members since resettlement began and about one-third experienced no change. Thirteen percent were thought to have had an increase. An analysis of a resettlement area in Alexandria, Virginia, projected an average decline in black housing occupancy of 85 households per year between 1975 and 1980. Many of these would be at or near retirement age (Hammer, Siler, George Associates, 1976).

Other neighborhood surveys have touched on the social effects of displacement but have been inconclusive about the costs of replacement housing for rental dislocatees. Estimates in a renovation neighborhood in St. Louis (Hu 1978) and in New Orleans (Ragas and Miestchovich 1977) concluded that about one-half of renovated homes in each had been vacant prior to renovation. Both implied that evictions for reinvestment purposes in these units do not appear to have occurred. Hu found that nearly all owner-households leaving the renovation area did so because of life-cycle factors related to "old age, illness, and family problems." However, his study could not determine the reasons for which renters left the area. Ragas and Miestchovich discovered that most outmigrating households had little difficulty locating another nearby rental unit of comparable quality and size but may have had to pay a higher rent. They concluded that about fifty to sixty persons were displaced in the neighborhoods each year.

Collectively, these studies suggest that the involuntary movement of households, usually low- or moderate-income ones, in response to private market rehabilitation of neighborhoods has grown significantly in the 1970s. Blacks and other minorities, as well as the elderly, appear to be disproportionately affected. Yet, there is little evidence that, except for a few cities, dislocation directly affects a very large number of households per year. Where middle-class rehabilitation proceeds at a moderate pace and where the vacancy rate in the existing housing stock approximates national averages, the impact of resettlement is likely to be modest. Nonetheless, it will be important, on both political and humanitarian grounds, for local governments to monitor the reinvestment process carefully. Where the social costs become excessive, planners and public officials should be prepared to respond with effective measures to mitigate the rate and intensity of displacement.

Implications for Policy

The primary significance of the present review is in its implications for urban planners and policy professionals concerned with central-city revitalization. First, it is clear that there has been a small but growing market among middle-class households in many urban areas for housing in older neighborhoods. However, it probably does not compose more than 25 percent of potential first-homebuyers in the twenties and thirties age groups currently living in central cities. Second, there is proportionately a much smaller market among suburbanites for such housing. In part, this may be due to poor information about inner-city housing opportunities and liabilities.

Third, those factors that most attract resettlers to buy an older dwelling—sales price and investment *potential*—obviously are least susceptible to manipulation by planners and public officials. Only the architectural and historical character of housing and neighborhoods and employment accessibility offer possibilities for policy intervention. Thus, preservation of such neighborhoods, adaptive reuse of older structures, careful blending of new and existing architecture, and improved public services and facilities may be the most promising programmatic activities for central-city planners. Just as important, although somewhat more difficult, is the attraction of new employment opportunities to the city and especially to the central business district. Unfortunately, neighborhood revitalization and economic development activities have sometimes been in conflict. This occurs when attractive older buildings in the CBD or in adjacent neighborhoods are demolished for higher density uses such as office, commercial, or industrial activities. Attracting both neighborhood revitalization and new employment generation, while achieving a proper balance between the two, continues to be one of the most compelling, yet difficult, challenges facing planners in the future.

A fourth implication of the present research is in the notion of a stage theory of resettlement. Certainly, the observations herein are tentative at present; yet, the logic of such a theory seems highly plausible. It suggests that neighborhood resettlement takes place in increments and that overlapping but relatively distinct demographic subgroups may enter such neighborhoods at different phases during the reinvestment process. Planners and policy makers, therefore, may want to view this as a kind of reverse filtering process. Hence, any strategy to attract middle-income households to older neighborhoods would concentrate first on younger singles and childless couples. Efforts to improve property values, such as historic districts and zoning, code enforcement, and public improvements, seem most appropriate at stage one.

However, efforts to attract families with children and those with long-term commitment to the neighborhood will encompass not only these, but other activities as well. Active and well-supported neighborhood advisory organizations are needed to encourage advocacy and political impact. The quality of public services—but especially education and crime control—will have to be enhanced. It seems apparent that any local government with a serious commitment to attracting and holding stage-two households will have to be able to compete with the quality of these services in at least some of the surrounding municipalities.

Nonetheless, the disruptive effects of resettlement on some low- and moderate-income households cannot be ignored, either. Two roles for planners are suggested. First, efforts should be made to monitor the extent and severity of displacement of low- and moderate-income households, especially renters, due to private reinvestment activity (Houstoun 1976). Second, where dislocation rates become excessive, displacement relief programs should be implemented (Gale 1978b; Weiler 1978). Certainly, some displaced households should be assigned a high priority for existing and future publicly subsidized units in programs such as Community Development Block Grants, section 8 and section 312.

Finally, thus far the present analysis has failed to ask, What happens to those central-city neighborhoods from which households migrate in order to settle in reinvestment areas? Will they decline? No evidence has been found by the author to suggest that the resettlement phenomenon is "robbing Peter to pay Paul." Most resettlers appear to have been renters prior to buying a home in an older neighborhood. They appear to be exercising normal life-cycle options in acquiring a first dwelling in their late twenties and thirties. In previous decades most would have purchased in the suburbs or in a more affluent neighborhood in the city. Meanwhile new renters, it would seem, move into the resettler's previous neighborhoods, replacing them. In other words, the resettlement phenomenon would seem not to affect these rental areas either positively or negatively. Admittedly, however, the position is only conjecture and more substantive comment will have to await further empirical research.

The Future of Neighborhood Resettlement

Thus far this discussion has been limited to the current extent and character of neighborhood resettlement in the United

States. What is the likelihood that this phenomenon will continue at the same rate or, perhaps, increase in the future? As the previous data indicate, most resettler households are composed of one or two members. Very few have children present and recent national statistics indicate that the number and proportion of these types of households have increased and are likely to continue doing so. The number of one-person households grew 29 percent between 1970 and 1975 while two-person households rose 19 percent. These two groups now comprise almost one-half of all U.S. households (U.S. Bureau of the Census, 1977a). The incidences of other demographic conditions such as the postponement of marriage and of childbearing, divorce rates, and cohabitation of unmarried couples have increased significantly in the 1970s (Population Reference Bureau, 1977). Many observers foresee a general continuation of these trends into the 1980s (Alonso 1977; Goetze 1976).

National demographic trends, however, present only one dimension of the possible future of neighborhood resettlement. Decline or growth in white-collar employment in central cities, the impact of urban real estate taxes and other exactions, and the extent and character of criminal activity will also influence this recently emergent phenomenon. The extent to which it can reach beyond young singles and couples and attract families with children is related primarily to the future quality of inner-city public education. At the present time, though, it is clear that resettlement is limited largely to childless households whose life-styles embrace careerism and consumerism rather than "familism" (Johnston 1972). Because increasing numbers of these persons are postponing childbearing or are having smaller families, they have more income and time to devote to other pursuits. It is not apparent from the present analysis that neighborhood resettlement, *in vacuo*, can reverse the tide of net outmigration from central cities to suburbs, which has continued since the post-war era. But it is reasonable to suspect that this movement, an anomaly in metropolitan residential mobility patterns, will continue to grow in most central cities in the ensuing decade. To that extent, then, it could help to mitigate some of the debilitating effects of suburban magnetism.

References

Advisory Commission on Intergovernmental Relations. 1977. *Trends in Metropolitan America.* Washington, D.C.

Alonso, 1977. *The Population Factor and Urban Structure.* Cambridge, Mass.: Center for Population Studies, Harvard University, Working paper no. 102.

Birch, D. L. 1971. "Toward a State Theory of Urban Growth." *Journal of the American Institute of Planners* (March), 37:78–87.

Black, J. T. 1975. "Private-Market Housing Renovation in Central Cities: A ULI Survey." *Urban Land* (November), 34:3–9.

Clay, P. L. 1978. *Neighborhood Revitalization: Issues, Trends, and Strategies.* Cambridge, Mass.: M.I.T., Department of Urban Studies and Planning.

Cousar, G. J. 1978. "Bulletin on HUD Estimates of National Displacement and Pertinent Program Information." Mimeographed, Washington, D.C.: U.S. Department of Housing and Urban Development.

Duncan, O. D. and B. Duncan. 1957. *The Negro Population of Chicago.* Chicago: The University of Chicago Press.

Firey, W. 1947. *Land Use in Central Boston.* Cambridge, Mass.: Harvard University Press.

Gale, D. E. 1976. "The Back-to-the-City Movement . . . Or Is It?: A Survey of Recent Homeowners in the Mount Pleasant Neighborhood of Washington, D.C." Occasional paper, Washington, D.C.: George Washington University, Department of Urban and Regional Planning.

—— 1977a. "The Back-to-the-City Movement Revisited: A Survey of Recent Homebuyers in the Capitol Hill Neighborhood of Washington, D.C." Occasional paper, Washington, D.C.: George Washington University, Department of Urban and Regional Planning.

—— 1977b. "The Unpredictable Reasons for Inner-City Living." *The Washington Post* (August 6), p. A17.

—— 1978a. "Dislocation of Residents." *Journal of Housing* (May), 35:232–235.

—— 1978b. "Neighborhood Resettlement and Displacement: People and Policies." Occasional paper, Washington, D.C.: George Washington University, Department of Urbans and Regional Planning.

Goetze, R. 1976. *Building Neighborhood Confidence.* Cambridge, Mass.: Ballinger.

Grier, G. and E. Grier. 1978. *Urban Displacement: A Reconnaissance.* Washington, D.C.: U.S. Department of Housing and Urban Development.

Grigsby, William G. 1963. *Housing Markets and Public Policy*. Philadelphia: University of Pennsylvania Press.

Hammer, Siler, George Associates. 1976. *Final N.E.A. Study Report to the City of Alexandria, Virginia*. Mimeographed, Alexandria, Va.: City of Alexandria.

Hoover, E. M. and R. Vernon. 1959. *Anatomy of a Metropolis*. Cambridge, Mass.: Harvard University Press.

Houstoun, L. O., Jr. 1976. "Neighborhood Change and City Policy." *Urban Land* (July–August), 35:3–9.

Hu, J. 1978. "Who's Moving In and Who's Moving Out—And Why." *Seller/Servicer* (May–June), 5:19–29.

Hunter, A. 1975. "The Loss of Community: An Empirical Test Through Replication." *American Sociological Review* (October), 40:537–558.

James, F. J. 1978. *The Revitalization of Older Urban Neighborhoods: Trends, Forces and the Future of Cities*. Washington, D.C.: The Urban Institute.

Johnston, R. J. 1972. *Urban Residential Patterns*. New York: Praeger.

Lipton, S. 1977. "Evidence of Central City Revival." *Journal of the American Institute of Planners* (April), 43:136–147.

Lowry, I. 1960. "Filtering and Housing Standards: A Conceptual Analysis." *Land Economics* (November), 36:362–370.

McWilliams, S. W. 1975. "Recycling a Declining Community: Middle Class Migration to Virginia-Highlands." Thesis, Georgia State University.

Meadows, G. R. and S. T. Call. 1978. "Combining Housing Market Trends and Resident Attitudes in Planning Urban Revitalization." *Journal of the American Institute of Planners* (July), 44:297–305.

National Urban Coalition. 1978. *Displacement: City Neighborhoods in Transition*. Washington, D.C.

New York Landmarks Conservancy. 1977. *Impacts of Historic District Designation*. New York.

Parkman Center for Urban Affairs. 1977. *Young Professionals and City Neighborhoods*. Boston: City of Boston.

Pattison, T. 1977. "The Process of Neighborhood Upgrading and Gentrification." Thesis, Cambridge, Mass.: M.I.T., Department of City Planning.

Population Reference Bureau. 1977. *Marrying, Divorcing and Living Together*. Population Bulletin (October), 32:1–41.

Ragas, W. R. and I. Miestchovich. 1977. *Summary Analysis of Households in the Lower Garden District*. New Orleans: University of New Orleans, Urban Studies Institute.

Urban Land Institute. 1976. *Private Market Housing Renovation: A Case Study of the Hill District of St. Paul*. Washington, D.C.

U.S. Bureau of the Census. 1977a. *Household and Family Characteristics, 1976*. Series P-20, no. 311, Washington, D.C.: GPO.

—— 1977b. *Population Characteristics, 1976*. Series P-20, no. 307, Washington, D.C.: GPO.

Weiler, C. 1978. *Handbook on Reinvestment Displacement*. Washington, D.C.: National Association of Neighborhoods.

Yezer, A. 1977. "Living Patterns: Why People Move into the Inner City." *The Washington Post* (June 25), p. A17.

5
Neighborhood Revitalization and Displacement: A Review of the Evidence

HOWARD J. SUMKA

IN THE PAST twenty-five years, few issues have presented so great a challenge to urban policy makers as the decline of the nation's central cities. During this period, large numbers of middle- and upper-income families chose to live in suburban communities. In large part, these trends reflect household preferences for the amenities of suburban life and the relatively low cost of land on the suburban perimeter. For many families the suburban dream was realized because of favorable mortgage terms offered by Federal Housing Administration and Veterans Administration programs. Similarly, the transportation cost associated with locating in suburban communities was greatly reduced by the construction of interstate highways under the National Defense Highway Act of 1954. Great new swaths of freeways through and around central cities carried suburban commuters to and from jobs in the urban core.

At the same time, suburban communities restricted entry

Reprinted with permission from *Journal of the American Planning Association* (October 1979), vol. 45.

to a relatively homogeneous class of "acceptable" neighbors through a variety of exclusionary techniques. These practices included restrictive zoning or building codes and concerted efforts to discourage, and in some cases to prohibit, the construction of subsidized housing under various federal housing programs. Augmented by outright racial discrimination, these restrictions helped to broaden the rift between the central city and its suburbs. As a result, the typical metropolitan area has become characterized by serious disparities in the distribution of public needs and resources among independent political jurisdictions.

Despite evidence that these trends are continuing, there are signs that considerable neighborhood revitalization is occurring in cities across the country. While one cannot conclude yet that this foreshadows a reversal of urban decline, a new sense of activity seems to be animating numerous neighborhoods in a variety of city types. To the extent that such activity is widespread, it offers some hope that cities may be beginning to attract and hold middle- and upper-income households which, in turn, may help to achieve such long-standing urban goals as improving the housing stock, increasing the tax base, attracting jobs and commercial activity, and improving the quality of services.

The potential for widespread revitalization, however, raises questions regarding who will bear the associated costs. Numerous observers of the urban scene argue that revitalization activity has caused the involuntary dislocation of lower-income residents from their neighborhoods. The result, it is claimed, is that the people who are least able to control their own destinies, those who have fewest choices, are being victimized by a phenomenon that benefits the middle classes.

Urban displacement has thus captured the attention of the popular press and prompted calls for new policies to help lower-income families remain in the revitalizing neighborhoods. A front-page article in the *New York Times* (Reinhold 1977) sharply contrasted the situation of a young professional couple who had purchased a home to rehabilitate in the Adams-Morgan neighborhood of Washington with the plight of a poor black woman and her young daughter, soon to be evicted from an $85-per-month apartment in the same neighborhood. Less than a month later, a *Times* editorial urged that federal and local programs be redirected toward minimizing the unanticipated side effects of the "miracle of revival in older city neighborhoods" (*New York Times* 1977). In the *Boston Globe,* an op-ed column highlighting price pressures in the North End expressed the fear that the neighborhood "will one day be Italian in flavor only" (Hartnett 1977). A follow-up editorial argued that to discourage reinvestment would be counterproductive, but that some federal assistance to help stabilize housing costs for low-income North Enders would be appropriate. It also noted that the acceptance of federal assistance would require residents to open their neighborhood to the "poor of other races" who had heretofore been excluded (*Boston Globe* 1977). One of the strongest antirevitalization pieces (Travis 1978) cast the image of hordes of middle-class whites converging on minority neighborhoods to reclaim "the prime land in the central areas of many of the nation's oldest cities." In contrast, the *Washington Star* (1978) acknowledged that "nothing is without its cost," but stated that the revitalization trend should be viewed at least as much as a "promise" as it is a "threat."

Although displacement has received much attention, remarkably little systematic knowledge exists about its magnitude or its effects on dislocated populations. Metropolitan-specific data on these questions are sparse, and national data are almost nonexistent. We have largely impressionistic views that are based on case studies of individual neighborhoods and affected by the biases of particular observers. This paper reviews this body of evidence with the intent of placing some perspective on the growing national debate and of assessing precisely what is and is not known about the displacement phenomenon.[1]

Trends in Urban Population Movement
and Neighborhood Revitalization

Extent of Revitalization

Despite the increasing evidence of reinvestment activity in cities throughout the country, national and metropolitan-specific data indicate that the central-city outmigration of 1950–1969 has continued through the first half of this decade. During the five-year period ending in 1975, net migration flows resulted in the loss of seven million people from central cities, with nearly six million of them moving to the suburbs and the remainder to nonmetropolitan areas (U.S. Department of Housing and Urban Development, 1978). Central cities, which contained nearly 39 percent of the U.S. population in 1950, housed less than 32 percent in 1970 and less than 30 percent in 1975 (Sternlieb and Hughes 1977). Central-city decline is particularly evident in the Northeast and North Central regions, which are victims of the recent Sunbelt development phenomenon (Sternlieb and Hughes 1977).

A recent detailed analysis of the intrametropolitan mobility in eleven large SMSAs presents further evidence that inner-city reinvestment has failed to produce a significant back-to-the-city movement (Nelson 1978). Although there is some evidence of increased central-city immigration among whites, especially among cohorts aged twenty to thirty-four, "the conclusion that central cities are becoming more attractive to whites is not supported by . . . other measures" (Nelson 1978:19). With the exception of Los Angeles, the net migration flow of whites continues to be from the central city to the suburbs. At the same time, the number of blacks migrating to central cities has been declining. Further, blacks moving to the suburbs from the central city tend to be upper-income, suggesting that this movement was more "a matter of choice rather than a result of displacement" (Nelson 1978:28). Given the apparent tendency for both blacks and whites to be moving out of the central city, "abandonment and lack of demand for central city housing units would appear to be a more pressing problem than displacement in the near future" (Nelson 1978:28).

These analyses pointedly suggest that the spontaneous revitalization of central cities is not yet imminent and that the problems of disinvestment and local fiscal imbalance are likely to persist through the near future.[2] In important ways, however, they do not directly address the displacement issue. A statistically obvious back-to-the-city movement is not a necessary precondition for the existence of displacement. Because of the geographical segmentation of urban housing markets, population trends that cannot be deciphered statistically at the city level may have severe impacts on specific central-city neighborhoods. Whether the movement is of returnees to the city or of households who elect to stay in the city rather than move to the suburbs, a trend that is small relative to the city population may in fact be substantial relative to the size of one or more particularly attractive neighborhoods.

Indeed, a growing body of evidence suggests that neighborhood renovation is occurring with increasing frequency across the country. A 1975 survey of local housing and planning officials conducted by the Urban Land Institute (ULI) documented such activity in nearly half the central cities with populations over fifty thousand (Black 1975). While that study was not designed to produce statistically reliable estimates of the extent of rehabilitation, it estimated that the total number of units undergoing renovation may be as high as fifty thousand dwellings. A similar survey of forty-four cities by the National Urban Coalition (1978) found widespread evidence of housing rehabilitation, regardless of city size or geographic location. Among the thirty largest central cities, Clay (1978) found evidence of revitalization in more than one hundred neighborhoods.

Despite the important insights provided by these surveys, they suffer from potential problems of unrepresentativeness. Each of these studies relied on a similar mail survey technique. Local officials were asked to supply information on the extent of private renovation in their cities, including the number, type, and location of houses being rehabilitated and the characteristics of the renovators. The ULI survey was mailed to 260 cities with populations of fifty thousand or more. The overall response rate of 55 percent ranged from 30 percent in the smaller cities to about 96 percent in the cities of more than 250,000 people. The Urban Coalition survey had a higher response rate, primarily because it was directed only to those cities where the coalition has local affiliates, associates, or other contacts.

More importantly, these survey techniques provide no assurance that the responses are consistent or reliable. The extent of rehabilitation reported by various respondents likely ranged from off-the-cuff estimates to hard data taken from systematic searches of building permit or other files. Apart from an effort to ascertain the characteristics of the pre- and post-rehabilitation occupants of the units, no attempt was made to determine the displacement effects of the renovation.

A systematic study of national statistics by Franklin James (1977) uncovered more conclusive evidence of heightened renovation activity in central cities. His findings were based on changes in house values and rents, in homeownership rates, and in home-improvement expenditures by central-city residents. Gregory Lipton (1977) measured inner-city revival in terms of the socioeconomic status of census tracts. The extent of revitalization in a city was indicated by the number of tracts within two miles of the central business district (CBD) in which the average income or educational level was above that for the entire SMSA. Among the twenty largest metropolitan areas, three (New York, Washington, and Boston) showed definite improvement from 1960 to 1970. Inner-city decline or stagnation was indicated in seven areas. While Lipton's work did not focus on displacement per se, two important conclusions were reached. First, revitalization is most evident in cities where a large portion of the employment base is in administrative or other white-collar jobs and where the CBD is far from outlying suburban areas. Second, a detailed analysis of San Francisco indicated that tracts contain a great deal of internal diversity; often they are the homes of both the very wealthy and of the poor who live in subsidized housing.

In addition to these multicity studies, a growing volume of anecdotal evidence and impressionistic accounts testify to increased renovation activity across the country. While these case studies are noncomparable and provide no basis for quantitative generalizations, the totality of the evidence indicates clearly that something is occcurring in many urban areas and, therefore, that the potential for displacement is widespread.

Cause and Location of Revitalization Activity

Some insights into the causes of spontaneous regeneration are provided by recent studies that have documented the characteristics of neighborhood inmovers. The overwhelming consensus is that the parents of revitalization are the children of the postwar baby boom, who entered the housing market at a time when the volume of new construction was low and the price of suburban housing very high (James 1977; Goetze et al. 1977). Not surprisingly, then, the revitalization of inner-city neighborhoods is the result of macro trends in housing-market economics and in demographic and life-style changes. Newcomers tend to be relatively affluent professionals between ages twenty-five and forty-four who live in childless households (Black 1975; Gale 1976; and Pattison 1977). In general, they can be classified according to the stage of revitalization at which they entered the neighborhood. Early entrants tend to be "risk oblivious," they are followed by the "risk takers" and, finally, by the "risk averse" (Pattison 1977:170). This suggests the possibility that the revitalization movement may persist only until these classes of homebuyers have been depleted.

Unfortunately, the literature provides little basis for predicting the locus of rehabilitation and thereby anticipating where displacement may occur. In the past, neighborhood research has concentrated on neighborhood decline, which is the result of normal market process (Hoover and Vernon 1959;

Public Affairs Counseling, 1975). As the housing stock aged and transportation and communications technology expanded metropolitan boundaries, upper-income households moved farther out of the city, leaving behind older, sometimes obsolete housing for lower-income migrants to the city. The spontaneous regeneration of these neighborhoods was, with a few notable exceptions, unheard of. As a result, virtually no theoretical or empirical research has attempted to explain systematically the revitalization process.

Renovation activity is apparently underway in a wide range of neighborhood and city types (Rogg 1977). In general, it appears to be more likely to occur in larger cities and in older cities in the Northeast and the South (Black 1975:6). Neighborhoods that have some intrinsic attractiveness—based on their proximity to downtown or other major focal points of activity or on the inherent value of the housing stock, no matter how deteriorated—are the prime candidates for renovation (Shur in U.S. Senate, 1977; National Urban Coalition, 1978:16).

Based primarily on a case study of Washington's Capitol Hill, James identified three more or less distinct geographic segments in revitalizing areas—the neighborhood core, the inner ring, and the outer ring (James 1977:125). The core area of Capitol Hill was almost completely revitalized between 1960 and 1970; by the end of that decade, restoration activity had spread to the inner ring around the core. In the outer ring area of Capitol Hill, neighborhood rehabilitation had not yet begun by 1975. This suggests that revitalization tends to concentrate in well-defined areas and to spread outward, rather than to occur in a scatter-shot fashion.[3]

Neighborhood Displacement:
The Empirical Evidence

Displacement is the most difficult aspect of revitalization to examine systematically. Although there have been some more or less careful studies of the extent, location, and processs of revitalization per se, the literature is virtually devoid of comparably insightful studies of displacement.[4] Yet, with an understanding of the process and dynamics of neighborhood revitalization, it may be possible to predict fairly accurately the areas where displacement is likely to be a future problem. The extent of revitalization and the geographic area it embraces can provide an indication of the potential seriousness of the displacement problem.[5] Equally important, however, is an understanding of the pattern of property transactions and price movements within revitalizing areas.

Although the process is likely to vary from one community to another, certain consistent patterns have been observed in many areas. The most dramatic evidence of displacement occurs when real estate speculators begin acquiring rental properties in areas they believe will soon become attractive to middle- to upper-income households. Speculative activity leads to the rapid turnover of recently obtained properties. A study of property transactions in Washington documented that 20 percent of the properties sold over a two-year period were sold more than once. Of these multiple sales, the great majority occurred within ten months of each other (cited in Goldfield and Hedeman 1978).

As speculators move into an area, the first to be affected are resident renters. Although actual renovation may not occur for several years, developers and speculators have no incentive to retain current tenants, even on an interim basis. Using New York City as an example, Schur (in U.S. Senate, 1977:49) argues that this occurs for a variety of reasons: current rents are too low even to cover operating and maintenance costs; the existence of housing code violations creates the possibility of legal action or rent strikes; and it is easier to dispose of the property if it is vacant.

Then as neighborhood revitalization proceeds, owner-occupants are likely to be affected. While no systematic research can be cited regarding the displacement of homeowners, two mechanisms are likely to operate. Presented with seemingly good offers, owners may sell too eagerly and rapidly, thinking that the neighborhood is still in decline. By not realizing the true value of their property, these home-owners may find it difficult to purchase housing other than in areas similar to their old neighborhoods. Second, as the neighborhood becomes more attractive to middle- and upper-income households, the surge in property values will corre-spondingly drive up tax assessments. This may serve to drive out owner-occupants whose incomes cannot cover the in-creased costs. Low-income elderly homeowners are particu-larly susceptible to being forced out for this reason. It should be noted, however, that the property tax burden of elderly homeowners is pervasive and has received considerable at-tention. Many states have enacted so-called "circuit breaker" or "homestead exemption" laws which substantially reduce the property tax liability of these families. Although not de-signed to avoid displacement per se, their application re-duces one problem of elderly homeowners in neighborhoods undergoing revitalization.[6]

Empirical Evidence of Displacement

Empirical studies of neighborhood revitalization raise more questions about displacement than they answer; at best they suggest hypotheses for further research. As noted ear-lier, the empirical research to date has focused primarily on revitalization, not its secondary effects. Second, the analysis of displacement raises difficult conceptual and measurement issues that no one has addressed systematically. Finally, the implementation of a displacement study is costly, time-consuming, and fraught with pitfalls, primarily because of the difficulty of tracing and locating movers.

However, relying on data from the Annual Housing Sur-vey, Cousar (1978) estimated that during the 1974–1976 pe-riod, over half a million households per year were displaced, about two-thirds being metropolitan households. To place this figure in perspective, it should be noted that the number of displacement moves did not exceed 4 percent of all moves in any of the years included in the study. More significantly, the data are subject to serious potential biases of an indetermin-able direction. For example, moves due to rent increases are excluded, although in some cases such increases may be the result of revitalization activity. On the other hand, evictions, which were categorized as displacement moves, may be the result of factors totally unrelated to revitalization.

A recent study by Grier and Grier (1978) offers some evidence that, in numerical terms at least, displacement due to spontaneous revitalization may be a smaller problem than is commonly believed. Although their reconnaissance of selected cities was not based on scientific sampling techniques, they estimated a "reasonable upper-bound" to the extent of reinvestment displacement. Their figures indicate that, in most large cities, fewer than one or two hundred households per year are likely to be affected. Even in Washington and San Francisco, where reinvestment activity is widespread, the number of displaced households was estimated to be relatively small.

Although the Urban Coalition study was specifically designed to examine the problem of displacement, its reliance on the opinions and perceptions of "informed" observers makes its conclusions difficult to evaluate. One is unable, for example, to attach significance to the statement that "80 percent of the neighborhoods reporting elderly residents indicated a decline in their number after rehabilitation" (National Urban Coalition, 1978:7).

The city of Portland, Oregon, concerned about the tightness of its housing market and the difficulty lower-income families had locating housing, commissioned two studies of residential mobility. The first, designed before displacement was perceived as a major concern, examined the broader issues of household mobility between and within the city and the surrounding suburbs. A displacement analysis constructed ex post was able to provide only limited insights into the problem (Lycan 1978).

The data indicated that slightly under 10 percent of the movers originally surveyed had moved involuntarily. Approximately 3 percent cited demolition or poor maintenance as the reason—more likely signals of disinvestment rather than revitalization. Another 2.3 percent could no longer afford the rent, but whether this was due to rent or income changes was not specified. Finally, 3.2 percent had moved either because the house was sold or the owner decided to move into it. Without additional elaboration, even these moves cannot be attributed unequivocably to revitalization. All told, it was estimated that 1.7 percent of Portland's households move involuntarily each year due to factors as disparate as disinvestment, revitalization, and idiosyncratic market factors.

In an effort to gain better insights into the displacement problem, the second Portland study focused on neighborhoods where some reinvestment was occurring (McGrath and Ohman 1978). For the purposes of the study, displacement was defined as the eviction of tenants due to the conversion of a renter-occupied unit to owner occupancy. While this definition obviously excludes much displacement that does not result in a tenure change, it is not a totally unreasonable first approximation.

Efforts were made to interview a sample of new owners of properties sold during 1977. Under the strained assumptions of the study, it was estimated that 13.5 percent of the recent movers had been displaced. No attempt was made to contact the prior renters to ascertain why they had moved. The only effort made to determine the characteristics of the previous renters involved asking the current owners. Only twelve respondents were willing to venture guesses as to the income and occupational status of the "displaced" households, and this information is so suspect it is not worth reporting here.[7]

As yet, no reliable mobility data have been collected from surveys of outmovers from revitalizing areas. Two sources of data which do exist, however, suggest that the prospect of moving out of revitalizing areas may appeal to neighborhood residents. Although 74 percent of those responding to a survey of three neighborhoods in Washington indicated that they "feel a part of (the) neighborhood," two-thirds stated that they would move out of the neighborhood "if it were possible" (Washington Urban League, 1978:41). Similarly, in his study of Bay Village and West Cambridge in Boston, Pattison (1977:137) reports that most residents saw revitalization as an opportunity to fulfill a long-term goal of moving to the suburbs.

One should hasten to add, however, that this information can hardly be taken as indicative of the sentiments of all inner-city residents. The Boston data are not representative even of the neighborhoods that were studied. Pattison's methodology consisted of interviewing households whose names were obtained from various "leads." These respondents were then asked to suggest the name of other residents who would be amenable to interviews. As a result, respondents tended to be people who were active in the local neighborhood association, which suggests serious bias in the results.

Depending on the extent that residents view revitalization in such positive terms, however, the measurement of displacement will be even more difficult. Very little is known about the characteristics of displacees beyond the obvious point that those who suffer most from displacement are lower-income households. A study of Capitol Hill in Washington found that of sixty-five identified displacees, thirty were families with three or more children and most were black. The remainder included a large portion of elderly families (James 1977:258–260).

One must be particularly careful about these data, however; the Capitol Hill statistics are based on records maintained by Friendship House, a neighborhood service organization. These households are not likely to be representative of all the families who have left Capitol Hill during renovation. Rather, they indicate the types of families most severely affected by displacement and who seek some form of assistance in relocating.

More systematic information on displacees is available from a recent study of persons who moved from apartment buildings undergoing condominium conversion in Washington (Development Economics Group, 1976). Although conversion is only one manifestation of neighborhood reinvestment, it is a fairly common response to the increasing operating costs of rental housing and to the expanding demand for central-city housing among middle- and upper-income families. Among the outmover households interviewed in this study, 45 percent were elderly, 82 percent contained one or two persons, and more than two-thirds had incomes (in 1975) of less than $15,000. Slightly over half of the households responded that they chose to move rather than purchase their apartments because it would have been too expensive to stay. Another 20 percent were not interested in becoming condominium owners. As the study documented, the cost concerns were justified; for three typical household types (elderly; small, middle-aged; and small, young) monthly housing expenses would have doubled following conversion from rental to owner status.

Combined with the basic problem of defining precisely who has been displaced, the difficulty of tracing mover households makes follow-up studies of those displaced both tedious and costly. Yet this aspect of displacement is crucial to understand, for only by carefully documenting the post-move circumstances of displacees can one fully understand the dimensions of the problem. For individual households, it is important to be able to compare housing, neighborhood, and accessibility characteristics of the residents' new and former locations. From the broader perspective of the overall impact of neighborhood regeneration, follow-up studies are required to estimate the redistribution of costs and benefits among the central-city and suburban jurisdictions due to regeneration and displacement. The 1976 study of the Development Economics Group of condominium conversions provides the only systematic analysis of displacees.

Although the households affected by condominium conversions are not typical of all households threatened by displacement, it is instructive that these families fared fairly well in their search for replacement housing. By and large they were able to locate homes of similar cost and size in areas near those they left. Nearly 90 percent of the families remained in the city, and more than three-quarters of this group relocated in the same or an adjacent neighborhood.[8] More than two-thirds were able to find a new home within one month of beginning their search.

Beyond this work, only scattered evidence is available from a few case studies. These data are not based on carefully designed sampling plans, nor do they contain sufficient detail about the housing circumstances of those displaced to allow for any strong inferences to be drawn. What they do provide is a basis for generating hypotheses around which to design more comprehensive and reliable research.

Two general patterns are implied by these case studies. First, displaced persons tend to move very short distances. For example, displacees from the Adams-Morgan area of Washington often locate in the immediate environs. Those who have left the area have not severed their social ties to the neighborhood, often returning for religious or social gatherings on weekends and evenings (Smith 1977). Similarly, half of the sixty-five families tracked by Friendship House on Capitol Hill relocated to other apartments within the neighborhood, while another 40 percent moved to other row-house neighborhoods within the city (James 1977:260). The Urban Coalition report supports these impressions, based not only on its study of Capitol Hill, but also on information from St. Louis.

The second, and related, point is that dislocated families often move more than once as the boundaries of the revitalizing area expand. The Adams-Morgan study documented that some families had moved as many as three times since they were first dislocated (Smith 1977). Likewise, one would expect that the families who have elected to remain in Capitol Hill will, in the not too distant future, be forced to move again (James 1977).

Some observers suggest further that those displaced by current private market revitalization are the same families who, in the past, were former displacees from the urban renewal areas that were redeveloped with public funds in the last two decades (Weiler, in U.S. Senate, 1977; Myers and Binder 1977).

Contrary evidence is provided by Pattison's study of the Bay Village area in Boston. There, many homeowners realized sufficient capital gains from the sale of their properties to fulfill a long-standing goal of moving to the suburbs. Others were able to retain their properties and convert them to rentals that generated income sufficient to allow them to move to the suburbs (Pattison 1977:138).

Summary

The major conclusion from this survey of studies of displacement in revitalizing areas is that very little reliable information exists. The work that has been done can be characterized fairly as impressionistic and generally devoid of carefully constructed research designs. More importantly, a large portion of the work has been done in Washington, D.C., a city that is probably an extreme case. This is true for a number of reasons. First, Washington's revitalization movement has been spearheaded by young professional households. In no other city in the country is such a large proportion of the work force engaged in white-collar employment. Second, Washington has one of the lowest housing vacancy rates in the country. Despite a consistent twenty-year trend of declining population in the district, the rental vacancy rate is critically low. This suggests that many housing units are being absorbed by small families, and that dwelling unit merging may be an important aspect of the revitalization process. In part, the vacancy rate also reflects the slowdown in suburban housing construction caused by Virginia and Maryland suburban development moratoria of recent years. No hard information exists to indicate whether displacement is equally severe in other housing markets where vacancy rates are higher and where suburban growth has proceeded more rapidly. This does not discount the seriousness of the displacement problem in Washington but merely cautions that it may represent a distorted microcosm of what is happening across the country.

Given the current state of knowledge about displacement, calls for a broad and far-reaching national policy appear to be premature. To be sure, families who are displaced likely suffer serious problems in locating new housing and adjusting to unfamiliar environments. As a matter of equity, no single class of households should be made to bear the full brunt of the costs of urban revitalization to the extent that it is occurring. Forced relocation is, therefore, an important concern of local planners and program administrators, whether the ultimate source is private or public action.

Nonetheless, there are numerous broader issues to consider.[9] Indiscriminate policies to stem displacement may slow or erase the trickle of middle-class movement back to the central city. Keeping in mind that these families may help restore some fiscal balance to urban economies, all the poor residents of the city would suffer. Ultimately, what is required is a careful analysis of the magnitude of displacement along with a consideration of the benefits of revitalization. Until we have such information, amelioration of the displacement problem should appropriately be left to local officials familiar with local problems. The role of the federal government should be restricted to making available program resources that local governments can apply sensitively to mitigate the problem without stifling the potential of inner-city revitalization.

Notes

1. This paper is limited to a review of the available information on displacement in neighborhoods experiencing private market revitalization. Displacement may also result from other causes, including disinvestment and abandonment of the housing stock as well as public actions (Grier and Grier 1978). Similarly, the body of literature emerging from the relocation problems associated with urban renewal and other direct government actions in the late 1950s and 1960s is not discussed. No attempt is made to recommend policies for neighborhoods where displacement is already an obvious problem. Discussions of policy and program options may be found in Kollias (1977) and Weiler (1978). Stephens (1978) reviews the antidisplacement strategies of local government and community groups in Washington, D.C.

2. The dimensions of disinvestment are suggested by the estimate from Annual Housing Survey data that 242,000 central-city dwelling units were removed from the inventory annually during 1973–1976. Of these, 194,000 were occupied (Dolbeare 1978:18).

3. This is consistent with the general theory of neighborhood externalities, which so far has been applied primarily to negative effects (Davis and Whinston 1961).

4. Even defining "displacement" causes some problems. Grier and Grier (1978) and Dolbeare (1978:5) define displacement as an involuntary move precipitated by environmental changes over which the family has no control. Although conceptually adequate, the definition is not sufficiently operational for authoritative research.

5. Clay (1978) distinguishes between "incumbent upgrading" and "gentrification." It is the latter that involves widespread changes in the neighborhood's residents and, consequently, may create a displacement problem.

6. Myers (1978) discusses the particular problems and needs of the elderly in the revitalization context.

7. McGrath and Ohman (1978) also tried to interview absentee owners who had recently purchased property in the neighborhood. The response rate was so low that no results were reported.

8. As a cautionary note, it should be pointed out that there may be some bias in these results, given the relative ease of locating those who made the shortest move.

9. Sumka and Cincin-Sain (1979) provide a conceptual framework for viewing the revitalization and displacement phenomena in cost-benefit terms. They also outline a research strategy for addressing the as yet unanswered questions regarding these issues.

References

Black, J. 1975. "Private-Market Housing Renovation in Central Cities: A ULI Survey." *Urban Land* (November), 34:3–9.

Boston Globe. 1977. "Pressures on the North End." (June 11), p. 6.

Clay, P. L. 1978. *Neighborhood Revitalization: The Recent Experience in Large American Cities.* Cambridge, Mass.: M.I.T., Department of Urban Studies and Planning.

Cousar, G. J. 1978. "Bulletin on HUD Estimates of National Displacement and Pertinent Program Information." Mimeographed, Washington, D.C.: U.S. Department of Housing and Urban Development.

Davis, O. A. and A. B. Whinston. 1961. "The Economics of Urban Renewal." *Law and Contemporary Problems* (Winter), 26:105–117.

Development Economics Group. 1976. *Condominiums in the District of Co-*

lumbia. Report to the Office of Housing and Community Development, Government of the District of Columbia.

Dolbeare, C. N. 1978. *Involuntary Displacement: A Major Issue for People and Neighborhoods.* Washington, D.C.: National Commission on Neighborhoods.

Gale, D. E. 1976. "The Back-to-the-City Movement . . . Or Is It?: A Survey of Recent Homeowners in the Mount Pleasant Neighborhood of Washington, D.C." Occasional paper, Washington, D.C.: George Washington University, Department of Urban and Regional Planning.

———1977. "The Back-to-the-City Movement Revisited: A Survey of Recent Homebuyers in the Capitol Hill Neighborhood of Washington, D.C." Occasional paper, Washington, D.C.: George Washington University, Department of Urban and Regional Planning.

Goetze, R., K. W. Colton, and V. F. O'Donnell. 1977. "Neighborhood Dynamics: A Fresh Approach to Urban Housing and Development Policy." Prepared for HUD, Office of Policy Development and Research. Cambridge: Public Systems Evaluation.

Goldfield, D. and P. E. Hedeman. 1978. "Neighborhood Redevelopment and Displacement in Washington, D.C." Manuscript.

Grier, G. and E. Grier. 1978. "Urban Displacement: A Reconnaissance." Washington, D.C.: U.S. Department of Housing and Urban Development.

Hartnett, K. 1977. "Tracking the Return of the Gentry: The Bad Side of Central-City Chic." *Boston Globe* (May 28), p. 7.

Hoover, E. M. and R. Vernon. 1959. *Anatomy of a Metropolis.* Cambridge, Mass.: Harvard University Press.

James, F. J. 1977. *Back to the City: An Appraisal of Housing Reinvestment and Population Change in Urban America.* Washington, D.C.: The Urban Institute.

Kollias, K. 1977. Internal memorandum, Office of Neighborhoods, Voluntary Associations and Consumer Protection, U.S. Department of Housing and Urban Development.

Lipton, S. 1977. "Evidence of Central City Revival." *Journal of the American Institute of Planners* (April), 43:136–147.

Lycan, R. 1978. "Displacement of Residents of Portland Due to Urban Reinvestment." Report prepared for the Office of Planning and Development, Portland, Ore.: Center for Population Research and Census, Portland State University.

McGrath, L. and C. Ohman. 1978. "Residential Displacement: Portland 1977." Report to the Office of Planning and Development, Policy Development and Research Section, Portland, Ore.

Myers, P. 1978. "Neighborhood Conservation and the Elderly." Washington, D.C.: The Conservation Foundation.

Myers, P. and G. Binder. 1977. *Neighborhood Conservation: Lessons from*

Three Cities, an Issue Report. Washington, D.C.: The Conservation Foundation.

National Urban Coalition. 1978. *Displacement: City Neighborhoods in Transition.* Washington, D.C.

Nelson, K. P. 1978. "Movement of Blacks and Whites Between Central Cities and Suburbs in Eleven Metropolitan Areas, 1955–1975." Annual Housing Survey working papers, report no. 2, Washington, D.C.: Office of Economic Affairs, U.S. Department of Housing and Urban Development.

New York Times. 1977. "When City Revival Drives out the Poor." (July 1):A22.

Pattison, T. 1977. "The Process of Neighborhood Upgrading and Gentrification." Master's thesis, Cambridge, Mass.: M.I.T., Department of City Planning.

Public Affairs Counseling. 1975. *The Dynamics of Neighborhood Change.* San Francisco: U.S. Department of Housing and Urban Development, Office of Policy Development and Research.

Reinhold, R. 1977. "Middle-Class Return Displaces Some Urban Poor." *New York Times* (June 5), p. 1.

Rogg, N. H. 1977. *Urban Housing Rehabilitation in the United States.* Washington, D.C.: United States League of Savings Associations.

Smith, F. 1977. *Rip-off and Reinvestment: A Report on Speculation in Washington, D.C.* Washington, D.C.: Public Resource Center.

Stephens, M. L. 1978. "Strategies to Deter Real Estate Speculation and Neighborhood Displacement in the District of Columbia." Chapel Hill, N.C.: Department of City and Regional Planning, University of North Carolina.

Sternlieb, G. and J. W. Hughes. 1977. "New Regional and Metropolitan Realities of America." *Journal of the American Institute of Planners* (July), 43:227–240.

Sumka, H. J. and B. Cincin-Sain. 1979. "Displacement in Revitalizing Neighborhoods: A Review and Research Strategy." In *Occasional Papers in Housing and Community Affairs,* vol. 2. Washington, D.C.: Office of Policy Development and Research, U.S. Department of Housing and Urban Development.

Travis, D. J. 1978. "How Whites Are Taking Back Black Neighborhoods." *Ebony* (September).

U.S. Department of Housing and Urban Development. 1978. *A New Partnership to Conserve America's Communities: A National Urban Policy.*

U.S. House of Representatives, Committee on Banking, Currency, and Housing. 1976. "Hearings: The Rebirth of the American City." (September 20–October 1).

U.S. Senate, Committee on Banking, Housing, and Urban Affairs. 1977.

"Hearings: Neighborhood Diversity, Problems of Dislocation and Diversity in Communities Undergoing Neighborhood Revitalization Activity." 95th Congress, 1st session, July 7 and 8.

Washington Star. 1978. "Renovation as Threat." (August 18).

Washington Urban League. 1978. *SOS 1976: Speakout for Survival.* (June).

Weiler, C. 1978. "Reinvestment Displacement: HUD's Role in a New Housing Issue." Paper prepared for the Office of Community Planning and Development, Washington, D.C.: U.S. Department of Housing and Urban Development.

P A R T   T H R E E

Population Growth in Rural Localities

EDITOR'S NOTE:

FUGUITT AND ZUICHES present opinion polls that show the popularity, irrespective of where people actually live, of rural places over large cities. Such a preference, however, is contingent on living in commuting distance to large urban places and appears to be driven by a belief that the quality of life is better in small places. Christenson tests the proposition as to whether small places actually have better community conditions than urban places. The evidence suggests that community sentiments are more positive while service quality is not. This suggests that growth now occurring in nonmetropolitan places may lead to more resident satisfaction, since rural places may gain in services to add to already strong feelings of community attachment. Morrison links nationwide demographic patterns with rising public concerns about citizens' "rights of access" to communities of their liking. Case studies are drawn from rapidly growing energy boom towns and growth-limiting municipalities. The circumstances brought about by either of these extremes raise troubling questions about who should live where, by what criteria, and decided by whom.

6
Residential Preferences and Population Distribution

GLENN V. FUGUITT
AND JAMES J. ZUICHES

RECENT SOCIAL TRENDS relating to the decline of central cities, urban sprawl, rural depopulation, and disparities among communities have served to focus attention on the need for population distribution policies in the United States (see, for example, Ad Hoc Subcommittee on Urban Growth, 1969; Advisory Commission on Intergovernmental Relations, 1968; Beale 1972; Commission on Population Growth and the American Future, 1972; Fuguitt 1971; Hansen 1970; Morrison 1970; National Goals Research Staff, 1970; President's National Advisory Commission on Rural Poverty, 1967). Specific recommendations have included proposals to develop depressed rural areas, to encourage migration to middle-sized cities, and to plan for more orderly urban expansion. Various strategies also have been suggested to redistribute the population away from metropolitan areas and to retain population in nonmetropolitan areas.

An important element figuring in this discussion is con-

Reprinted with permission from *Demography* (1975), vol. 12, no. 3, Population Association of America. Tables and figures and text references to tables and figures are omitted due to space constraints. These are available from the authors.

cern about public preferences and attitudes on desirable places to live. A policy that provides community and housing options compatible with preferences should have a greater chance of success and could be expected to lessen any discrepancy between the actual and ideal distribution of the population. That such a discrepancy exists is one argument used by proponents of population deconcentration. For more than a decade, national public opinion surveys have found a decided preference for living in small towns and rural areas as contrasted to larger cities. Thus the coincidence of public interest and private preference is pointed to as a positive reason for a population dispersal policy since, "except for the economic pressures, many city dwellers would eagerly move to the country" (National Goals Research Staff, 1970:54).

Despite this stated dissatisfaction with large cities, there has been no major exodus to medium-sized cities, small towns, and rural areas of nonmetropolitan counties. In fact, during the 1950s over 1,400 nonmetropolitan counties experienced such heavy out-migration that they declined in population, and about 1,300 nonmetropolitan counties declined in the 1960s. Since 1960 a number of formerly declining nonmetropolitan areas have begun to grow (see Hansen 1973; Beale 1974), and since 1970 a net migration gain has been reported for the nonmetropolitan sector as a whole. Nevertheless, Current Population Survey results (U.S. Bureau of the Census, 1974) indicate that between 1970 and 1973 the rate of net migration gain for metropolitan areas outside central cities was three times the rate for the nonmetropolitan United States.

In this paper, we offer evidence that this paradox between expressed public opinion and actual migration can be explained at least in part by the way residential preference questions have been asked in earlier surveys. Whereas previous studies have generally considered only the size of place in which respondents prefer to reside, we have further distinguished places according to proximity to large cities. Our initial work (Zuiches and Fuguitt 1972) was based on a survey of Wisconsin residents. This paper reports the results of a nationwide sample survey which allow us to draw conclusions relating to preferences by city size and proximity to a metropolitan center for the adult population of the continental United States.

Previous Research on Residential Preferences

Some previous results on preferences by size of community are first reviewed. Because of differences in the questions asked, these distributions are not precisely comparable; yet the findings are broadly similar, showing that (1) most respondents would like to live in small towns and rural areas and (2) the proportion having this preference exceeds that currently residing there. All of these studies, however, have a common limitation: they fail to distinguish certain key relational characteristics of places people claim to prefer. Among these, nearness to a large city may be of paramount importance. Failure to distinguish proximity differences could well mix, on the one hand, the respondent who prefers the small town or country milieu of, say, Philadelphia's suburban Main Line with, on the other hand, the respondent who has a small town in central Nebraska in mind. The same "small town" descriptor on the survey can have quite different meanings to different respondents.

This potentially misleading effect was first examined in our statewide survey of Wisconsin in 1971. After an initial size-of-place question, we asked respondents not preferring a large city whether or not they would prefer to live within thirty minutes of a large city. Judging from the initial question, our results broadly agreed with those of Gallup, the Population Commission, and others. The distance-qualifying question, however, showed that well over one-half of the 79 percent preferring to live in small towns and rural areas stated that they would like their residence to be within thirty miles of a city over fifty thousand in size. This finding shed considerable light on the paradox noted above: the realization of these preferences would result in a net movement out of central cities and nonmetropolitan areas and into metropolitan rings, which is consistent with the overall trends that prevailed in Wisconsin at least through 1970 (Zuiches and Fuguitt 1972).

A study by Dillman and Dobash (1972) done at about the same time in Washington State also casts doubt on the interpretation of earlier surveys that a high proportion of citizens would prefer to live in small towns and rural areas away from large cities. Their questions, however, were worded quite differently.

Questions and Sample

The data reported here are from a nationwide study building on our earlier work for Wisconsin. Basic questions very similar to those included in the Wisconsin 1971 survey were included in NORC's Amalgam Survey of the total noninstitutional U.S. population eighteen and over conducted in November 1972. The questions were worded as follows:

> First, we are interested in the kind of community you would prefer to live in now, if you had your choice.
> 1. In terms of size, if you could live in any size community you wanted, which one of these would you like best?
>   A large metropolitan city (over 500,000 in population)
>   A medium-sized city (50,000 to 500,000 in population)
>   A smaller city (10,000 to 50,000 in population) (ASK A)
>   A town or village (under 10,000 in population) (ASK A)
>   In the country, outside of any city or village (ASK A)
>   Don't know
>   A. *If smaller than medium-sized city:*
>   In terms of *location*, would you like that place to be within 30 miles of a large or medium-sized city, or would you rather be farther away from such a city?
>   Within 30 miles
>   Farther away
>   Don't know/doesn't matter

Similar questions yielded classifications with the same categories for present residence and residence at time of birth.

In addition, we obtained information on the respondent's view of specific aspects of communities as related to his preferences and a ranking of preferred locations. These were analyzed giving particular attention to the relation between actual and preferred residence.

Those interviewed appeared to have little difficulty responding to specific questions on distance from a large city and size of place. To get an impression of how accurately respondents could determine whether or not they live within thirty miles of a city over 50,000, the sample segments, usually census tracts, were classified by distance edge-to-edge to places of that size. We found that 64 respondents who were in PSUs more than forty miles from a large city reported being within thirty miles of such a place, and 23 respondents who were in PSUs less than twenty miles from a large city reported living more than thirty miles away. These 87 were less than 6 percent of the total number interviewed, so we concluded that estimating distance is not a serious problem. Similarly, we compared reported present location with a classification of PSUs by size of place and found only 14 percent of the respondents differed by more than one class interval. Moreover, inspection shows that most of these deviant responses were plausible as, for example, some who reported being in large cities appeared to be in rural territory adjacent to a large city according to the PSU designation based on the 1970 census.

The NORC sample is a multistage area probability sample down to the block level, where quota sampling is used. The primary sampling units are SMSAs and nonmetropolitan counties. Because of the quota feature, tests of significance are not appropriate. For details of the sampling procedure, see King and Richards (1972).

Residence and Preferences

Actual residence is next compared with preferred residence according to both size of place and proximity to a large city.

Almost one-half of the respondents in a nationwide survey reported living in cities of over 50,000 population, one-third within thirty miles of a city of 50,000 or more, and 20 percent in more distant locations. If everyone were to live in the location that he preferred, however, the distribution of population would look somewhat different. Under those conditions only one-quarter would live in large cities, and over one-half would be in easy commuting distance of such places. The proportion living more distant, however, would remain almost the same. The largest drop in percentage, were such a shift to come about, would be for cities over 500,000, and the largest gain would be for rural areas near large cities.

Our results accord well with previous survey findings if proximity to a large city is ignored. The Gallup and Harris surveys of 1970 and 1972, for example, show 55 and 47 percent, respectively, wanting to live in small towns or on farms. The Population Commission study and both our Wisconsin and U.S. surveys show almost two-thirds to three-fourths of the respondents preferring small cities and towns or rural areas.

Our data, however, reveal a key *relational* prerequisite for desiring to live in small towns and rural areas: only 9 percent of all respondents in the nationwide survey would prefer to live in rural areas, and another 10 percent in small and medium-sized towns, if these locales were more than thirty miles from a large city. (Comparable percentages for Wisconsin are 14 and 16.) Many people respond positively to the idea of rural living, but not where it would entail disengagement from the metropolitan complex. This suggests a clear desire to have the best of both environments—which may include proximity to metropolitan employment, services, schools, and facilities, along with the advantages of the smaller local-residential community for familial and neighborhood activities.

A complete cross-classification of respondents by their reported current and preferred residence was also examined.

In only two residence categories (places under 10,000

within thirty miles and rural areas within thirty miles) do current and preferred residences coincide for more than one-half the respondents. For communities within the thirty-mile zone, there is also a systematic inverse relationship between size of residence and preference for this residence. Only 36 percent of the residents in cities over 500,000 selected this type as their preferred location, but 67 percent of near (less than thirty miles) rural residents selected near rural areas as preferred. The least "popular" locations, as measured here, are large cities and medium and small towns away from a large center.

Most of the differences between actual residence and preferences indicate a desire for smaller and/or more remote locations. Overall, however, the data show the predominance of suburban and fringe-type locations in residential preferences. These are the categories with the highest agreement between residence and preferences and the categories most preferred by people currently living elsewhere.

This generalization is shown clearly by combining the categories of residence and preference into three groups: cities over 50,000; smaller places and rural areas near large cities; and smaller places and rural areas away from large cities. Of people currently living in cities over 50,000, 52 percent would prefer smaller places. Conversely, of people not currently living in large cities, only eight percent would prefer to do so. More than three-fourths of those now living in smaller places near large cities would prefer this type of location, as would 42 percent of those not now living there. Of those more than thirty miles from a large city, over one-half preferred to live nearer. But only 13 percent of the people living near or in a large city chose a more remote location. Figure 6.1 is the cross-classification of current and preferred residences using this trichotomy of residence types. The remainder of the analysis is based on data grouped in this way, with the three categories referred to as "big city," "near" and "away," for convenience. (Whether a city of 50,000 is indeed big depends, of course, on one's viewpoint.)

Origins and Residential Preferences

Is a respondent's residential preference related to where he
grew up or formerly lived?

Comparison of origin with current residence indicates the
movement from more remote areas into big cities and their
peripheries which has taken place over the last generation. If
the preferred residences were realized, however, there would
be a reverse shift out of cities, so that the proportion of residents in large cities and in rural areas would be less than the
proportion born there; whereas the periphery of large cities
would again capture an increasing proportionate share.

Next we considered the association of place of origin as
well as current residence with the preferences given for each
of the three general residence types.

Current residence has an important effect in that people
who live in an area are more likely to prefer it than people
who do not, regardless of origin. But place of origin, representing an influence that may be more remote in time, also
has a smaller but consistent effect on people's preferences for
those preferring to live in a big city, near a big city, or farther
away. Mazie and Rawlings (1972) reported similar results with
their residence categories.

Reasons for Preferences

After stating their preference for a community size and location, respondents were read a list of reasons people might
have for preferring to live in one kind of community or another and asked whether or not each was one of their reasons.
The percent of people reporting each reason was tabulated
by the three location types and graphed in Figure 6-1. In order to clarify the distinction between locations, the reasons
were ordered by the percent of people reporting them who
preferred to live away from a big city. These ranged from 13

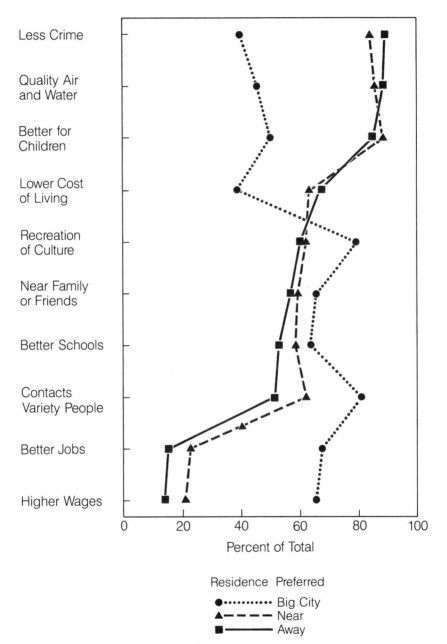

FIGURE 6.1. Proportion of respondents stating a reason is important in their residential preference by type of preference. Reasons have been ranked according to proportion of mention by respondents who prefer an "away" location.

percent for higher wages to 89 percent for less crime and danger.

This ordering gives a clear discrimination between big city and other preferences. Those preferring small towns and rural areas near big cities have almost the same pattern of response as persons preferring more remote locations. People who want to live near big cities, then, seek the same qualities as those preferring to live farther away; but both groups differ markedly from those who prefer large cities. This latter group differentially seeks higher wages or salaries, better job opportunities, the possibility of contacts with a variety of people, better schools, nearness to family or friends, and recreation or cultural facilities.

Almost all those preferring more rural locations mentioned quality of life factors often associated with the country: less crime, quality air and water, better place for children. On the other hand, only about 20 percent favored more rural locations because of better job opportunities or higher wages there. These five reasons showed the maximum differences between the urban and rural preference groups.

The analysis of reasons was extended by controlling for present location. Present location made little difference, however, in comparison to the differences between preferences for big cities and more rural areas. The people wanting to live in a different area thus respond in terms of the same qualities as those already there who wish to remain.

Tables of reasons also were constructed separately by categories of age, income, and sex, but differences were small and not systematic. Perhaps people are simply responding to generally recognized stereotypes concerning the types of residences they prefer. The fact that over 40 percent of those preferring big cities gave reasons of less crime and danger there, and better quality of air and water, suggests that many respondents were simply assenting to factors desirable in any community. Nevertheless, systematic differences did emerge between those preferring big cities and those preferring other locations. A thorough analysis of possible reasons would require considerably more interview time than was available to us for detailed questions tailored to specific preferences.

The Ranking of Preferences

An unanswered question is whether the basic preference pattern described in our data is for the metropolitan area itself (with the smaller city or open country therein viewed as a more pleasant living alternative); or whether basic preference is really for small towns or rural areas themselves (with proximity to a big city representing a kind of cost paid for urban advantage). In an effort to ferret out this subtle distinction, we asked respondents to rank in order of preference three types of location: a city over 50,000, a smaller city or rural area within thirty miles of a city over 50,000, and a smaller city or rural area more than thirty miles from a city over 50,000.

The first-rank choices to these questions show a somewhat lower proportion preferring large cities (19 versus 25 percent) and a somewhat higher proportion preferring remote rural areas (26 versus 20 percent) than the trichotomous classification of responses based on the two initial residential preference questions. Such response differences are to be expected in survey research, and the general conclusions of the study are the same with either preference measure.

The pattern of first and second choices is of interest here. Whereas 43 percent of the respondents ranked a near location first and a more rural location second, only 12 percent ranked a near location first and a big city second. In all only 32 percent ranked the big city either first or second, whereas 71 percent ranked a distant location either first or second, and 97 percent ranked the near location first or second. Such results indicate that the desire for a small town or rural setting is extremely pervasive and that most respondents view the advantages of living in such a setting even at some distance from a large city as preferable to living in a large city.

Discussion and Summary

Antiurbanism in America appears to be qualified: although many people do not prefer to live in big cities, few want to live far from one. Previous survey data on residential preferences considerably overestimated the popularity of nonmetropolitan rural environments by failing to define them precisely in people's minds. When respondents are allowed to express a preference for the degree of proximity to a large city of over 50,000 population, they favor the peripheral metropolitan ring areas that have, in fact, been gaining rapidly in population.

These findings have a direct meaning for policy, since they call into question arguments for population dispersal into nonmetropolitan areas based on public preferences alone. Other worthy objectives may be served by such a national goal, but the proportion of people eager to move to a remote nonmetropolitan setting appears to be small and balanced by an equal number already in nonmetropolitan areas who want to move closer to a big city.

The findings illuminate an issue of population distribution policy which, like the controversy about whether or not voluntary family planning can suffice to achieve lowered growth rates, hinges on the matter of what voluntarism would produce. Our research suggests that, if people were to sort themselves out into the kinds of residential environments they claim to prefer, there would be no massive exodus to remote areas. Americans' residential preferences, when properly interpreted, lend no credence to the view that measures aiding dispersal to nonmetropolitan areas would simply be satisfying a large unmet public need, although such measures may be justified on other grounds.

Despite the massive movements into metropolitan areas during this century, we found little evidence of a desire by migrants to return to their place of rural origin. We found that origins influence preferences but that present location is considerably more important. Furthermore, this small origin effect prevailed for those born in all three types of location considered, not just in rural areas. As Mazie and Rawlings (1972) point out, the place-of-origin effect may move aggregate preferences toward big cities for later generations having higher proportions born there.

These conclusions should not minimize the favorable orientation to rural and small-town life expressed by the respondents on this as well as previous surveys. The reasons given here for preferences show that the commonly held advantages of rural life are believed to be present even within proximity of a large city. The ranking question showed that four out of five of the respondents who preferred to live near large cities as a first choice gave rural areas away from large cities as a second choice, rather than the large city itself. Among all respondents two-thirds ranked the large city least desirable of the three options.

The discrepancy between preference and current residence which we found is consistent with trends in U.S. population redistribution over the past several decades. But as yet there is little direct evidence concerning the interrelations between residential preferences and migration behavior or between both of these and other attitudinal variables such as community satisfaction. Such knowledge would increase our understanding of population movements and is needed by those interested in formulating and attempting to implement population distribution policies on a national or local level.

References

Ad Hoc Subcommittee on Urban Growth. 1969. *Population Trends.* Hearings for use of the Committee on Banking and Currency, House of Representatives. Washington, D.C.: U.S. Government Printing Office.

Advisory Commission on Intergovernmental Relations. 1968. *Urban and Rural America: Policies for Future Growth*, report A-32. Washington, D.C.: GPO.

Beale, C L. 1972. "Rural and Nonmetropolitan Population Trends of Significance to National Population Policy." In S. M. Mazie, ed., *Population, Distribution, and Policy*, pp. 665–677. Commission on Population Growth and the American Future, vol. 5. Washington, D.C.: GPO.

—— 1974. "Rural Development: Population and Settlement Prospects." *Journal of Soil and Water Conservation,* 29:23–27.

Commission on Population Growth and the American Future. 1972. *Population and the American Future.* Washington, D.C.: GPO.

Dillman, D. A. and R. P. Dobash. 1972. *Preferences for Community Living and Their Implications for Population Redistribution.* Washington Agricultural Experiment Station, Bulletin 764. Pullman: Washington State University.

Fuguitt, G. V. 1971. "The Places Left Behind: Population Trends and Policy for Rural America." *Rural Sociology,* 36:449–470.

Hansen, N. M. 1970. *Rural Poverty and the Urban Crisis: A Strategy for Regional Development.* Bloomington: Indiana University Press.

—— 1973. *The Future of Nonmetropolitan America: Studies in the Reversal of Rural and Small Town Population Decline.* Lexington: Lexington Books.

Louis Harris and Associates, Inc. 1970. *A Survey of Public Attitudes Toward Urban Problems and Toward the Impact of Scientific and Technical Developments,* Study no. 2040. New York: Louis Harris and Associates.

King, B. F. and C. Richards. 1972. "The 1972 NORC Probability Sample." Unpublished preliminary draft. Chicago: National Opinion Research Center.

Mazie, S. M. and S. Rawlings. 1972. "Public Attitude Towards Population Distribution Issues." In S. M. Mazie, ed., *Population, Distribution, and Policy,* pp. 599–615. Commission on Population Growth and the American Future, vol. 5. Washington, D.C.: GPO.

Morrison, P. A. 1970. *The Rationale for a Policy on Population Distribution.* Santa Monica: RAND Corporation.

National Goals Research Staff. 1970. *Toward Balanced Growth: Quantity with Quality.* Washington, D.C.: GPO. Printing Office.

President's National Advisory Commission on Rural Poverty. 1967. *People Left Behind.* Washington, D.C.: GPO.

U.S. Bureau of the Census. 1974. *Mobility of the Population of the United States: March 1970 to March 1973.* Current Population Reports, series P-20, no. 262. Washington, D.C.: GPO.

Zuiches, J. J. and G. V. Fuguitt. 1972. "Residential Preferences: Implications for Population Redistribution in Nonmetropolitan Areas." In S. M. Mazie, ed., *Population, Distribution, and Policy,* pp. 617–630. Commission on Population Growth and the American Future, vol. 5. Washington, D.C.: GPO.

7
Urbanism
and Community Sentiment:
Extending Wirth's Model

JAMES A. CHRISTENSON

WHAT ARE THE effects of urbanism or rurality on people's well-being? This question has stimulated the development of both urban and rural sociology and remained a focus of these subdisciplines. Fischer (1975:70) observes that, in most societies, different ways of life are ascribed to people in the city and in the country. Even in an advanced industrial society such as the United States, differences exist between the condition of people living in urban and rural areas in services, educational attainment, housing, and espousal of various beliefs, attitudes, and mores (Hines et al. 1975; Fischer 1973, 1975; Willits et al. 1973). While considerable empirical research has documented differences between people in rural and urban areas for various purposes, Wirth's (1938) theory "remains the most explicit, seminal, and comprehensive theory of the rural-urban continuum, and still provides the preeminent framework for the study of community and personality" (Fischer 1975:72).

Wirth was concerned with the effects of structural conditions on the feelings and relationships of urban residents. Studying under Park and influenced by the Chicago School, Wirth used the term "sentiment" to reflect the normative integration achieved through common values, local loyalties, shared tradition, and individual interactions. Community sentiment indicates residents' subjective feelings toward one another and their community as a whole. Using Homans' terminology (1950), the psychological sentiment of a community (that is, the positive feelings that group members develop toward one another and the group) is one of the major elements of the internal system of a community. The idea that smaller or rural communities foster stronger community sentiment both is accepted as a common truism and is a key component of theories relating to urbanism or rurality. Tönnies (1887) suggested such a relationship with the concepts *Gemeinschaft* and *Gesellschaft*. Simmel (1905) wrote of the effect of urbanism on mental health. Durkheim (1933) presented two types of solidarity exemplified in rural and urban societies. It is Wirth's theory (1938), however, that provides the most commonly used assessment of the effect of urbanism on individual well-being.

Wirth (1938:1) defines urbanism as a relatively large, dense, and permanent settlement of heterogeneous individuals. These three structural conditions—size, density, and heterogeneity—generate a deterioration and loss of community sentiment, as manifested through such social-psychological conditions as isolation, anonymity, impotence (powerlessness), impersonality, and malaise (see Fischer 1972). For example, Wirth suggests that the larger the number of inhabitants in the community, the greater the likelihood of segmented and impersonal human relationships leading to blasé outlooks and a sense of malaise (compare Fischer 1973).[1] As the human density of a community increases, Wirth suggests that friction, irritation, powerlessness, and loneliness increase. Likewise, increased heterogeneity in a community stimulates insecurity, isolation, and exploitation. In this manner, Wirth attempts to explain the fate of residents in different sizes and types of communities.

Wirth's theory is limited, first, because it considers only the population characteristics of urbanism and emphasizes the negative consequences of urbanism on people's feelings of well-being. His model excludes the economic aspect of urbanism. Wirth (1938:22–23) discusses briefly the consequences of urbanism on the economic life of the individuals, focusing specifically on income, but he excludes any structural measure of the "marketplace." For Weber, size or density were not sufficient as criteria for urbanism, but were necessary conditions for the market or economic activity. Other writers have suggested a relationship among level of economic activity, income, and social-psychological well-being (compare Bauer 1966; Gerson 1976; Dillman and Tremblay 1977). Dillman and Tremblay (1977:117) observed that economic growth has given most Americans substantially greater purchasing power, thus giving them the ability to acquire more material goods and services that contribute to public well-being.

Second, Wirth's theory, while touching on the implications of urbanism in relation to services, does not incorporate services in his model. Bell (1973) argues that services are characteristic of the city in contemporary U.S. society, with service employment now accounting for nearly two of every three persons in the labor force. Bell characterizes urban areas as becoming service centers, providing a wide range of commercial, public, and social amenities. Bell's characterization of the city as a service center seems to suggest a positive or desirable aspect of living in urban areas.

The purpose of this paper is to extend Wirth's model of urbanism by including considerations of economic activity and public services and to study the relationship of these aspects of urbanism with community sentiment. The article will treat certain social-psychological correlates of urbanism on people. This analysis does not deal with behavioral consequences of urbanism such as deviance. A central question is

the extent to which these additional characteristics of urbanism can explain community sentiment and how the relationships are affected in a multivariate context. It is expected that
Wirth's predictions concerning the negative effect of
size/density or heterogeneity on sentiment will be supported
in a bivariate context; but the inclusion of economic activity
and services in the multivariate model of urbanism will show
some of the limitations of Wirth's view of the effects of urbanism on community sentiment.

The Model

Community sentiment is conceptualized as a subjective measure of individual well-being aggregated in a community
context. It falls under the larger label of "Quality of Life"
measures, the validity of which Campbell and associates
(1976) assert rests in the eye of the beholder. This evaluative
emphasis differentiates this study from studies of social or
material well-being that have used objective conditions such
as suicide rates, percent unemployed, Consumer Price Index,
or related measures to assess the human condition in a community context (compare Bauer 1966; Liu 1975). These are
objective conditions related to, but independent of, people's
subjective appraisals of their community.

Wirth (1938) wrote of urban malaise, anonymity, powerlessness, and impersonality as examples of the deterioration
or loss of community sentiment. Recent research on quality
of life or satisfaction studies have found similar results. For
example, less dissatisfaction, despair, or unhappiness is reported by residents in rural as opposed to urban areas (Johnson and Knop 1970; Rossi 1972; Durand and Eckart 1973;
Gallup Opinion Index, 1974; Marans and Rodgers 1975;
Goudy 1977). However, Fischer (1973), focusing specifically
on urban malaise (unhappiness, despair), found only a very
weak relationship between malaise and city size in his American data.

Anonymity in the sense of indifference toward community or lack of community attachment (Berry and Kasarda 1977; Goudy 1977), or transitoriness in the sense of willingness to move (Durand and Eckart 1973; Kasarda and Janowitz 1974), has been reported more often by people in larger cities as opposed to smaller cities. In the same vein, impotence is positively related to urbanism (Johnson and Knop 1970) and impersonality in the context of interpersonal ties, relations, and opportunities for social interaction has been identified with urbanism (Rossi 1972; Goudy 1977). These four aspects—malaise, anonymity, impotence, and impersonality—will comprise the elements of a community sentiment index that will serve as the dependent variable.

Size or density is often related to various types of community sentiment.[2] Summarizing a wide range of empirical research on size/density, Dillman and Tremblay (1977) point out that people living in different-sized cities differ on generalized feelings of well-being, with rural respondents reporting higher levels of satisfaction. This review also suggests that more rural respondents, in recent years, feel that their communities are becoming more enjoyable places in which to live than do residents of cities and suburbs. However, Berry and Kasarda (1977:65), using large-scale community surveys, find that population size and density have relatively weak and, for the most part, insignificant effects on their indicators of community sentiment. Nevertheless, the weight of previous research seems to support Wirth's position.

Heterogeneity is more difficult to conceptualize. Fischer (1972:192) notes problems in defining the many possible forms of heterogeneity (such as age, race, sex, ethnicity, lifestyle, occupational differentiation and/or specialization). In his articles testing Wirth's theory (1972, 1973, 1975), Fischer ends up discarding the variable heterogeneity because of ambiguity. While agreeing with Fischer on the difficulty of concept delineation, heterogeneity will be treated so that Wirth's model can be tested, but the variable will be limited to cultural heterogeneity.[3] Wirth's theory suggests a negative relationship between heterogeneity and community sentiment.

Homogeneous groups are considered to rate higher on various measures of community sentiment. For example, research indicates a weak negative relationship between race (percent nonwhite) and feelings of community involvement or measures of satisfaction with locality (Campbell et al. 1976:226; Marans and Rodgers 1975:303).

Economic activity usually means the exchanged goods and services for equivalent value in a standard monetary system (Lowenthal 1977). If economic activity is defined as per-capita income, then research suggests a strong positive relationship between economic activity and size/density (Molotch 1976; Berry and Kasarda 1977) and a modest positive relationship between economic activity and services (Campbell and Sacks 1967). It is also expected that economic activity would have a positive relationship with community sentiment or related indicators of community satisfaction (Rojek et al. 1975; Clemente and Sauer 1976; Campbell et al. 1976; Marans and Rodgers 1975; Goudy 1977).

Services will be limited to those provided through the public sector (such as police, education, libraries) and the effect of public services on community sentiment. Services are directly affected by size/density and economic activity (Niederfrank 1971). Usually, costs or expenditures for services decrease as population density increases. In a few cases, service costs are shown to rise with density. But when this occurs, it is often due to variations in the quality of services (Hawley 1971:133). Researchers have generally substantiated the direct positive relationship among density, per-capita income, and per-capita expenditures on services (Berry and Kasarda 1977:221–223; Campbell and Sacks 1967). Likewise, service quality has been positively related to community satisfaction (Rojek et al. 1975). Empirical research suggests that perceived satisfaction with public services is positively associated with individual social-psychological well-being and is considered a major determinant of satisfaction with locality (Rojek et al. 1975; Marans and Rodgers 1975; Goudy 1977). Overall, services are expected to be a positive function of size/density and economic activity, and an intervening vari-

able between and a postive determinant of community sentiment.

Procedure

This study entails a macroanalysis of these characteristics of
urbanism with community sentiment for the one hundred
counties in North Carolina. The state is noted for its large
number of counties and their relatively small size. With only
a few exceptions, one community (usually the county seat)
tends to dominate the county, being both the commercial hub
and service center. Some researchers may question the equat-
ing of county and community; however, Arensberg (1955),
Fuguitt (1965), and Seiler and Summers (1974) argue that the
community and county can be equated in the South, where,
for historical reasons, the county seat was located approximately at the center of each small county to serve the hinterland.

North Carolina provides a useful but limited measure of
urbanism. The state ranks seventeenth in the United States in
terms of population density but has only sixteen counties that
are labeled SMSA (U.S. Bureau of the Census, 1973:15, 912–
916). The state has no city the size of Chicago, New York, or
Los Angeles (Charlotte, N.C., having one-half million people). But the state does provide a comparative assessment of
middle-range urban centers to very small rural places.

Because of the interrelation $(r = .89)$ between size and
density, only density will be used in the following analysis.
Density (people/square mile) is based on calculations from
1975 population estimates for the hundred counties.[4] Heterogeneity is the proportion of nonwhites in the county. The
nonwhites category mainly includes blacks (near 90 percent)
with American Indian being the next largest group. North
Carolina has a sizeable nonwhite population varying from 1
to 59 percent across the hundred counties.

Economic activity will be measured by per-capita income. Clark (1973) considers the level of a community's

wealth probably the best predictor of the population's material well-being. Both Clark (1973) and Eberts (1973) use income as an indicator of the economic aspects of community. Per-capita income is commonly used by economists as an indicator of economic activity.

Selecting appropriate measures of service is difficult because, ideally, public services exist in all counties. In terms of urbanism, the quantity and quality of services seem to be the issues. Two measures are used. The first is per-capita expenditures (total for county includes cities). This provides a quantitative measure of services. The second is citizen evaluation of service quality. A public services index in the form of a Guttman scale was developed to test the relationship of the quality of common public services with community sentiment. All eight services were available in all counties: libraries, elementary and secondary schools, county and city law enforcement, medical services and facilities, cultural opportunities, public parks and playgrounds, recreational facilities, and child-welfare services. In brief, if the majority of respondents in a county rated a particular service as good, then the county was accredited as having quality service on that item. The services scale scores the counties according to this type of quality rating on eight services.[5] Coefficients of reproducibility and scalability exceed minimum bounds established by conventional criteria. Detailed procedures for this scale and the data collection are available elsewhere (Christenson 1976; Dillman et al. 1974).

Data for this scale came from a 1975 statewide mail survey conducted in all one hundred counties of North Carolina. Based on a proportionate and over-sampling procedure, 8,882 respondents returned usable questionnaries for a response rate of 66 percent. An average of 89 respondents from each county was included in this sample.

The community sentiment index contains four social-psychological measures which seem to encompass major components of community sentiment as related to Wirth's theory (such as malaise—more than 50% lack enjoyment in community; anonymity—more than 50% indifference toward community; impotence—more than 50% no voice in government; impersonality—more than 50% lack social interaction). While these items are not precisely comparable to Wirth's labels, it can be argued that the scale items tap these dimensions and also relate to the other quality of life/satisfaction measures used in past research. The proposed index manifests the hierarchical implications of Guttman scaling with items ranging in order of increasing difficulty from enjoyment of community, to pride in community, to perceived voice in community, to perceived opportunity for social interaction. Scale scores for the counties ranged from 0 to 4. Thirteen counties did not score on any of the items. The data for the scale came from the mail survey conducted in the one hundred counties of North Carolina.

Findings

A correlation matrix, along with means and standard deviations, was calculated. Quality of services and heterogeneity have the strongest bivariate relationships with community sentiment, though no variable in the matrix has a correlation with community sentiment larger than 0.48. And with the exception of the density-income relationship, all zero-order correlations in the matrix are below 0.57.

A final model of significant ($p \leq .05$) path coefficients for the extension of Wirth's model was calculated. It provides an algorithm for decomposing the total correlation between the dependent and independent variables and for assessing both the direct and indirect effects of each exogenous variable on the dependent variable. Per-capita expenditures for services was dropped from the model because of insignificant relationships with the quality of services index and community sentiment.

The relationship between density and the community sentiment index is important because of the very weak zero-order correlation, but the very strong direct effect in the multivariate analysis. This suggests that *ceteris paribus,* less populated areas would have higher scores on the community sentiment index than more heavily populated areas. However, for this situation to exist, adjustments would have to be made for the variation in the heterogeneity, economic activity, and services variables. In other words, rural areas would have to have about the same level of income, racial mix, and service quality as urban areas. Thus, existing variation between densely populated and sparsely populated areas would have to be altered considerably.

This provides an explanation for some of the contradictory findings of past research. Rural areas have tended to rate much lower than urban areas on such measures as income, services, and various amenities (Hines et al. 1975). Yet, when people were asked to indicate their satisfaction with, attachment to, or sentiments toward their locality, rural people appeared to be generally happier and more satisfied than urban people (Dillman and Tremblay 1977). However, the indirect effect of density (+.30) through the service quality index shows a positive indirect relationship with the community sentiment index. This suggests that more densely populated localities score higher on measures of community sentiment if the issue is formulated within the context of public service quality. The findings indicate that both rural and urban areas can have positive scores on community sentiment, but the conditions for the existence of each vary.

Density and economic activity are the major predictors of the service quality index. The service quality index and density were the major predictors of community sentiment, with services having a strong positive effect and density having a strong negative effect. Economic activity did not have a significant direct effect on community sentiment but did have a weak indirect effect (+.18) on sentiment. Heterogeneity had a weak negative effect on sentiment. The variables accounted for 41 percent of the explained variance for the dependent variable.[6]

Implications

Neither density nor heterogeneity has large zero-order correlations with community sentiment, though both are in the direction that Wirth predicted. This is consistent with Berry and Kasarda (1977:65) and shows the limited explanatory ability of Wirth's theory. The addition, however, of two other characteristics of urbanism (economic activity and services) to Wirth's characteristics shows that all variables in the extended model have an effect on sentiment. Density and economic activity are major predictors of service quality, which itself is the major predictor of sentiment. Service quality seems to be the key to interpreting rural-urban differences in community sentiment. All things being equal, less heavily populated areas manifest more favorable community sentiments than more heavily populated areas. The indirect effect of density via service quality, however, suggests that more populated areas have an indirect positive score on the sentiment index when compared to less populated areas.

In a policy perspective it has been assumed that people have moved from less populated areas to live in or near large cities to obtain quality services (Dillman and Tremblay 1977). In the process, Wirth's theory suggests that people incur the costs of loss of community sentiment and social solidarity. Extending Wirth's model suggests what positive factors people get in return—that is, increased material well-being and quality services. In the past, the benefits of material well-being and quality of services seem to have offset loss of community sentiment. The findings suggest that perhaps people could have both. If the quality of services were increased in less populated areas, perhaps in small growth centers, people could have the best of both worlds—quality services, economic well-being, and community sentiment (that is, social well-being).

While Wirth posited only the negative consequences of urbanism on social-psychological well-being, the model presented here shows both the negative (size/density or heterogeneity) and positive (economic activity and services) sides of urbanism in relation to the aggregated sentiment index. This, we believe, presents a more realistic picture of urbanism. But this is just the first step. The findings are limited by the surrogate measures for heterogeneity, economic activity and services, in addition to the geographical location and single time period of the study. Future research should overcome these time and geographic limitations and also take into account other community variables such as structural influences (community political structure, equality, suburbanization), in addition to controlling for different types of cities and other amenities (employment, environment). It might also look closely at participation in social networks and its influence on community sentiment.

Fischer (1975:73) observes that theory in urban sociology is at an impasse (the same could be said for rural sociology). He comments that theories of the rural-urban continuum have not been adequately tested; nor have these theories, especially Wirth's, been modified or extended to take into account alternative approaches that treat the same central issue, the effect of urbanism/rurality on well-being. This paper has taken a tentative step in this direction by exploring the consequences of extending Wirth's conceptualization of urbanism in relation to community sentiment.

Notes

1. Hawley (1971:134–135) summarizes traditional criticism of Wirth's model. For example, he notes that opportunities for close associates and intimate friendships were at least as numerous in urban areas as they were in rural villages.

2. Size and density have been noted to be highly interrelated (Duncan 1957; Hawley 1971:135). In North Carolina, the counties are relatively small and uniform in size. The correlation between size and density is quite high ($r = .89$). Thus, the two variables will be discussed as one.

3. Wirth (1938:19–20) suggested four variables to tap heterogeneity: age, sex, race, and ethnic background. He observed that "cities contain a larger proportion of persons in the prime of life than rural areas which contain old and very young people" (Wirth 1938:19). In an earlier version of this paper, age dependency ratio and sex were included as indicators of heterogeneity. Also, the Gibbs and Martin (1962) measure of the degree of

division of labor was constructed to provide a slightly different measure of heterogeneity. Neither age dependency, nor sex, nor the Gibbs–Martin measure had a significant effect on the dependent variable (community sentiment) and, thus, were not included in the final analysis. Data on ethnic background were not available for 1975. In North Carolina, race seems to be an appropriate indicator of cultural heterogeneity and will be used as such.

4. County population density was based on 1975 population estimates divided by county land area (square miles) from the U.S. Department of Commerce, Bureau of the Census. Per-capita income estimates for 1975 were from the Bureau of Census. Percent nonwhite were 1975 estimates from data supplied by the Division of State Budget and Management, Research and Planning Services, Raleigh, North Carolina, 1978. The data for expenditures comes from the *Census of Government*, vol. 4, no. 3 (1972), pp. 157–161.

5. Respondents were requested to rate the quality of each of these eight services as (1) poor, (2) fair, (3) good, or (4) excellent. If the majority of respondents rated the service as good or excellent, the county was accredited as having quality services. The Guttman scaling procedure was used rather than a summated Likert procedure because with Guttman scales a researcher can know if his or her scale is internally consistent and valid (Clayton 1973:6). In Likert scales, all responses to individual items are lumped together, while Guttman scaling displays a unidimensional ordering that manifests the interrelationship between and among items. To insure that the adoption of a particular scaling technique did not alter the results, a summated Likert scale was constructed with the same eight items based on the four response categories. The correlation between the Likert scale and the Guttman scale was 0.80. Further investigation showed only slight changes in Beta weights on insertion of the Likert scale in the analysis. The findings remained substantially the same. The Guttman scale is used to maintain continuity with previous research employing the scale (Christenson 1976).

6. While the quality of services scale is grounded in the objective existence of the public services in all counties, both the measure of service quality and community sentiment are subjective, depending on residents' evaluations. Might not each measure actually represent the same thing, such as whether residents are happy or unhappy with their county? A colleague suggested this, but on further consideration, it seems unlikely. To begin with, the correlation of community services and community sentiment is 0.48, rather low for measures supposed to be tautologies. Moreover, community services correlate strongly with income and density, but community sentiment does not. Community services and community sentiment seem to be distinct empirically. Evidently, residents of the counties studied were able to distinguish the quality of a community's services from their evaluation of community sentiment.

References

Arensberg, C. M. 1955. "American Communities." *American Anthropologist,* 57:1143–1162.

Bauer, R. A., ed. 1966. *Social Indicators.* Cambridge, Mass.: M.I.T. Press.

Bell, D. 1973. *The Coming of Post-Industrial Society.* New York: Basic Books.

Berry, B. J. L. and J. D. Kasarda. 1977. *Contemporary Urban Ecology.* New York: Macmillan.

Campbell, A. K. and S. Sacks. 1967. *Metropolitan America: Fiscal Patterns and Governmental Systems.* New York: Free Press.

Campbell, A., P. Converse, and W. Rodgers. 1976. *The Quality of American Life.* New York: Russell Sage Foundation.

Christenson, J. A. 1976. "Quality of Community Services: A Macro-Unidimensional Approach with Experiential Data." *Rural Sociology* (Winter), 41:409–425.

Clark, T. N. 1973. "Community Social Indicators: From Analytical Models to Policy Applications." *Urban Affairs Quarterly* (September), 9:3–36.

Clayton, R. 1973. "Guttman Scaling: An Error Paradigm." *Pacific Sociological Review* (January), 16:5–26.

Clemente, F. and W. J. Sauer. 1976. "Life Satisfaction in the United States." *Social Forces* (March), 54:621–631.

Dillman, D. A., J. A. Christenson, E. H. Carpenter, and R. Brooks. 1974. "Increasing Mail Questionnaire Response: A Four State Comparison." *American Sociological Review* (October), 39:744–756.

Dillman, D. A. and K. R. Tremblay, Jr. 1977. "The Quality of Life in Rural America." *Annals of the American Academy of Political and Social Science* (January), 429:115–129.

Duncan, O. D. 1957. "Community Size and the Rural-Urban Continuum." In P. K. Hatt and A. J. Reiss, eds., *Cities and Society,* pp. 35–45. New York: Free Press.

Durand, R. and D. R. Eckart. 1973. "Social Rank, Residential Effects and Community Satisfaction." *Social Forces* (September), 52:74–85.

Durkheim, E. 1933. *The Division of Labor in Society.* Glencoe, Ill.: Free Press.

Eberts, P. R. 1973. "The Most Rural of the Planning Regions in New York State." Mimeographed, Ithaca, N.Y.: Cornell University, Department of Rural Sociology.

Fischer, C. S. 1972. "Urbanism as a Way of Life: A Review and an Agenda." *Sociological Methods and Research,* 1(2):187–242.

—— 1973. "Urban Malaise." *Social Forces* (December), 52:221–235.

—— 1975. "The Study of Urban Community and Personality." *Annual Review of Sociology,* 1:67–89.

Fuguitt, G. V. 1965. "County Seat as a Factor in Small Town Growth and Decline." *Social Forces* (December), 44:245–251.

Gallup Opinion Index. 1974. *Report No. 110* (August).

Gerson, E. M. 1976. "On 'Quality of Life.' " *American Sociological Review* (October), 41:793–806.

Gibbs, J. P. and W. Martin. 1962. "Urbanization, Technology, and the Division of Labor: International Patterns." *American Sociological Review,* 27(5):667–677.

Goudy, W. J. 1977. "Evaluation of Local Attributes and Community Satisfaction in Small Towns." *Rural Sociology* (Fall), 43:371–382.

Hawley, A. H. 1971. *Urban Society: An Ecological Approach.* New York: Ronald Press.

Hines, F. K., D. L. Brown, and J. M. Zimmer. 1975. *Social and Economic Characteristics of the Population in Metro and Nonmetro Counties, 1970.* Agriculture Economic Report no. 272, Washington, D.C.: U.S. Department of Agriculture.

Homans, G. 1950. *The Human Group.* New York: Harcourt, Brace and World.

Johnson, R. L. and E. Knop. 1970. "Rural–Urban Differentials in Community Satisfaction." *Rural Sociology* (December), 35:544–548.

Kasarda, J. D. and M. Janowitz. 1974. "Community Attachment in Mass Society." *American Sociological Review,* 39:328–339.

Liu, B.-C. 1975. *Quality of Life Indicators in U.S. Metropolitan Areas.* Washington, D.C.: U.S. Environmental Protection Agency.

Lowenthal, M. D. 1977. "The Social Economy in Urban Working-Class Communities." In R. Warren, ed., *New Perspectives on the American Community,* pp. 305–316. New York: Rand McNally.

Marans, R. W. and W. Rodgers. 1975. "Toward an Understanding of Community Satisfaction." In A. Hawley and V. Rocks, eds., *Metropolitan America in Contemporary Perspective,* pp. 299–352. New York: Russell Sage Foundation.

Molotch, H. 1976. "The City as a Growth Machine: Toward a Political Economy of Place." *American Journal of Sociology* (September), 82:309–332.

Niederfrank, E. J. 1971. "What and Where of Community Service." *Yearbook of Agriculture,* pp. 254–258.

Ostrom, E. 1972. "Metropolitan Reform: Propositions Derived from Two Traditions." *Social Science Quarterly* (December), 53:309–332.

Rojek, D. G., F. Clemente, and G. Summers. 1975. "Community Satisfaction: A Study of Contentment with Local Services." *Rural Sociology* (Summer), 40:177–192.

Rossi, P. H. 1972. "Community Social Indicators." In A. Campbell and P. Converse, eds., *The Human Meaning of Social Change,* pp. 87–126. New York: Russell Sage Foundation.

Seiler, L. H. and G. F. Summers. 1974. "Locating Community Boundaries: An Integration of Theory and Empirical Techniques." *Sociological Methods and Research* (February), 2:259–280.

Simmel, G. (1905) 1957. "The Metropolis and Mental Life." In P. K. Hatt and A. J. Reiss, eds., *Cities and Society*, pp. 635–646. New York: Free Press.

Tönnies, F. (1887) 1957. *Community and Society*. New York: Harper & Row.

U.S. Bureau of the Census. 1973. *Statistical Abstract of the United States*. Washington, D.C.: GPO.

Weber, M. (1921) 1958. *The City*, D. Martindale and C. Neuwirth, trans. and eds. New York: Free Press.

Willits, F. K., R. Bealer, and D. Crider. 1973. "Leveling of Attitudes in Mass Society: Rurality and Traditional Morality in America." *Rural Sociology*, 38(1):36–45.

Wirth, L. 1938. "Urbanism as a Way of Life." *American Journal of Sociology* (July), 44:1–24.

8
Migration and Rights of Access: New Public Concerns of the 1970s

PETER A. MORRISON

LAST FALL, MOST of the 236 residents of Hardenburgh, New York, attempted to exempt themselves from property taxes by becoming ministers in a church that offers divinity degrees by mail. Perhaps to their own surprise they succeeded, for they originally staged their action as a media event to dramatize Hardenburgh's financial plight for New York officialdom: over the past several years a number of tax-exempt groups have bought large tracts of land in the area, narrowing the tax base drastically. As a result, property taxes for Hardenburgh's residents, most of whom have modest or meager incomes, have tripled or quadrupled, threatening many of them with loss of their homes and farms.[1]

In northern California a year or so earlier, the Board of Supervisors of scenic, sparsely populated Plumas County voted unanimously to stop paying the county's share of state and federally mandated welfare programs. They took that action in protest against a welfare load whose proportions re-

Reprinted with permission from Rand Series P-5785 (1977), Rand Corporation. Table and text reference to table are omitted due to space constraints.

semble those of New York City: One in eight of the county's
residents (1,540 out of 21,700 total population) were receiving some kind of public assistance. Local residents blamed
the escalating welfare costs on an influx of "long hairs and
minorities" that followed the establishment of a small two-
year college in the area several years before.

A number of other places have rebelled in recent years
against ailments they blamed on "newcomers." Petaluma and
Livermore (in the San Francisco Bay area), Boulder, Colorado, and Boca Raton, Florida, are among the smaller cities
that have imposed population ceilings or enacted other measures to control growth from migration. In Hawaii, Governor
Ariyoshi recently proposed Federal legislation to control the
influx of migrants to his state.

These tax and welfare rebellions and no-growth ordinances are symptoms of fiscal, socioeconomic, and environmental stresses that arise partly from new patterns of population redistribution. Now, as in the past, people migrate for
reasons that are connected with the workings of the national
economy. Most of them do so to improve their lot in life,
defined chiefly in terms of job or income opportunities, and
therefore move from areas where jobs are dwindling to areas
where workers are needed.

Until quite recently, the trend of this movement was toward metropolitan areas or between them and was mostly due
to employment opportunities in those areas. But in the 1970s,
a number of economic trends—along with other forces harder
to pin down—have converged to alter this pattern of redistribution. In one of the noteworthy reversals in migratory patterns in the nation's history, more people are now moving
away from metropolitan areas than are moving to them, and
some of the places they are moving to have experienced little
or no growth for decades.

This new dispersal of population, coupled with a sharp
slowdown in overall growth due to a lower birth rate, has
altered local and regional population growth rates, and the
new patterns are having signficant social, fiscal, and political
repercussions. Suddenly, people are thinking about migra-

tion—a topic about which few Americans have thought it necessary to have any opinion whatsoever. Migration is gaining recognition as a powerful and unpredictable force. The essentially private and unregulated movements that make up migration flows are now being scrutinized for the newly perceived costs they create, both at origin and especially at destination.

This new sensitivity to the costs of migration is partly due to its new directions. When people move away from densely populated areas to sparsely populated ones, instead of the other way around, they cause two important asymmetries. One of them is arithmetic: migrants who move to or between cities for opportunities afforded by "bigness" enhance that bigness; but if large numbers of migrants move to the country for its "smallness," they may destroy what they seek. The second is a cultural asymmetry: the people who are descending on small cities and towns and creating settlements in virtual wilderness areas are a different breed from the relatively poor and uneducated migrants who flocked to the cities in the first half of this century. Many of them are comparatively affluent and well-educated urbanites who, for all their reported affection for "the simple life," are accustomed to urban living standards. For them, the dirt road that was so picturesque in autumn must be paved the minute winter snows and spring rains turn it into rutted mud.

These asymmetries have brought the right to migrate into conflict with the less well-defined rights of the population already living where migrants decide to go—or, in the case of unpopulated areas, with the public's right to conserve the wilderness. The pressure of population on limited spatial resources is producing an array of disputes over issues of access to places. The most notorious, perhaps, are arising between those who value the aesthetics of a space and those who have to pay taxes on it.

Historically, Americans have enjoyed the right to migrate anywhere in the country without any form of official sanction or intervention. Each citizen's right of access to the social, economic, and physical resources of the nation has been vested in the right to migrate and, for generations of migrants, geographical mobility has indeed meant upward social mobility. But an individual's access to social and economic well-being can be abridged by law, custom, prejudice, or disadvantage.

Today, an intensely rights-conscious society is transferring some of the burden of equalizing opportunity from the individual to the society. Opportunities once secured, if at all, by movement to a more hospitable or economically provident community are now secured by law. The "rights" of access to jobs, to welfare, to better schools and housing, and so forth are to be guaranteed in all places. But increasingly, the rights of migrants are being called into question by those who feel *their* rights are being impinged upon by migrants' traditionally unlimited access. The local manifestations are as diverse as the circumstances in Hardenburgh or Petaluma, but a common issue is being raised: Does the right to access include a right not to be "accessed"—that is, subjected to population growth or compositional change and all that it entails? So far the answer has been yes in some instances (Petaluma), no in others (Plumas County).

The Current Demographic Context

Population change in any given locale is by definition the net effect of changes in fertility rates, mortality rates, and migration rates (including rates of immigration and emigration). Currently, the U.S. population is undergoing some noteworthy transformations attributable to changes in two of these factors: fertility and migration.

The sharp decline in births, especially in this decade, has slowed the overall rate of population growth nationally. This slower growth rate has intensified the effect on the nation's major urban centers of a trend to net outmigration from metropolitan areas. This effect has been most noticeable in the large metropolitan areas, many of which now have a stable or declining number of residents. Fully ten of the nation's twenty-five largest Standard Metropolitan Statistical Areas (SMSAs) were declining as of 1974: New York, Chicago, Los Angeles-Long Beach, Philadelphia, Detroit, St. Louis, Pittsburgh, Cleveland, Seattle-Everett, and Cincinnati. All told, nearly one in six of all 259 metropolitan areas had fewer residents in 1975 than they had in 1970, and *one in three metropolitan residents was living in an area of population decline.*

This new dispersal pattern is multifaceted. First, migrants are gravitating increasingly toward the South and Southwest, producing a wave of growth that has spread throughout many formerly declining Southern areas and leaving behind a situation of population stasis throughout much of the Northeast. This shift, building for many years, reflects basic shifts in regional shares of national employment. The differences in growth rates among regions are due less to the relocation of firms than to the different growth rates of firms that stay put[2]—which perhaps accounts for recent allegations that federal spending and regulation have systematically short-changed the Northeast.

Second, more Americans are now moving *away* from metropolitan areas than are moving *to* them, reversing a long-established urbanization trend. Each year between 1970 and 1975, for every 100 people who moved to a metropolitan area, 131 moved out. As a result, net migration gains occurred in nearly two-thirds of all nonmetropolitan counties, compared with only one-quarter in the 1960s. This reversal is affecting distinctly remote nonmetropolitan areas as well as those adjacent to metropolitan centers; it cannot, therefore, be explained away semantically as just more metropolitan sprawl or "spillover." For now, at least, nonmetropolitan areas have become more attractive, both to their residents and to outsiders, whereas metropolitan areas have become less so.[3]

It is unclear whether this reversal will be a temporary or a long-term phenomenon. (The shift coincided with, and may be due in part to, the severe economic recession of the past several years.) Its immediate effects, however, are palpable and real. The by now familiar problem of population decline in older central cities has spread outward. Suburbs that were accustomed to resisting the "negative" aspects of growth—higher taxes, higher-density zoning, crowded streets and classrooms—are now dismayed by the loss of the "positive" aspects of growth—rising employment, an expanding tax base, and general prosperity. On the other hand, rural areas that failed to grow despite years of federal economic development subsidies are now growing spontaneously, but not always in beneficial ways.

Together, lower fertility and changed migration patterns have made for surprising—in some cases disturbing—shifts in regional and local fortunes. Over time, economic trends and federal policies give rise to forces that attract migrants to some areas and repel them from others. Federal policies that exert a powerful and largely undirected influence include, for example, oil depletion allowances, federal purchases of goods and services, energy price regulation, and income redistribution (principally through welfare programs and Social Security). Individual states or local jurisdictions, which in the past have had little say about the effects of these policies, are now organizing to exert more control over their own economic welfare.[4]

One currently prominent instance of how national policy may have highly visible location-specific effects is energy-related industrial development. A new variant of the rapid-growth-through-migration syndrome—the "energy boom town"—has appeared in numerous places throughout the Rocky Mountain and Northern Great Plains states.

The Energy Boom Town

The sudden congregation of migrants in some isolated place is not a new phenomenon in the United States. The instant city is an ancient form, as is its special variant, the energy boom town. A rhyme appearing in the June 9, 1866, Meadow

Lake *Morning Star* in Nevada County, California, foreshadowed contemporary developments:

> But one short year since first these mines were known,
> Behold, like magic, lo! a town is shown.

In many places in the Rocky Mountain and Northern Great Plains states where large-scale projects are underway to develop energy supplies, the 1970s genre of boom towns is sprouting up: Gillette, Wyoming; Colstrip, Montana; and others like them. The energy boom town—brought to life by the lure of sudden treasure and exposed to a freewheeling interplay of social, economic, and political forces—draws people motivated by personal gain to sites possessing few of the standard prerequisites for urban greatness.[5]

Today's instant cities, like the earlier boom towns, are characterized by a transient, largely male population and the "Four Ds"—drunkenness, depression, delinquency, and divorce. Several of their distinctive features are of special significance in the contemporary context.[6]

For one thing, the areas in which they have appeared are sparsely populated, by and large, and possess no sizable indigenous labor pool from which workers can be drawn. Most of the work force must come from outside the surrounding region and their influx constitutes a relatively large population increase.[7] Unlike most other types of rural industrialization, which tend to attract a commuting work force, the energy boom towns consist of newly arrived migrants, a sociologically distinct type of human community.

No less significant than the relative magnitude of population change is its duration and pattern. Sharp fluctuations of employment occur as construction commences and then ends, giving way to long-term operation over a twenty- to sixty-year period. The construction phase of a large-scale energy project may last from several months to several years; generally, there is little overlap in personnel or skill requirements once construction is finished and operation begins.

The extreme disparity in numbers of employees between

these two separate phases is suggested in the following estimates from a recent Rand Corporation study of coal development in the Northern Great Plains.[8] Construction of a 1,000-
megawatt electric generating plant uses 1,250 to 2,500 employees at the peak of activity, whereas operation of such a
plant requires only 150 to 200 employees. Construction of a
large synthetic natural gas plant (250 million cubic feet per
day) is likely to require a peak work force of 2,000 to 4,000,
but only 600 to 800 operating employees thereafter.

The typical energy boom town is, in fact, a succession of
two different communities. The first, fast-growing but imper-
manent, consists largely of a temporary construction work
force that may number upwards of several thousand people.
The second consists of the far smaller group of personnel who
will operate the facility afterwards. Numbers and timing may
vary from place to place, but the pattern is typical.

Demands for additional classroom space, health care facilities, a larger police force, and other "necessities of life"
crop up as soon as newcomers move in, but the finances do
not; moreover, construction workers' taxes rarely pay for the
instantaneous demands their presence creates, since many of
them live in mobile homes with relatively low assessed val-
uations. In the end, the beleaguered community may well be
left with a far smaller population that has to shoulder the
long-term debt resulting from these front-end costs for
schools, medical clinics, and the like, which by then may
stand half empty.

A third distinguishing feature of the energy boom town
is the disparity between newcomers and old-timers. Typically, the newcomers are younger and better paid, and are
natives of other places, possibly urban. They are likely to
judge the adequacy of local services by different standards,
and to expect a higher level of services than do the native
residents they join.

Migrant influx is never easy to absorb, but both the locale and the phasing of development make it especially disruptive for the typical energy boom town. Local governmental units in sparsely settled areas are ill equipped to cope

with increased demands for basic community services, which are typically marginal before development. They lack manpower and fiscal resources, and these difficulties may be compounded by confusion about the relative responsibilities of local, state, and federal governments.

The post-1970 experience of Gillette, Wyoming, and other communities like it is a foretaste of the stresses in store for other places that undergo sudden increase through migration. Like their predecessors, today's energy boom towns demonstrate that the populations that make instant cities do not make instant citizens.

The Emerging Concern with Access

The issue of access has aroused increasing concern at the local level. Outsiders enjoy a constitutionally guaranteed freedom of entry, and local officials have felt frustrated over their inability to affect the external forces that attract migrants or to regulate directly the numbers and types of arriving newcomers. The result may be high rates of growth (which provoked growth-control ordinances in Boulder, Petaluma, and Livermore); or a heavy burden on the pocketbooks of local residents (which prompted religious ordination in Hardenburgh, New York, and unilateral withdrawal from federal welfare in Plumas County, California). The visibility of migrants seems to have made them a ready focus of territorial issues concerning access.

Cities and towns that have felt inundated by new settlers are now stubbornly challenging certain basic, heretofore inalienable rights in actively seeking to regulate further increases in population. Recent years have seen a proliferation of local efforts to impose population ceilings. These have taken various forms: restricting the number of new dwelling units that can be built; making new residential construction contingent on the provision of additional education, sewage-disposal, and water-supply facilities; or simply legislating a maximum allowable population (without specifying the fate of the next arriving migrant). Whatever the stratagem, the impetus is a stiffening local reluctance to accept the costs of demographic excess. This reluctance can only grow, with the new pattern of migration away from large centers to small places and the arithmetic asymmetry whereby sheer numbers inevitably destroy "smallness."

The right to enact such growth controls has generally been denied by the courts on the grounds that citizens have a constitutional right not to be discriminated against in choosing a place to settle. But communities' growing reluctance to accept more migrants highlights a vexing proposition: If the Constitution prohibits discriminatory barriers against people settling where they wish, then a community has to make room for newcomers without limit.

If issues of territoriality are to be settled rationally, the legal aspects of access will have to be informed by a better understanding of the demographic *mechanism* of access. In attempting to control its growth, does a community abridge the freedom of outsiders to move in? Interestingly enough, the legal aspects of access may be moot for demographic reasons: explicit growth-control policies would not necessarily eliminate migrants' access to certain locales. Even if Petaluma, Livermore, and Boulder are allowed to continue the growth control measures they have enacted or proposed, the demographic evidence suggests that they will not seriously curtail *access* through inmigration. The reason is that net migration figures offset inmigrants against outmigrants, showing only the resulting number following what amounts to a large exchange of individuals.

Evidence on this point derives from newly available data on contemporary domestic migration flows into and out of local jurisdictions.[9] The data furnish a remarkably high-resolution view of local migration flows into and out of individual cities. These figures call into question the contention that population ceiling ordinances necessarily abridge individuals' right of access to a community.

Estimated migration rates for several illustrative localities, which are of two contrasting types, were gathered. The first are five growth-limiting cities, in which efforts have been under way to curtail migratory influx during the 1970s: Petaluma, Livermore, Boulder, St. Petersburg, and Boca Raton. The second type are five comparison cities, each with roughly the same size population as one of the growth-limiting cities but without major growth through migration: San Pablo (roughly Petaluma's size), Redlands (Livermore's size), and Waterloo, Tampa, and Urbana.

The first noteworthy feature underlying these data is the rapid rate at which migrants come and go. Annually, the growth-limiting cities gain anywhere from 9 to 16 inmigrants per hundred residents; the comparison cities tend to be somewhat lower. Rates of departure are nearly as high, ranging from 6 outmigrants per hundred residents in Waterloo to 15.5 per hundred in Urbana.[10] These figures serve as a reminder that the American city is not so much a place as a process—a flow of people coming and going. In the course of a decade, then, the total number of *different* people residing in most of these cities could be easily twice the entire number there at any one point in time.

The annual rates of net migration into the growth-limiting cities are generally lower for 1973–1975 than for 1970–1973, perhaps reflecting the enactment (or simply threat) of local growth controls.[11] (Changes in net migration for the comparison cities are, for the most part, nominal.)

What is more significant for the issue at hand, though, is the consistently high rate of migratory *outflow*. Changes in net migration, by comparison, are quite small. The principal factor determining access from outside, then, is the impermanence of current residents and the rate at which their departure opens up places for newcomers. Net migration is misleading as an index of accessibility. For example, annual net migration to Petaluma was sharply lower during 1973–1975 than during 1970–1973, but access by outsiders was still high: between 1973 and 1975, no less than one Petaluma resident in ten could claim to have taken up residence just last year in this supposedly "closed" community.

Zero net migration, whether spontaneously attained or

deliberately induced, does not abridge the right of access to a community, because inmigration and outmigration typically produce considerable population change, even without growth. Demographically stable localities remain accessible from outside because each year a sizable percentage of residents choose to depart.

Who Gets to Live Where?

Submerged beneath the contemporary concerns with migration, and the often unwelcome access it confers on destination areas, are more profound legal and political issues. The question, "Who gets to live where?" immediately raises the equally vexing question, "Who is to decide, and by what criteria?" Whether or not society poses these questions explicitly, it does not avoid providing implicit answers.

Those answers are provided by a host of private and public decisions that together amount to a rationing system that controls local settlement patterns. When government agencies build highways, regulate energy prices, and choose sites for federal installations, they simultaneously redistribute employment growth and alter incentives for private investment. Although these and other government programs and activities are nominally unrelated, they exert a powerful undirected influence on migration patterns.

Within an individual metropolitan area, residence in many, if not most, communities is allocated by rationing mechanisms of one sort or another. The type and diversity of available housing is one such mechanism, with values set by zoning and adjusted by market forces. The legitimacy of this mechanism is reflected in the Supreme Court's recent decision that zoning rules in Arlington Heights, Illinois, which bar multifamily dwellings, are not unconstitutional unless discriminatory intent is shown. Jobs are also rationing mechanisms, and by choosing to welcome or oppose a prospective employer a community exercises some control over the number of available jobs and hence job-holders. Some cities like

Chicago go so far as to impose residency requirements on municipal employees: to work for the city, you must live in it. Here, too, the Supreme Court has upheld the propriety of municipal residency rules that, in effect, give a reply to the question, "Who is to live where?"

The right to live where one wishes, then, is not as unlimited as Americans have casually assumed; it is strongly modified by the workings of economic and social systems. The legal issues arising out of the no-growth controversy not only raise profound legal and political questions concerning individual rights, but also introduce the idea of tinkering with the vast and complex system by which population and economic changes occur throughout the country. The hazard is that there is no clear place for such tinkering to stop.

In Hardenburgh, New York, newly tax-exempted old-timers now greet each other with the question, "Reverend, have you seen the light?" The way this particular town overcame "the system" is amusing but also disturbing, for it rivets attention on the much thornier question of access that is troubling many different sorts of places throughout the nation. It is a question for which there is, as yet, no consistent answer.

Notes

1. A tax assessor granted tax exemptions to Hardenburgh's newly ordained clergy early last December, according to the *New York Times*. What began as a media event has spread in recent months to other neighboring Catskill area communities, most recently Carmel, New York.

2. R. J. Vaughan, *The Impacts of Federal Policies on Urban Economic Development*, the Rand Corporation, R-2025-KF, forthcoming.

3. See: C. J. Tucker, "Changing Patterns of Migration Between Metropolitan and Nonmetropolitan Areas in the United States: Recent Evidence," *Demography*, 13 (1976):435–443; P. A. Morrison, "Rural Renaissance in America? The Revival of Population Growth in Remote Areas," Population Bulletin, 31 (Washington, D.C.: Population Reference Bureau, 1976).

4. See: "The Second War Between the States," *Business Week* (May

17, 1976):92–114; and "Federal Spending: The North's Loss is the Sunbelt's Gain," *National Journal* (June 26, 1976):878–891.

5. G. Barth, *Instant Cities: Urbanization and the Rise of San Francisco and Denver* (New York: Oxford University Press, 1975). The rhyme above is cited by Barth.

6. W. R. Freudenberg, "The Social Impact of Energy Boom Development on Rural Communities: A Review of Literature and Some Predictions," paper prepared for the annual meeting, American Sociological Association, Section on Environmental Sociology, New York City, August 31, 1976; J. S. Gilmore, "Boom Towns May Hinder Energy Resource Development," *Science,* 191 (1976):535–540; B. Christiansen and T. H. Clack, Jr., "A Western Perspective on Energy: A Plea for Rational Energy Planning," *Science* 194 (1976):578–584.

7. The population of the town of Colstrip, Montana, for example, increased from 423 in 1970 to 2,682 in 1975. (Data are from Christiansen and Clack, "A Western Perspective.")

8. R. Nehring et al., *Coal Development and Government Regulation in the Northern Great Plains: A Preliminary Report,* the Rand Corporation, R-1981-NSF/RC (1976), pp. 120–121.

9. The data in table 8.1 are special tabulations based on U.S. Bureau of the Census migration files, and refer only to internal migration (they exclude international migration). The Census migration files, prepared in conjunction with its population estimation program, are based on individual federal income tax returns filed in each of several years. For the tabulations shown here, rates of migration have been developed for a given geographic area over two intervals of time: 1970–1973 and 1973–1975 (referring to a three-year and two-year migration interval, respectively).

The Bureau of the Census uses the following general procedure to estimate these migration rates: (1) IRS files containing individual tax returns for calender year i (e.g., 1969) are matched by Social Security number with their counterparts for calendar year j (e.g., 1972); (2) matched records, sorted by geographic area, serve as the base for calculating migration rates into or out of the area. Our special tabulations were designed to show gross rates of migration.

Migration rates furnished by the Bureau refer to areas only and contain no information about the entering and departing migrants themselves. For further information, see U.S. Bureau of the Census, *Current Population Reports,* series P-25, no. 576 (or comparable issues) and no. 640, p. 12.

10. Although scaled to an annual basis, the 1970–1973 and 1973–1975 rates are not strictly comparable because the migration intervals are not the same. Multiple moves (e.g., by a migrant who arrives at time 1 and departs at time 2) are less likely to be recorded the longer the migration interval, which leads to a downward bias. Shorter migration intervals register a larger percentage of all moves that are made. Accordingly, the 1973–1975 rates are subject to somewhat less downward bias than are the 1970–

1973 rates. Therefore, we expect the former to be higher (i.e., closer to correct) than the latter when each is scaled to an annual basis, other things being equal.

11. Interpretation here is complicated by a concurrent sharp reduction in housing construction. Around 1973, considerable capital being pumped into suburban housing construction by real estate investment trusts dried up. As a result, some places where growth control measures have been enacted are now awaiting the arrival of growth.

PART FOUR

Renewed Interest in Residential Crowding

EDITOR'S NOTE:

GALLE AND GOVE review the extensive literature on the effects of extremes in population distribution—that is, overcrowding and isolation—on humans and other animals. Studies of human overcrowding are beset with numerous problems—defining overcrowding, separating out social structural variables, and measuring effects—and have lacked consistent results. The authors' own studies, which use resident surveys and statistics on urban area characteristics, suggest that household crowding has small but consistent effects on well-being. Gillis, in examining a different type of overcrowding, considers the effects of high-rise housing on mental strain. Surveys indicate that there are sex differences in reactions to high-density living. The fact that women have more strain than men suggests that social factors, role positions, and personal expectations may result in varying responses to difficult housing conditions.

9
Overcrowding, Isolation, and Human Behavior: Exploring the Extremes in Population Distribution

OMER R. GALLE AND WALTER R. GOVE

THE EXISTENCE OF some optimal level of population size and density, above or below which a population may exhibit deleterious effects, has been an intriguing and recurring notion in both animal and human population studies. In the late nineteenth century Durkheim (1933) and Spencer (1879–1882) came to rather different conclusions about the structural and behavioral consequences of increasing size and density of human populations. Even before this, Verhulst (1845) had observed positive correlations between the death rate and the population density of specific populations. Sociologists (and others) have also been impressed by the severe effects of the other end of the population distribution continuum: extreme isolation (Davis 1940; Spitz 1945, 1946; Spitz and Wolfe 1946). In this paper we review the evidence on the behavioral consequences of the two extremes of pop-

Reprinted with permission from K. Taeuber, L. Bumpass, and J. Sweet, eds., *Social Demography* (New York: Academic Press, 1978). Sections were deleted because of space constraints.

ulation distribution—overcrowding and high population density on the one hand, and isolation on the other.

Ecological Studies of Overcrowding and Isolation in Human Populations

In our review of ecological studies of human populations, we begin with a review of the effects of high density and over-crowding; this is followed by a brief discussion of the effects of isolation. There are many more studies of the effects of high density and overcrowding than of isolation. We group high density and overcrowding together for, although we have specified the conceptual differences between the two con-cepts, this distinction is not always made in the literature.

High Density and Overcrowding

Theoretical support for an effect of population density on social relationships rests on the notion that the number of social actors per unit of area affects the potential contacts, both for a given individual and within the aggregate. Fre-quencies of contact and communication are potentially mul-tiplied exponentially as density increases. These contacts and communications create the possibility of increases in coop-eration and/or conflict. On an aggregate level, high-density settlements and the large number of contacts each individual may make have been assumed to create a preponderance of secondary and segmental role relationships (Simmel 1957; Wirth 1938).

At the individual level, density may affect one's health and level of well-being. Most of the theoretical literature on the experience of crowding focuses on two analytically dis-tinct but interrelated concepts: an excess of stimulation and a lack of privacy. For example, Desor (1972) defines crowd-ing as "receiving excess of stimulation from social sources." Other investigators who have emphasized stimulus overload in the experience of crowding are Rapoport (1973), Galle et al. (1972), Wohlwill (1974), and Milgram (1970). Perhaps the best theoretical discussion of the effects of the environment on behavior is the book by Altman (1975). Altman, while recognizing the importance of stimulus overload, feels that the concept of privacy is the key to understanding crowding. We would note that there is a fairly extensive *conceptual* literature dealing with the nature and importance of privacy (for example, Altman 1975, 1976; Bates 1964; Chermayeff and Alexander 1965; Fischer 1975; Jourard 1966; Kelvin 1973; Marmor 1972; Pastalan 1970; Pennock and Chapman 1971; Schwartz 1968; Shils 1966), and that privacy is typically related to aspects of the physical environment, such as the number of persons per room in a household (for example, Chapin 1951; Schwartz 1968; Smith et al. 1969). There has been, however, virtually no empirical investigation of the effects of a lack of privacy (Altman 1975:6).

The National Academy of Sciences (1971) reports that crowding increases the incidence of infectious disease mainly through a greater opportunity for the spread of infection. The NAS report cites evidence that crowding also has other injurious health effects that occur primarily when the degree and extent of crowding are rapidly increasing. Thus the rapidity of growth and accompanying urbanization may be more deleterious to health than population density per se. The NAS report claims that animal experiments and experience with humans confirm that social stresses due to crowding produce physiological disturbances that in turn increase the susceptibility to disease. The relationship may be far more complex than this. Crowding under some circumstances appears to be clearly associated with poor health states, while under other circumstances it may be neutral or even beneficial (Taylor and Knowelden 1957). Indeed microbial disease is not necessarily acquired through exposure. In many cases disease occurs as a result of factors that upset the balance between ubiquitous organisms and the host that harbors them (Dubos 1965).

A number of studies of the effects of crowding have utilized urban-residential neighborhoods as their units of analysis. A study of 42 census tracts in Honolulu for 1960 utilized five measures of population density: population per acre; proportion of dwellings with 1.5 or more persons per room; average household size; proportion of "doubled up" families; and proportion of dwelling units in structures with five or more units (Schmitt 1966). These measures were then correlated with nine indicators of pathology: death rate, infant mortality rate, suicide rate, tuberculosis rate, and rates of venereal disease, admissions to mental hospitals, illegitimate births, juvenile delinquency, and adult crime. After controls for social class, persons per acre correlated much more strongly with the nine pathology measures than did any of the other component measures of density. Unfortunately, when Schmitt attempted to control for social class he dichotomized his variables (education and income) instead of treating them as continuous measures, which tended to weaken their effects and thus our faith in his results.

A negative relationship between gross density and general mortality was found across Chicago community areas for 1950, after controlling for socioeconomic status, quality of housing, and migration (Winsborough 1970). Negative associations also were shown for public assistance rates and tuberculosis rates. However, a positive relationship obtained between gross density and the infant mortality rate (after controls). Winsborough's negative results, however, may be due to including the percentage of dwellings with 1.5 or more persons per room as one of his controls (a measure of housing quality). This measure is very closely related to persons per room, which was later shown to be more closely associated with pathology than the gross density measure Winsborough employed (Galle et al. 1972).

In another analysis of data for Chicago community areas, this time for 1960, we (Galle et al. 1972) attempted a roughly approximate rendition, in a natural human setting, of Calhoun's well-known study (1962) of population density and pathology in rats. A measure of gross density (persons per acre) was shown to be related slightly to five measures of "pathological behavior": standardized mortality rates, general fertility rates, juvenile delinquency rates, rates of admissions to mental hospitals, and rates of public assistance to persons under eighteen years of age. Indices of social class and ethnicity were constructed in an attempt to take the complex human social structure into account. The density effects were reduced to insignificance when the controls for social class and ethnicity were introduced.

We then decomposed gross density into four component parts—persons per room, rooms per dwelling unit, dwelling units per structure, and structures per acre. On the basis of this decomposition we concluded that, after social class and ethnicity are controlled for, there appears to be a small but significant effect of overcrowding (persons per room) on rates of pathological behavior. However, the effects of density and social structure are so intertwined at the ecological level that it is extremely difficult to separate the two effects. For example, of the total variance in mortality, fertility, and juvenile delinquency explained by density and social structural measures taken together, over 90 percent is variance held in common by density and social structure, and it cannot be allocated independently to either density measures or social structural factors. This finding of high collinearity between measures of overcrowding and other relevant social structural controls appears in most of the ecological studies; unambiguous interpretation of any of these studies is inappropriate. However, the problem of collinearity has been lost in the debate over whether or not overcrowding is an important factor in the determination of behavior in human populations.

The complexity of the data and their interrelations also have caused a number of methodological questions to be raised about our Chicago study. The specific indices of social class and ethnicity have been questioned (Ward 1975) along with the use of ratio measures for density (Schuessler 1974). In addition, it has been suggested that the use of measures of central tendency (such as average persons per room) should have been replaced by measures of extremes of the distribution under examination (for example, percentage of housing units with more than one person per room [Ward 1975]). Finally, the cross-sectional, one-point-in-time nature of the analysis has been criticized (McPherson 1973). In a more recent analysis (Galle and Gove 1974) we considered each of these criticisms and examined each census period from 1940 through 1970 for Chicago. Extreme measures of each variable were used: Percentage of housing units with more than one person per room and percentage of housing units in structures with more than five housing units were our measures of overcrowding and structural density; percentage non-white, percentage of families with low incomes, percentage with less than eight years of education, and percentage of labor force in lower blue-collar occupations were our measures of social structure. For all time periods between 1940 and 1970 and for all "pathologies" (mortality, fertility, juvenile delinquency, and marital instability) the two density variables are able to account for an average of 6.6 percent of variation independently. Social structure is able to account for slightly more—12.3 percent—of variation independently. The amount of explained variance held in common by the two sets of variables, however, is much larger—57.7 percent (Galle and Gove 1974).

Several recent studies using cities as units of analysis have attempted to examine the effects of overcrowding on murder rates. A positive relationship between a set of density variables and homicide rates was found for 171 U.S. cities in both 1950 and 1970, although the relationship was greatly reduced after social class and racial controls were introduced (McCarthy et al. 1975). Using a larger sample of U.S. cities (n = 389) Gove et al. (1976a) found overcrowding and city size to be positively correlated to homicide. The relationship for overcrowding (but not city size) was reduced to insignificance after controls were introduced. Among an even larger set of U.S. cities (n = 656) Booth et al. (1976) found a small relationship between density and a variety of personal and property crimes. Density had more effect on large than on small cities. Their study, however, suffered from a severe methodological problem: They used census data from 1960 and crime data from 1967. The analysis by McPherson (1973) suggests the time lag was great enough to distort the relationship they found.

The effect of population density and crowding on health and social behavior was assessed among 145 economic-geographical regions in the Netherlands (Levy and Herzog 1974). After economic status and population heterogeneity were controlled for, density was positively associated only with age-adjusted death rates. Weak or inverse relations were found between crowding (persons per room) and measures of age-adjusted male heart disease rate, admissions to general hospitals, admissions to mental hospitals, delinquency, illegitimate births, and divorce.

A study by Collette and Webb (1974) looked at the effects of density (persons per acre) and crowding (persons per room) in the eighteen urban areas of New Zealand; unfortunately, no socioeconomic controls were used. New Zealand, however, has a system of free public hospital care that greatly diminishes class-related differences in health care utilization. A fairly strong positive relationship was found between density and psychological disorder, but the relationship of density with physical disorder was negative. In general, weak and inconsistent relationships were found between crowding and the dependent variables.

In a study using census tracts in Edmonton, after controls for income and national origin, building type (that is, multiple-unit dwellings) had a strong positive association with juvenile delinquency and social allowance (public assistance), but the relationships of those dependent variables with density and overcrowding were nonsignificant (Gillis 1974).

A study of Peoria used city blocks rather than census tracts, controlled for a large set of other variables, and examined the relationship among measures of density and crime and mortality (Choldin and Roncek 1976). Compared to the effect of some of their control variables, that of density was relatively weak; however, it was significantly related to child and infant mortality and the general crime rate and more strongly to the violent crime rate.

Booth and Welch (1974) looked at the relationship be-

tween areal density and civil disorder using sixty-five nations as their units of analysis. They found that "household
crowding and, to a far less extent, areal density are linked to
the emergence of civil strife" (p. 153). It is noteworthy that
household overcrowding had a much greater explanatory
power than did measures of industrialization, urbanization,
and discrimination. Fischer et al. (1975:416, note 10) refer to
this study and a similar one by Factor and Waldron (1973)
that use national averages of density, including countries
composed largely of uninhabited territory, as "representing a
reductio ad absurdum, so much so that one is tempted to
suspect they are purposeful caricatures." In a subsequent
study of cities in the United States Welch and Booth (1975)
found a much weaker relationship between density and civil
disorder; most of the variance in the civil disorder measure
was accounted for by the size of the black population.

In sum, ecological studies of overcrowding, high population density, and various rates of "pathological" behavior
show very mixed results. Part of the difficulty of generalizing
from these studies arises from confusion among the several
aspects of high population density, particularly overcrowding versus structural density. Also contributing to the mixed
results are the different ways of managing and interpreting
the high degree of collinearity between density variables and
control variables. Our summary assessment is a cautious affirmation of a positive relationship between crowding and
some rates of "pathological" behavior. Although social structural factors are highly interrelated with high levels of structural density and interpersonal crowding, there does appear
to be a small but significant amount of explained variance in
certain rates of behavior, which can be attributed to density
and/or overcrowding factors independently of other social-
structural factors.

Isolation

There have been surprisingly few ecological studies of
the relationship between isolation and behavior. In fact we
know of only two studies, both of which are recent. One study

is based on a survey of all pharmacists in the forty-five New Zealand urban areas with populations of over ten thousand (Webb and Collette 1975). Use of stress-alleviate drugs (tranquilizers, antidepressants, and so on) was found to be very strongly related to living alone.

The second study is our own, and we shall review briefly our conceptualization as well as our findings (Gove et al. 1976a). Those who live alone (our measure of isolation) are less likely to be firmly integrated into social networks. The literature on integration and isolation suggests the following premises. First, if one is integrated into a set of social networks one's life tends to take on meaning and value, whereas if one is isolated life tends to be meaningless and empty. Second, social control of behavior requires social interaction, and the individual who lives alone, lacking such control, will be free to act in deviant ways. Third, when one confronts a problem the social support and feedback of others put the problem into perspective and often suggest ways of handling it; isolated individuals tend to lack such support and feedback. Fourth, living alone is characterized by an environment that lacks the input and structure that tend to involve the individual in the daily affairs of life; individuals in such a situation may withdraw into a fantasy world and, if they are emotionally disturbed, this may lead them to brood about and thus magnify their problems. A fifth issue, which has received very little attention in the literature, is the fact that if others are present there is a high probability they will intervene (see, for example, Gove and Howell 1974). In the case of suicidal behavior, for example, if others are present generally they will act to prevent the prospective suicide. All five of these factors suggest a positive relationship between the percentage of the population living alone in a given areal unit and the suicide rate.

A positive relationship also may be anticipated between the percentage of the population living alone and the death rate due to cirrhosis of the liver (a measure of alcoholism). This expectation is based on two factors that play a role in a person's drinking behavior. First, drinking is highly regulated by social norms (Bacon 1957; Bales 1946; Blacker 1966; Larsen and Abu-Laban 1968; Patrick 1952; Pittman 1967; Pittman and Snyder 1962; Roman and Trice 1970; Skolnick 1958; Snyder 1962; Ullman 1958; Whitehead and Harvey 1974; Wilkinson 1970). Second, many persons drink in reaction to a stressful situation that produces feelings of discomfort and distress (Alexander 1963; Borowitz 1964; Chafetz et al. 1962; Greenberg 1963; Pearlin and Radabaugh 1975; Seely 1959; Strauss 1971; Trice 1966; Washburne 1956). Living alone would appear to be related to both of these factors, for many of the same reasons just cited linking isolation to suicide. Persons who live alone tend, almost by definition, to be largely removed from the social control of others. The environment associated with living alone may produce a desire for alcohol. And, for the problem drinker, living alone tends to prevent other persons from intervening or procuring help, thus increasing the probability of death from cirrhosis of the liver.

Utilizing a sample of all U.S. cities with populations of fifty thousand or more in 1970, we have tested the relationships of suicide rate and death rate from cirrhosis of the liver with the percentage living alone, while controlling for a number of social-structural factors, namely age, race, education, income, and unemployment. Percentage living alone was by far the most powerful predictor of both suicide and alcoholism.

In summary, the effect of residential isolation on humans has received relatively little attention in empirical research. However, the proportion of persons living alone is increasing in our society and the limited ecological evidence that is available suggests that this mode of residence has a number of undesirable effects.

Surveys on Overcrowding, Isolation, and Human Behavior

The studies reviewed in the preceding section took areas—census tracts, city blocks, entire cities, even nations—as the units of analysis. The measures of density and crowding as well as the measures of outcome behaviors and control variables all were calculated to describe populations of areas. This is a legitimate and useful research approach, but it has limitations when the conceptualization is based on individual behavior. This is because relationships that occur at the aggregate level are not necessarily the same ones that occur at the level of the individual (Hannan 1971). Because individual inferences from aggregate data have inherent limits, to establish relations truly for individuals it is necessary to utilize data obtained from individuals. In the studies reviewed in this section, the outcome and control variables are typically measured for individuals, while the density measure may refer to an aggregate index (persons/area) or specifically to the individual living circumstances (persons/room, living alone).

In 1970 Marsella et al. published a study on the effect of dwelling density on the mental health of a small sample (n = 99) of Filipino men. They found that high levels of density were assoiciated with poor mental health; however, their results are difficult to interpret because there were no controls on socioeconomic factors.

The following year Mitchell (1971) published the results of a large survey on overcrowding in Hong Kong. The degree of household crowding in Hong Kong is extremely high by American standards. Mitchell found that high levels of crowding were related strongly to complaints about lack of space and lack of privacy. These complaints were particularly common among those who shared their dwelling unit with another household. The level of general unhappiness and amount of worrying also were strongly related to crowding, but under controls for income these relationships were only maintained among the poor. Two indices of more serious psychiatric impairment, an indicator of emotional illness (generally composed of psycho-physiological symptoms) and an index of hostility, were unrelated to levels of overcrowding. The index of emotional illness was related positively to floor of residence when there were two or more households per unit; the index of hostility also was related to floor of residence, and the effects were compounded when there were two or more households per unit. Overcrowding was found to affect husband-wife communication and emotional happiness, but not quarrels. Respondents in overcrowded households were much less likely to know where their children were, and this relationship was not particularly affected by controls for the education of the respondent.

Booth and his associates conducted a major survey in Toronto in which they looked at the effects of overcrowding. These results are available in a series of papers (Booth 1975a, 1975b; Booth and Cowell 1976; Booth and Edwards 1976; Booth and Johnson 1975; Edwards and Booth 1975; Johnson and Booth 1975; Welch and Booth 1975) and a book (Booth 1976). Booth's data were obtained from a stratified multiple-stage probability sample of Toronto families. All of the thirteen census tracts used in the Toronto study "were selected for their potential in yielding a large number of families residing in dwellings in which the number of people exceeded the number of rooms" (Booth and Edwards 1976:310). Furthermore, from those census tracts "nearly 17,000 screening interviews [were held which] yielded 862 eligible households. In 560 of these we were able to obtain interviews with one or both parents for a 65% completion rate" (Booth and Edwards 1976:311). Booth and Edwards (1976:311) go on to state "the majority (80%) of the household heads were employed in blue-collar occupations, typically ones requiring only modest skills. Only 23 percent had completed high school; however, more than half had completed the eighth grade." Thus they had a very atypical sample and one that was very homogeneous on both crowding and social characteristics. As a consequence of this homogeneity, one would expect little variation on most variables and that the relationships found would be very modest.

In their analysis Booth and his associates controlled for age, education, occupational status, and ethnicity. In almost all their analyses these control variables were entered first and their crowding terms were entered as a second step. Thus they allocated any variance associated with their crowding variables that was collinear with their control variables to the control variables. This form of analysis "represents an extremely conservative test of crowding" (Booth and Cowell 1976:211). Throughout their analysis they used four measures of crowding, (1) objective neighborhood crowding, (2) subjective neighborhood crowding, (3) objective household crowding, and (4) subjective household crowding, and in addition they at times used a "rooms deficit" measure; in Booth and Edwards (1976) they also used persons per room and households per block.

The major focus of the Toronto study was on the relationship between crowding and physical health. The presence of communicable infections or stress disease was based on responses to a set of forty-two symptomatic questions, information obtained from an interview and examination by a nurse and physician, and data based on tests of urine and blood samples taken at the time of the medical examination (Booth and Cowell 1976). Unfortunately, between the initial interview and the subesequent medical examination there was a 49 percent attrition rate, and this attrition included a number of persons who were physically ill. In their analysis they looked at physiological indicators of stress, stress-related illnesses, communicable diseases, physical trauma (bruises), and reports of illness. On all five of these indices household crowding tended to be associated with poor physical health. The relationships were weak, however, and most did not reach statistical significance. In general the relationships were stronger for objective household crowding than for subjective household crowding and they were stronger for men than for women. Physical health was generally unrelated to either measure of neighborhood crowding.

Crowding, by itself, explained only a very modest portion of the variance in sexual behavior (Edwards and Booth 1975; Johnson and Booth 1975). The data indicate, however, that (1) subjective crowding was related to reports that lack of privacy prevented intercourse, and (2) under very special conditions crowding was related to high levels of marital intercourse. There was some very limited evidence that crowding was related to extramarital involvement and sexual deviation.

Booth and Edwards (1976) looked at the effect of crowding on marital relationships, relationships with children, and sibling relationships. With or without controls, the relationships with crowding were generally weak. Their view of the magnitude of their relationships is perhaps best captured in their discussion where they refer to "the minute effect of crowding revealed in our analysis" (Booth and Edwards 1976:319). Nevertheless, some of their relationships were statistically significant; for example, among wives subjective household crowding was related to a love decrement scale, arguments with spouses, and threats to leave spouses, while among men it was related to the love decrement scale and the physical striking of children.

Booth and Johnson (1975) found that crowded household conditions had a small adverse effect on the physical and intellectual development of children, with crowded children tending to be somewhat small for their age and slightly behind in school.

In summary, Booth and his associates found neighborhood crowding generally was unrelated to their dependent variables. Subjective household crowding was related slightly to poor family relations and to a variety of sexual experiences. Objective and, to a lesser extent, subjective household crowding were related weakly to poor physical health. Household crowding was related to retarded intellectual development and physical stature of children.

Booth (1976:1) concludes that "perhaps the most important finding of this study, contrary to our expectation before we began the study, is that crowded conditions seldom have any consequences and even when they do their effects are very modest." Such a conclusion, however, should be viewed with a great deal of caution. As we have already noted, their sample is very atypical, which makes generalization a rather hazardous procedure. It is also very homogeneous, with the independent variables having relatively little variance, which decreases the likelihood of finding strong relationships. Furthermore, as Booth himself notes, their analysis tends to be very conservative. However, as is noted in detail in Gove et al. (1976b), not only is their analysis (generally) very conservative, but it also contains serious flaws. There are, for example, a number of problems with the scales they use. Perhaps the most serious problem is that throughout virtually all of the analysis when they are looking at the effects of a crowding variable, they not only control for various demographic variables but they also control for all of their other crowding variables. Thus to the extent that one measure of crowding relates to another (that is, they both measure crowding), they are actually controlling for the effects of the very variables they are looking at. After going over the Toronto study in great detail, looking especially at the zero order relationships, we (Gove et al. 1976b) feel that "perhaps the most that can be concluded [from the data produced by the Toronto study] is that household crowding has at least as much effect as, and possibly more than, some of the traditional demographic variables considered by sociologists when looking at the dependent variables under consideration."

We have recently completed a survey of 2,035 residents of Chicago (Gove et al. 1976c). Approximately twenty-five interviews were gathered from each of eighty selected census tracts within the Chicago city limits. Equal numbers of tracts were selected from each of four different categories: (1) tracts with low levels of crowding and low levels of socioeconomic status, (2) tracts with high levels of crowding and low levels of socioeconomic status, (3) tracts with high socioeconomic status and low crowding, and (4) high socioeconomic status tracts that also had high levels of crowding. For each combination of crowding and socioeconomic status we selected five predominantly black tracts, five racially mixed tracts, and ten predominantly white tracts. Households were randomly selected from each census tract, and a randomly selected adult was interviewed from each of the selected households.

Of the 2,035 respondents interviewed, 453 or 22 percent were living alone. As we were initially screening by households and since the proportion of households in the United

States where persons were living alone in 1970 was 19 percent and rising rapidly (Carnahan et al. 1974:70), this is about
the proportion one would expect. As persons living alone
cannot be crowded in their homes (using a measure of persons per room), we have excluded them from our analysis.
An analysis of the data that include those who live alone
shows that by excluding these persons from our analysis we
are weighting the analysis against the overcrowding hypothesis.

The levels of crowding in our full sample are very similar to those of both the nation as a whole and central cities
in 1970, and they are considerably less than those of the nation as a whole and central cities in 1950. As a consequence
our results, unlike those of the Toronto study, have very broad
generality for most persons living with others in the United
States.

In the analysis we introduced controls for family income,
education, race, sex, age, and marital status. Statistical significance was tested *after* these variables were controlled for.

The literature on crowding emphasizes the need to consider the subjective experience of crowding. While in the
household the number of persons per room probably tends to
be the key determinant of the experience of crowding in that
setting, it is clear that other factors are important. First, due
largely to cultural and experiential factors, there is wide variation in the extent to which persons experience a particular
situation as crowded (for example, Altman 1975; Booth 1976;
Hall 1966; Mitchell 1975). Second, the organization of activities in the home will vary greatly by household. As a consequence, in some households there may be a great deal of
time spent in a crowded room, whereas in other households
with the same ratio of persons per room, there may be very
little time spent in a crowded room. Thus the indices of the
experience of crowding may be, in some cases, a more accurate measure of the amount of actual crowding than the more
objective measure, persons per room (Booth 1976; Fischer
1975).

In our analysis we introduced two measures: (1) a social

demands scale, which measured an excess of social stimulation, and (2) a lack of privacy scale. These involve measures of the two key concepts that have been the theoretical bases for the explanation of the subjective experience of crowding. To our knowledge this is the first time there has been an attempt to measure these experiences in a household study. We would note that the demands scale and lack of privacy scale are fairly strongly related to persons per room. Furthermore, when these measures are used as controls they tend to "interpret" or "explain" the relationships between persons per room and the various dependent variables.

Mental Health

It would seem that, if overcrowding has adverse effects on the individual, it would almost have to be related to poor mental health.

After controls, the crowding variables are related to experiencing psychiatric symptoms, a lack of positive affect, having a nervous breakdown, manifest irritation, feeling alienated, having low self-esteem, and feeling unhappy. These relationships are statistically significant for all mental health items with all the crowding indices, except for the relationship between felt demands and positive affect. Taking an overall average shows that the crowding variables independently account for 40.4 percent of the total explained variance and the five control variables independently account for 41.3 percent, with 18.3 percent being collinear. Taken as a composite, these results provide strong support for the hypothesis that crowding has a substantial negative effect on a variety of aspects of mental health.

Social Relations in the Home

If overcrowding has an adverse effect on social relations, it would seem that this would be primarily manifested in the home. Our data on marital relations show that, after controls, the three indices of crowding are significantly related to a lack of positive marital relations, the presence of negative relations, a low score on the marital relations balance scale, and not feeling close to one's spouse. Regarding the respondents' relationships with (1) their children and (2) others living in the home, the data showed that persons per room is unrelated to, while lack of privacy and felt demands have significant adverse effects on, such relationships. Crowding also is significantly related to arguments and physical violence in the home.

Comparing the effects of crowding with those of the five control variables shows that crowding tends to explain more variance. On the average, the crowding variables independently account for 57.0 percent of the total explained variance and the control variables independently account for 34.6 percent, while 8.4 percent is collinear.

Social Relations Outside the Home

It would seem that crowding in the home would have a relatively slight effect on social relationships outside the home, particularly in comparison to its effect on social relations in the home. If, as our data suggest, however, crowding has an effect on the mental state of the individual, we would expect it to have some effect on social relationships outside the home. In all cases at least some, and in some cases all three, of our crowding indices show a significant effect on the respondents' relationships with relatives and neighbors and on the number of close friends the respondents had. Some of the crowding variables are also positively related to arguments and physical violence outside the home. Overall, however, the data indicate that the effect of crowding on social relations outside the home is minor compared to that of the social structural variables.

Physical Health

Our study did not focus on physical health and, lacking a physical examination, we have only a crude measure of the respondents' physical health. However, we had one innovation that allowed us to shed light on the relationship of crowding to physical health. The literature assumes that, if crowding is related to physical health, it is because persons

in crowded households are physically rundown, more susceptible to infectious disease, and, when sick, tend to be involved in the flow of activities, cannot get a good rest, and
are not well cared for (for example, Galle et al. 1972). In the
interview we obtained information on all of these presumed
relationships, and the data indicate crowding is strongly related to two of them. In contrast, the effect of crowding on
the respondents' evaluation of their overall health is relatively minor, although significant.

Fertility

Data on fertility-related behavior were collected only from
married respondents. They indicate that (1) crowded respondents had more children than they wanted, (2) crowding
has a slight relationship with ineffectual family planning, (3)
crowding at least occasionally inhibits sexual intercourse, and
(4) crowding is not related to hypersexuality. Support for one
of the recurrent themes in the literature, that crowding is related to fetal mortality, is provided by the data that show that
crowding is related to having a pregnancy end in stillbirth,
miscarriage, or abortion.

Care of Children

Our data show a mixed pattern in the effect of crowding
on parental care. Crowded parents feel hassled by their children, and they are relieved when the children are out of the
house, tend not to get along well with their children, and do
not like the way their children behave. Furthermore, they tend
not to know their children's friends or the parents of their
children's friends. However, crowding is relatively unrelated
to parents' supportive or punitive behavior toward their children, and it is unrelated to juvenile delinquency.

To date we have made only a very preliminary analysis
of the effects of structural density (primarily the number of
housing units per structure) and the effects of living alone.
This analysis suggests (with a few important exceptions) that
these variables are not nearly as important as overcrowding.
The number of housing units per structure has a strong neg-

ative relationship with one's being satisfied with where he or she lives. Increase in housing units per structure, particularly the shift from single-unit to multiple-unit structure, is significantly associated with three indicators of poor mental health: unhappiness, symptoms, and alienation. In general, housing units per structure appears to be largely unrelated to social relations inside the home, physical health, and fertility-related behavior. Consistent with the finding by Gillis (1974), the number of housing units per structure is significantly related to juvenile delinquency. Among residents in multiple-unit structures, there is a strong association between juvenile delinquency and floor of residence: If the floor of residence is the first floor the rate of delinquency is low; if it is other than the first floor the rate of delinquency is high.

Now let us briefly look at the respondents who live alone and compare them to respondents who live with others. The respondents who live alone do not differ significantly from the other respondents in their satisfaction with their living arrangements or on any of the indicators of mental health. They are less likely to act overtly aggressive, probably due to the fact that there is no one at home to act aggressively toward. They do tend to report better physical health than the other respondents. Our ecological analysis of cities over fifty thousand suggested that persons who live alone were likely to have a drinking problem. This relationship held up in the survey. Respondents who live alone are much more likely to drink heavily and to manifest problems associated with drinking.

With the Chicago survey data we looked at the interactive effects of number of persons per room, number of housing units per structure, and floor of residence. Persons who live in households with more than one person per room and in structures with more than forty housing units are particularly likely (1) to be dissatisfied with their living arrangements, (2) to be in poor mental health, (3) to be in poor physical health, and (4) to have children who have participated in delinquent activities. Similarly, persons who live in homes with more than one person per room and who live above the

fifth floor (our upper category for floor of residence) are particularly likely to be (1) dissatisfied with their living arrangements, (2) in poor mental health, (3) in poor physical health,
and (4) aggressive. A tentative finding is that women are more
reactive to crowding than are men, which is consistent with
the fact that women typically spend a greater proportion of
their time at home than do men.

Concluding Remarks

We have been exploring the idea that either end of the population distribution continuum—either very high or very low
density—may have deleterious effects on the behavior of human populations. Evidence from various animal studies suggests that overcrowding and isolation have negative effects
on a variety of species, although the specific effect and the
mechanisms bringing about that effect vary across species.
Evidence from studies of human populations, including both
ecological analyses and survey data, is not as rich, but several general themes emerged in our review. First, the concepts of high population density and overcrowding are substantially more complex for human than for animal
populations, but this fact has sometimes been obscured in the
studies reviewed. Future studies ought, at least, to distinguish between structural density—the way an area is built
up—and interpersonal crowding, for many studies indicate
that these two aspects of density have somewhat different relationships to behavior. The same might be said for the other
end of the population distribution continuum. The percentage of the population living alone is a measure of isolation,
but those persons who are living alone in urban settings are
in fact living in the midst of many other humans. In this case
human contacts are not obviated by living alone, but the frequency and character of contacts are probably quite different
from those of persons living with others. Similarly, those living alone in an isolated environment probably have very dif-

ferent social relationships from those of persons living alone
in a city.

Our review of the literature on density suggests that it
probably has some effect on "pathology," but that such an
effect has not been conclusively demonstrated, and it appears
unlikely that with further research density will emerge as a
variable of major substantive importance. Most of the studies
that have looked at the relationship between overcrowding
and human behavior have relied on ecological data. There is
some problem in interpreting the results, for the studies are
essentially concerned with individual experiences and behavior, while the items of analysis are usually large aggregate
units. Furthermore, crowding tends to be highly related to
class and race, and collinearity cannot be avoided in such
studies. Taken in toto the areal aggregate studies indicate that
crowding probably is related positively to "pathological" behavior but that the strength of the relationship is unclear.

The three major surveys also show a mixed pattern. We
take Mitchell's study in Hong Kong as suggesting crowding
has a very discernible but not a huge effect. However, in part
because of the mode of analysis and measures used, but primarily because the study involves such a very different culture, it is not clear what implications this study has for Western society.

The general conclusion reached by those involved in the
Toronto study is that crowding has very little effect. However, as we have noted here and discussed at greater length
elsewhere (Gove et al. 1976b), the sample is so atypical and
homogeneous and the measurement and analysis so flawed
that it is difficult to draw any conclusions about the effect of
crowding. (There is, of course, the possibility that our perspective leads us to a biased interpretation, and we recommend that the reader look at the works by Booth and his associates—keeping our comments in mind.)

The only other survey is the one we did in Chicago. We
managed to avoid the problem of collinearity between class,
race, and crowding, and our levels of crowding are very similar to those in the United States as a whole. We used one

objective measure of crowding (persons per room) and two subjective measures (a social demands scale and a lack of privacy scale) that tap the two concepts that the theoretical literature has linked to the subjective experience of crowding. We found crowding to be related strongly to poor mental health of the respondents and to poor social relationships in the home. It also is related strongly to certain aspects of physical health, fertility-related behavior, and child care. It has only a weak relationship with social relationships outside the home. We take our results as indicating that crowding in the home is a major variable that has a substantial impact on a varied set of behaviors. Of course, one should not consider the issue settled on the basis of one study. There has been a striking lack of studies of social isolation. What little research there is on social isolation (as indicated by living alone) suggests that it may be an important variable, and it is clear that it deserves more attention than it has received.

References

Alexander, F. 1963. "Alcohol and Behavior Disorder—Alcoholism." In S. P. Lucia, ed., *Alcohol and Civilization*, pp. 130–141. New York: McGraw-Hill.

Altman, I. 1975. *The Environment and Social Behavior*. Monterey, Calif.: Brooks/Cole.

—— 1976. "Privacy: A Conceptual Analysis." *Environment and Behavior* (March), 8:7–29.

Bacon, S. 1957. "Social Settings Conducive to Alcoholism." *Journal of the American Medical Association* (May), 164:177–181.

Bales, R. F. 1946. "Cultural Differences in Rates of Alcoholism." *Quarterly Journal of Studies of Alcohol* (March), 6:480–499.

Bates, A. 1964. "Privacy—A Useful Concept?" *Social Forces* (May), 42:429–434.

Blacker, E. 1966. "Sociocultural Factors in Alcoholism." *International Psychiatry Clinics* (Summer), 3:51–80.

Booth, A. 1975a. "Crowding and Social Participation." Manuscript.

——1975b. Final report submitted to Department of Urban Affairs, Ottawa, Canada.

—— 1976. *Urban Crowding and Its Consequences*. New York: Praeger.

Booth, A. and J. Cowell. 1976. "The Effects of Crowding Upon Health." *Journal of Health and Social Behavior* (September), 17:204–220.

Booth, A. and J. N. Edwards. 1976. "Crowding and Family Relations." *American Sociological Review* (April), 41:308–321.

Booth, A. and D. R. Johnson. 1975. "The Effect of Crowding on Child Health and Development." *American Behavioral Scientist* (July–August):736–749.

Booth, A. and S. Welch. 1974. "Crowding and Urban Crime Rates." Paper presented at the Annual Meetings of the Midwest Sociological Association, Omaha, Nebraska.

Booth, A., S. Welch, and D. R. Johnson. 1976. "Crowding and Urban Crime Rates." *Urban Affairs Quarterly* (March), 2:291–307.

Borowitz, G. H. 1964. "Some Ego Aspects of Alcoholism." *British Journal of Medical Psychology*, 37:257–263.

Calhoun, J. B. 1962. "Population Density and Social Pathology." *Scientific American* (February), 206:139–148.

Carnahan, D. L., W. Gove, and O. Galle. 1974. "Urbanization, Population Density, and Overcrowding." *Social Forces* (September), 53:62–72.

Chafetz, M. E., H. W. Demone, Jr., and H. Soloman. 1962. *Alcoholism and Society*. New York: Oxford University Press.

Chapin, S. F. 1951. "Some Housing Factors Related to Mental Hygiene." *Journal of Social Issues*, 7:164–171.

Chermayeff, S. and C. Alexander. 1965. *Community and Privacy: Toward a New Architecture of Humanism*. New York: Doubleday.

Choldin, H. and D. Roncek. 1976. "Density, Population Potential and Pathology: A Block Level Analysis." *Public Data Use* (July), 4:19–30.

Collette, J. and S. Webb. 1974. "Urban Density, Crowding, and Stress Reactions." Paper presented at the meeting of the Pacific Sociological Association, San Jose, California.

Davis, K. 1940. "Extreme Social Isolation of a Child." *American Journal of Sociology* (January), 45:554–565.

Desor, J. A. 1972. "Toward a Psychological Theory of Crowding." *Journal of Personality and Social Psychology*, 21:79–83.

Dubos, R. 1965. *Man Adapting*. New Haven: Yale University Press.

Durkheim, E. 1933. *The Division of Labor in Society*. Translated with an introduction by George Simpson. New York: Macmillan Company.

Edwards, J. and A. Booth. 1975. "Crowding and Human Sexual Behavior." Manuscript.

Factor, R. and I. Waldron. 1973. "Contemporary Population Densities and Human Health." *Nature*, 243:381–384.

Fischer, C. S., M. Baldassare, and R. Ofshe. 1975. "Crowding Studies and Urban Life: A Critical Review." *Journal of the American Institute of Planners* (November), 41:401–418.

Fischer, C. T. 1975. "Privacy as a Profile of Authentic Consciousness." *Humanitas* (February), 2:27–43.

Galle, O. and W. Gove. 1974. "Crowding and Behavior in Chicago, 1940–1970." Manuscript.

Galle, O., W. Gove, and J. McPherson. 1972. "Population Density and Pathology: What Are the Relationships for Man." *Science* (April), 176:23–30.

Gillis, A. R. 1974. "Population Density and Social Pathology: The Case of Building Type, Social Allowance and Juvenile Delinquency." *Social Forces* (December), 53:306–314.

Gove, W., O. Galle, J. McCarthy, and M. Hughes. 1976a. "Living Circumstances and Social Pathology: The Effect of Population Density, Overcrowding and Isolation on Suicide, Homicide and Alcoholism." Manuscript.

Gove, W. and P. Howell. 1974. "Individual Resources and Mental Hospitalization: A Comparison and Evaluation of the Societal Reaction and Psychiatric Perspectives." *American Sociological Review* (February), 39:86–100.

Gove, W., M. Hughes, and O. Galle. 1976b. "Some Comments on the Toronto Study." Manuscript.

—— 1976c. "Overcrowding in the Home: An Empirical Investigation of Its Possible Consequences." Paper presented at the meeting of the American Public Health Association, Miami.

Greenberg, L. A. 1963. "Alcohol and Emotional Behavior." In S. Lucia, ed., *Alcohol and Civilization*, pp. 109–121. New York: McGraw-Hill.

Hall, E. 1966. *The Hidden Dimension*. New York: Doubleday.

Hannan, M. 1971. *Aggregation and Disaggregation in Sociology*. Lexington, Mass.: Lexington Books.

Hoover, E. M. and R. Vernon. 1962. *Anatomy of a Metropolis*. Garden City, N.Y.: Doubleday.

Johnson, D. R. and A. Booth. 1975. "Crowding and Human Reproduction." Manuscript.

Jourard, S. M. 1966. "Some Psychological Aspects of Privacy." *Law and Contemporary Problems* (Spring), 31:307–318.

Kelvin, P. 1973. "A Social-Psychological Examination of Privacy." *British Journal of Social and Clinical Psychology* (September), 12:248–261.

Larsen, D. and B. Abu-Laban. 1968. "Norm Qualities and Deviant Drinking Behavior." *Social Problems* (Spring), 15:441–450.

Levy, L. and A. Herzog. 1974. "Effects of Population Density and Crowding on Health and Social Adaptation in the Netherlands." *Journal of Health and Social Behavior* (September), 15:228–240.

McCarthy, J., O. Galle, and W. Zimmern. 1975. "Population Density, Social Structure, and Interpersonal Violence: An Intermetropolitan Test of Competing Models." *American Behavioral Scientist* (July–August), 18:771–791.

McPherson, J. M. 1973. "A Question of Causality: A Study in the Application of Regression Techniques to Sociological Analysis." Ph.D. dissertation, Vanderbilt University.

Marmor, J. 1972. "Mental Health and Overpopulation." In S. T. Reid and

D. L. Lyon, eds., *Population Crisis: An Interdisciplinary Perspective*. Glenview, Ill.: Scott, Foresman.

Marsella, A., M. Escudero, and P. Gordon. 1970. "The Effects of Dwelling Density on Mental Disorders in Filipino Men." *Journal of Health and Social Behavior* (December), 11:288–294.

Milgram, S. 1970. "The Experience of Living in Cities." *Science*, 167:1461–1468.

Mitchell, R. E. 1971. "Some Social Implications of High Density." *American Sociological Review* (February), 36:18–29.

—— 1975. "Ethnographic and Historical Perspectives on Relationships between Physical and Socio-Spatial Environments." *Sociological Symposium* (Fall), 14:25–40.

National Academy of Sciences. 1971. *Rapid Population Growth*. Baltimore: Johns Hopkins University Press.

Pastalan, L. A. 1970. "Privacy as an Expression of Human Territoriality." In L. A. Pastalan and D. H. Carson, eds., *Spatial Behavior of Older People*. Ann Arbor: University of Michigan Press.

Patrick, C. 1952. *Alcohol, Culture, and Society*. Durham: Duke University Press.

Pearlin, L. and C. Radabaugh. 1975. "Economic Strains and the Coping Function of Alcohol." Manuscript.

Pennock, J. R. and J. W. Chapman, eds. 1971. *Privacy*. New York: Atherton Press.

Pittman, D. J. 1967. *Alcoholism*. New York: Harper & Row.

Pittman, D. J. and C. Snyder. 1962. *Society, Culture, and Drinking Patterns*. New York: Wiley.

Rapoport, A. 1973. "An Approach to the Construction of Man-Environment Theory." In W. F. E. Preiser, ed., *Environmental Design Research*, vol. 2, pp. 124–136. Stroudsburg, Penn.: Dowden, Hutchinson and Ross.

Roman, P. and H. Trice. 1970. "The Development of Deviant Drinking Behavior: Occupational Risk Factors." *Archives of Environmental Health* (March), 20:424–433.

Schmitt, R. 1966. "Density, Health, and Social Disorganization." *Journal of the American Institute of Planners* (January), 32:37–40.

Schuessler, K. 1974. "Analysis of Ratio Variables: Opportunities and Pitfalls." *American Journal of Sociology* (September), 80:379–396.

Schwartz, B. 1968. "The Social Psychiatry of Privacy." *American Journal of Sociology* (May), 73:741–752.

Seely, J. R. 1959. "The W.H.O. Definition of Alcoholism." *Quarterly Journal of Studies on Alcohol* (June), 20:352–358.

Shils, E. 1966. "Privacy: Its Constitution and Vicissitudes." *Law and Contemporary Problems* (Spring), 31:281–306.

Simmel, G. 1957. "The Metropolis and Mental Life." In P. K. Hatt and A. J. Reiss, Jr., eds., *Cities and Societies: The Revised Reader in Urban Sociology*, pp. 635–646. New York: Free Press.

Skolnick, J. R. 1958. "Religious Affiliation and Drinking Behavior." *Quarterly Journal of Studies on Alcohol* (September), 19:452–470.

Smith, R. H., D. B. Downer, M. T. Lynch, and M. Winter. 1969. "Privacy and Interaction Within the Family as Related to Dwelling Space." *Journal of Marriage and the Family* (August), 31:559–566.

Snyder, C. 1962. "Culture and Jewish Sobriety." In D. J. Pittman and C. Snyder, eds., *Society, Culture, and Drinking Patterns*, pp. 616–628. New York: Wiley.

Spencer, H. 1879–1882. *Principles of Sociology.* 2 vols. in 5. New York: Appleton.

Spitz, R. A. 1945. *Hospitalism: An Inquiry Into the Genesis of Psychiatric Conditions in Early Childhood.* In The Psychoanalytic Study of the Child. New York: International Universities Press.

—— 1946. "Hospitalism: A Follow-up Report." In The Psychoanalytic Study of the Child, pp. 113–117. New York: International Universities Press.

Spitz, R. A. and K. M. Wolfe. 1946. "Anaclitic Depression: An Inquiry into the Genesis of Psychiatric Conditions in Early Childhood." In The Psychoanalytic Study of the Child, pp. 313–342. New York: International Universities Press.

Strauss, R. 1971. "Alcohol." In R. Merton and R. Nisbet, eds., *Contemporary Social Problems*, 3rd ed., pp. 236–280. New York: Harcourt Brace Jovanovich.

Taylor, I. and J. Knowelden. 1957. *Principles of Epidemiology.* Boston: Little, Brown.

Trice, H. *Alcoholism in America.* New York: McGraw-Hill.

Ullman, A. D. 1958. "Sociocultural Backgrounds of Alcoholism." *Annals* (January), 315:48–54.

Verhulst, P. E. 1845. "Recherches mathématiques sur la loi d'accroissement de la population." *Nouveaux mémoires de l'Academie R. des Sciences de Bruxelles,* 18:1–38.

Ward, S. K. 1975. "Methodological Considerations in the Study of Population Density and Social Pathology." *Journal of Human Ecology,* 3(4):275–286.

Washburne, C. 1956. "Alcohol, Self, and Group." *Quarterly Journal of Studies on Alcohol* (March), 17:108–123.

Webb, S. and J. Collete. 1975. "Urban Ecological and Household Correlates of Stress-Alleviating Drug Use." *American Behavioral Scientist* (July–August):750–770.

Welch, S. and A. Booth. 1975. "Crowding as a Factor in Political Aggression: Theoretical Aspect and an Analysis of Some Cross-National Data." *Social Science Information,* 13:151–162.

Whitehead, P. and C. Harvey. 1974. "Explaining Alcoholism: An Empirical Test and Reformulation." *Journal of Health and Social Behavior* (March), 15:57–65.

Wilkinson, R. 1970. *The Prevention of Drinking Problems: Alcohol Control and Cultural Influences.* New York: Oxford University Press.

Winsborough, H. H. 1970. "The Social Consequences of High Population Density." In T. R. Ford and G. F. DeJong, eds., *Social Demography,* pp. 84–90. Englewood Cliffs, N.J.: Prentice-Hall.

Wirth, L. 1938. "Urbanism as a Way of Life." *American Journal of Sociology* (July), 44:1–24.

Wohlwill, J. F. 1974. "Human Adaptation to Levels of Environmental Stimulation." *Human Ecology,* 2:127–147.

10
High-Rise Housing and Psychological Strain

A. R. GILLIS

HOUSES ARE BOTH art forms and machines designed by architects to lighten "the stress of life" and take "the raw environmental load off man's shoulders" (Fitch 1972:9). The success of a structure depends in part on the degree to which it facilitates the desired activities of its occupants. Buildings that score high in facility effectively lighten "the stress of life," while low-scoring structures fail to alleviate stress significantly, or may even contribute to it. Further, a dwelling that satisfies the needs of one person may fail to satisfy the needs of another. For example, traditional sex roles impose different activities on men and women, particularly with respect to the home environment. Women and men, then, may differ in the functional (and perhaps aesthetic) demands they make on dwellings. Therefore, a particular structure could indeed take "the raw environmental load off man's shoulders" but fail to do so for women.

Social scientists have long been concerned with the relation of housing to people's health, attitudes, and behaviors (see Gutman 1975, for an excellent discussion on the relation of architecture and sociology and a review of sociological re-

Reprinted with permission from *Journal of Health and Social Behavior* (December 1977), vol. 18, American Sociological Association. Figures and tables and text references to figures and tables were omitted because of space constraints.

search on housing), and are showing an increased interest[1] in the nonhuman environment as a variable. Unfortunately, this interest seems largely confined to the relationship between certain types of population density and a vague collection of behaviors and conditions known as "social pathologies." Little attention has been given to high-density housing, the type of population density that has come to symbolize urban life.

Building density (persons or dwelling units per structure) has been identified as one of three types of population density (Michelson 1970) and, like the other types of density, has been found to be a significant predictor of some variables that have been regarded as indicative of "social pathology" (Gillis 1974). Students of population density, however, have confined their research to external density (persons per square mile or acre) and internal density (persons per room or square feet per person). (For detailed discussions of many of these studies, see Fischer et al. 1975; Freedman 1975; Loo 1974.)

Population density essentially involves the separation (or lack of separation) of people from other people (Michelson 1970); the importance of building density would seem to lie in the separation of households from one another by the walls, floors, and ceilings they share.[2]

High-density housing contains vertically and horizontally stacked dwelling units, so that the wall of one unit is also the wall of another, the floor of one unit is the ceiling of another, and so on. The number of barriers shared by a specific dwelling unit varies by the design of the building (for example, row housing is single-story, so units can share neither ceilings nor floors), and location (end units share one less wall than do centrally located dwelling units). Both the design of the building and the location of one's dwelling unit in it, then, should affect the impact building density has on residents.

High Living and Psychological Strain[3]

Perhaps the most widely recognized characteristic of high-density housing is height. A consequence of vertical stacking, and most dramatically expressed in the high-rise design, floor level may also affect some people. Fanning (1967) found that different physical ailments and psychological strain (psychosomatic symptoms) not only varied with building design (single, detached houses, and walk-up apartments), but that psychological strain among apartment dwellers varied directly with the floor level on which their dwelling units were located. Further, since the subjects of Fanning's study were people who had been unable to choose their dwelling units, the possibility of a selection factor producing these relationships was eliminated.

Fanning observed that subjects who suffered from strain and inhabited the upper stories had a tendency to report feeling lonely, and concluded that isolation and loneliness intervenes between high-rise living and psychological strain.

This explanation is consistent with Fanning's data as well as with the popular notion that high-rises contain people with an aversion to neighboring, and with the idea that isolation results in psychological strain (Faris 1939:32; Lemkau 1955). No attempt was made by Fanning, however, to test this model by controlling for the intervening variable to see if the original relationship between floor level and strain would be attenuated. This is unfortunate, because confinement and loneliness may result from psychological strain rather than cause it.

Mitchell's (1971) extensive research on high-density housing in Hong Kong provides additional support for the notion that floor level causes psychological strain. Of the several housing characteristics examined by Mitchell, floor level was the only direct correlate of "emotional strain." This relationship held, however, only for respondents in households containing more than one family, and for the sample as a whole, dwelling level and strain were unrelated.

Like Fanning, Mitchell suggested that the inhabitants of upper stories are more confined to their dwelling units than are residents of the lower floors. Rather than hypothesize, however, that confinement results in loneliness and then strain, Mitchell suggested that confinement results in enforced interaction with the members of one's household,

which becomes translated into strain if the household contains individuals who are not kin.

While the Fanning and Mitchell studies are substantially
similar, they differ in important respects. Both studies controlled for various housing characteristics, but neither examined elements of high-density design apart from floor level
(such as shared walls, floors, and ceilings). The two studies
also converge in finding that psychological strain is correlated with the floor level of respondents' dwelling units. Both
researchers suggested confinement as an intervening variable, but neither Fanning nor Mitchell was able to test this
empirically.

The two studies diverge with respect to the *conditions*
under which floor level is related to psychological strain. As
pointed out earlier, Mitchell did not observe this relationship
for his total sample, which contained both men and women.
The sample for which Fanning found floor level to be related
to psychological strain, however, contained no men. This
suggests that sex interacts with floor level on psychological
strain.[4]

Sex

The notion that men and women respond in different ways
to their environments has both empirical and logical support.
In a laboratory setting, internal density is a better predictor
of aggressive behavior in men than in women (Freedman et
al. 1972; Freedman 1975), and recent surveys of population
density and psychological strain have found external density
to be a better predictor of strain for men than for women
(Booth and Cowell 1976; Collett and Webb 1974).

Although these studies suggest that men more than
women are adversely affected by internal and external population density, there is reason to believe that women may be
more affected by building density and height than are men.

Traditional sex roles confine women more than men to
the home. Because of this, one might reasonably expect the

residential environment to have a greater effect on women than on men. Also, traditional sex roles require their incumbents to make different use of the home environment. For women, the home environment is more a place of work than it is for men, and some residential environments seem more suitable than others for child supervision, one of the central status-roles women have traditionally occupied. For example, Wallace (1952) and others have noted that the supervision of children who are playing outside is a difficult, if not impossible task from the upper stories of a high-rise. Perhaps as a result, preschoolers who live in high-rises spend more time in their dwelling units than do their lower-living counterparts (Kumove 1966), and their mothers struggle to inhibit their activities in order to prevent neighbors from being disturbed by the sounds of their playing (Willis 1955). The alternatives, accompanying young children every time they go outside or allowing children to go outside unsupervised, could be as distressing as keeping young children inside; the former because this pattern would impair household-centered duties, and the latter because of the worry it could produce in the parent and the vandalism that could occur in and around the high-rise (Newman 1972; Rainwater 1966, 1970; Yancey 1972). The ideal structure would seem to be the single, detached house, sharing no walls, floor, or ceiling: the sounds of children and adults cannot pass through to disturb neighbors, and parents can remain inside but at the same time maintain surveillance on their children playing outside.

To summarize, it may be difficult for women who occupy a traditional wife-mother status to perform their roles in modern, man-made environments.

The Present Study

Several questions emerge from the preceding discussions. For example, is psychological strain associated with high-density design factors, and if so, which ones? Are women more likely than men to experience strain in conjunction with high-level living, and if so, why? These are the questions that will be addressed by this research.

Specifically, this study is an investigation of the relationship between the elements of high-density design (shared walls, shared floors, shared ceilings, floor level of dwelling unit), internal density (persons per room) and external density (persons per acre), and psychological strain, with sex as an interacting variable. Three clusters of factors are examined as possible intervening variables. These factors, derived from the preceding discussions, are: (1) child supervision variables, (2) confinement variables, and (3) social isolation variables.

Child supervision variables include: (1) parents' estimates of the amount of time they know where their children are (broken down by three age groups of children), (2) the degree of satisfaction associated with this level of knowledge of their children's whereabouts, (3) parents' reports concerning the degree to which their children cause them problems, and (4) parents' desire to be alone more often.

Confinement variables include measures of the degree to which respondents stay in their dwelling units, respondents' level of satisfaction with the amount of leisure time they enjoy away from home, and reports of respondents' general level of boredom.

Social isolation, the intervening variable suggested by Fanning (1967), is represented by three indicators: reported loneliness, reports on how easy it is to meet neighbors, and the proportion of respondents' friends who are neighbors.

Research Methods

Data for this study were collected from a sample of the residents of public housing projects in Calgary and Edmonton, Canada. This population is particularly appropriate for a study of this nature. Variation in income is limited by a maximum income rule, and rent is based on family income rather than on the type or location of dwelling units, as often is the case with housing on the private market.

Because of this, and the wide variety of different building designs in these housing projects, multicollinearity be-tween income and housing characteristics, a problem plagu-ing much of the previous research on population density (Fischer et al. 1975; Ward 1975), can be avoided.

A stratified probability sample was drawn from all thirty-nine public housing developments in the two cities, with the dwelling unit as the sampling unit. A sliding scale to assure adequate representation of the various building designs was used.

Respondents in each city were motivated to participate through a lottery with a hundred-dollar prize. The response rate was just under 90 percent, resulting in a sample of 442 public housing residents, all of whom were adults with chil-dren living at home.[5]

On the average, respondents inhabit projects with an ex-ternal density of 107.5 persons per acre (s.d. = 84.9), build-ings containing 30.2 units (s.d. = 56.2), and dwelling units containing .76 persons per bedroom (s.d. = .20).

Respondents' dwelling units ranged in location between the ground and the sixteenth floor, with a mean location be-tween the third and fourth floors (s.d. = 1.28). The average dwelling unit shares 1.85 walls (s.d. = .82), and the means for shared floor and ceiling are .23 (s.d. = .27) and .27 (s.d. = .44), respectively.

Most of the data were provided by respondents' answers to questions on an interview schedule. Where possible, ob-servational data and documents were collected and used in-stead of respondents' answers. For example, the housing data (number of rooms in a dwelling unit, shared walls, floors, ceilings, floor level, external density,[6] and so on) were col-lected through the examination of project blueprints, floor plans, housing commission records, and site visits.

Two scales are used in this study. These are the Indik et al. (1964) scale for measuring psychological strain,[7] and the socioeconomic index constructed by Duncan (1961).

Most variables are interval or better in level of measure-ment, and nominal level variables are coded as dummy vari-ables.[8] Stepwise regression is used to analyze the data, with

interaction terms represented in equations by dummy variables (see Blalock 1972; Kerlinger and Pedhazur 1973, for
discussions on this technique).[9]

Results

Internal density, external density, and the characteristics
of high-density housing design are all poor predictors of psychological strain. Only sex is a significant correlate of strain,
indicating that women are more likely than men to experience psychological strain. This is consistent with previous
research concerning psychological strain (U.S. Department of
Health, Education, and Welfare, 1970).

A multiplicative version of the above additive model was
calculated. Sex × internal density represents the difference
between the slopes of psychological strain on internal density for women and for men; sex × external density represents the difference in the slopes of strain on external density
for women and for men and so on.

The most striking characteristic is the strong positive relationship shown between sex × floor level and psychological strain ($b = .684$). This indicates that the partial slope for
psychological strain on floor level differs significantly between men and women. Among women this partial slope is
positive and for men, negative. The weak relationship between floor level and strain for both sexes then, is the result
of two reasonably strong forces, one positive and the other
negative, each canceling out the other.

These data show that women tend to experience psychological strain in conjunction with high living. On the other
hand, if men indeed find that their family status-role is little
more than "star boarder" in conjunction with high-level living (Wallace 1952; Rothblatt 1971), they appear not to find
this situation distressing. On the contrary, men tend to thrive
as they move up in the world.

Sex also interacts with shared floor on psychological
strain ($b = -.347$). Women in dwelling units with a shared
floor tend to report lower levels of psychological strain than
do women in units without a shared floor. Among men,

shared floor is not a significant correlate of psychological strain. A close examination of the variables and partial slopes reveals that the relationship between floor level and strain is not only nonadditive but nonlinear as well. Shared floor is associated with psychological strain among women. The only dwelling units without a shared floor are located on the ground floor.[10] All other units have shared floors. Hence, women living on the ground floor have higher rates of psychological strain than have their higher-living counterparts. The linear relationship between floor level and strain, then, holds only for women in dwelling units located above the ground floor.

Equations containing variables typically used as controls by social scientists are next presented. Even when five different indicators of socioeconomic status[11] are included in the equation, the difference between partial slopes for men and for women for psychological strain on floor level remains relatively unchanged. Also, when selected demographic variables[12] are included in the equation, the original relationships between psychological strain and floor level and shared floor are sustained for both men and women.

To summarize, floor level is a strong, direct, and durable predictor of psychological strain among women, and a weaker, though as persistent, negative predictor of strain among men. Shared floor is a weak negative correlate of psychological strain among women. The introduction of other variables into the equation adds to the predictive power of the equation, but the nature of the relationships remains unchanged.

These relationships persist, further, to the point of defying explanation. The *beta* weights for psychological strain on sex, shared floor, floor level, sex × shared floor and sex × floor level show that differences between men and women regarding strain experienced in conjunction with shared floor and floor level are significant beyond the .05 level.

Variables pertaining to household composition were included in the equation to locate the existence of a selection factor based on household composition. It is reasonable to expect that tenants may self-select or be placed by the Housing Authority in particular dwelling units on the basis of household composition, which in turn may be independently related to psychological strain. The data however, indicate that this is not the case. The introduction of the household composition variables into the equation has almost no effect on the relationships.

It is doubtful that child supervision intervenes between floor level and psychological strain. If this were the case, we might reasonably expect the *beta* coefficient for strain on high living to have been reduced by controlling for children. The data clearly show that variables associated with the supervision of children do not intervene between floor level and strain among women.

The effects of adding the confinement variables to the regression equation are that the regression coefficient for strain on sex $\times$ floor level, although attenuated, remains strong, with $b = .529$, $p < .01$.

It is interesting to note that work hours away from home is a negative correlate of strain, while leisure hours away is a positive predictor of this variable. One might have expected the opposite, especially considering Marxist views of work and alienation. A closer examination, however, found that the negative relationship between work hours and strain disappears when one controls for employment status. Neither work nor leisure hours away from home reduces strain, then, and if anything *all* time away from home seems to either contribute to or reflect psychological strain.

Taking weekend trips is a significant negative correlate of psychological strain. This may mean that getting away for extended periods every now and then reduces strain. On the other hand, this correlation may simply indicate that neurotics tend not to go on weekend trips.

The zero-order correlations between loneliness and sex $\times$ floor level and loneliness and psychological strain are $r = .194$ and $r = .353$, respectively. These correlations are in accord with Fanning's discoveries, and suggest that loneliness may indeed intervene between floor level and strain among women. This is not the case, however. None of the variables associated with social isolation significantly attenuates the relationship between level of floor and psychological strain.

A regression equation for psychological strain on the independent variables and all control variables that were significant ($p \leq .05$) predictors of this dependent variable was calculated. The inclusion of these variables does not greatly attenuate the relationships of strain on sex × shared floor ($b = .283$) or sex × floor level ($b = .515$).

The interaction terms for sex and all potential intervening variables were included in other equations. The addition of these terms into the equations had little or no effect on the relationships between psychological strain and shared floor and floor level for either sex.

The use of dummy variables representing interaction terms in multiplicative regression models is in some ways unsatisfactory. The individual variables used to construct the product terms are of necessity highly correlated with the product terms, and this multicollinearity can reduce the stability of the estimates of partial slopes (Althauser 1971; Blalock 1963; Hartnagel 1974).[13] Although multicollinearity most often distorts slopes in a conservative direction, some conditions can produce *inflated* estimates of slopes (Althauser 1971), a less tolerable bias in explanatory research.

The zero-order correlations between sex, shared floor, floor level, sex × shared floor, and sex × floor level that the correlation coefficients for individual variables and their product terms are strong, although only two are greater than .70. Nevertheless, seven of the ten correlations between these "independent" variables exceed .50, and this could inflate the estimates of the partial slopes.

In view of the possibility that slopes may have been inflated by multicollinearity, we split the sample into males and females and regressed psychological strain on shared floor and floor level for each subsample. This allows the comparison of the slope of strain on each independent variable across the subsamples, giving an estimate of the interaction of sex with the other variables on strain. That is unbiased by multicollinearity.

Floor level is a significant ($p \leqq .05$) positive predictor of psychological strain among women ($b = .185$), and a significant negative predictor of strain among men ($b = -.224$). The difference (.409) is moderately strong and statistically significant (both slopes are opposite in sign and significant beyond the .05 level).

Shared floor also interacts with sex on psychological strain. The difference between slopes ($-.382$) is significant and only slightly smaller than the difference across subsamples for strain on floor level.

Both the dummy variable and subsample analyses indicate that sex interacts with floor level and with shared floor as predictors of psychological strain. The strength of the interactions are moderate to strong, and are significant ($p \leqq .05$).

Discussion

The principal findings of this study are that floor level is a positive predictor of strain among women, and shared floor is a negative predictor of strain among women. These relationships resist efforts to attenuate them by controlling for household composition variables, socioeconomic status, selected demographic characteristics, and three plausible intervening factors: confinement, social isolation, and problems with child supervision.

Although I was unable to find empirical support for explanations of the relationships between high-level living and shared floor and psychological strain, several post-factum explanations are plausible and should be investigated in subsequent research. For example, there is reason to believe that the negative relationship between shared floor and strain among women may result from insecurity experienced by women living on the ground floor.[14] Several women expressed a preference for second floor dwelling units because they felt "vulnerable" on the ground floor, containing the only dwelling units without shared floors. We were unable to find out whether this anxiety involves fear of physical attack, burglary, or merely the fact that ground-floor units afford their occupants less privacy. The nature of this feeling of vulnerability, how widespread it is among women, and whether it indeed intervenes between shared floor and psychological strain should be assessed empirically. In addition, care should be taken to see if this anxiety occurs in women outside of public housing projects. Public housing has a relatively high crime rate (U.S. Department of Housing and Urban Development, 1975), so the vulnerability felt by ground-floor residents in public housing projects may not be experienced by their counterparts in private housing. It is noteworthy that in Fanning's (1967) sample, women on the ground floor had the lowest rate of psychological strain.

Perhaps the most obvious explanation for relationships between the physical environment and social or psychological variables is selection. In the case of psychological strain and floor level, for example, it is possible that neurotic women tend to choose high living. If this is the case, we would not expect to find confinement, isolation, or child supervision problems acting as intervening variables.

The selection hypothesis fits well with the data in this study, and, although the demand for public housing exceeds the supply and there are waiting lists to get in, the possibility that our respondents were able to choose their dwelling units cannot be eliminated.

The selection hypothesis cannot be used to explain Fanning's results, however, because his population included only people who had been unable to choose the type or location of their dwelling unit; and to argue that such similar findings (mine and Fanning's) have different causes violates the norm of parsimony. It seems preferable, then, to assume that something other than selection produces the relationships between floor level and psychological strain among women in both Fanning's population and ours.

The differences between men and women with respect to floor level and strain may reflect sex differences regarding the *aesthetics* rather than the function of design. For example, men may be attracted to high-level living, seeing it as symbolic of upward social mobility (rent in high-rise apartments is frequently a direct correlate of floor level) and, from a man's perspective, the "good life" (it is noteworthy that a well-known "men's" magazine is called *Penthouse*). On the other hand, women may find high living less meaningful and unaesthetic. The high-rise may merely be a constant and dramatic reminder to women that they fail to occupy a single, detached house, an important goal to the occupants of traditional wife-mother status roles. Michelson (1970) and Fischer (1973) point out that disjunctures between actual and idealized environments can have potentially important consequences, and Maslow and Mintz (1972) and Mintz (1972) found aesthetic variation in the appearance of rooms affected the well-being of their subjects. Housing is a "symbolic form which is an extension of one's own person" (Schorr 1963). It may be "home—the symbol" rather than "home—the machine," then, that produces different responses to high-level living by women and men.

The different relationships between high living and strain for women and for men could also reflect a greater susceptibility to vertigo or acrophobia among women.[15] Sex-role socialization patterns may allow or even encourage boys more than girls to climb fences, trees, and the like, and therefore to become comfortable with height, while girls may experience more down-to-earth play schedules. The fear of falling associated with living in a tall building (Izumi 1970), then, may be more intense in women than in men.

Summary and Conclusions

The foregoing is highly speculative and should be the subject of subsequent investigations. As it is, the contributions of this paper are limited to the empirical demonstration that sex interacts with both floor level and shared floor on psychological strain, and that child supervision, confinement, and social isolation factors cannot be used to explain the relationships.

It is impossible to argue that the population for this study is typical. Our respondents were residents of public housing in Edmonton and Calgary, Alberta. Public housing residents differ in important respects from the general population (Michelson 1970), and Alberta is not representative of the world. The extent to which our findings can be generalized, then, is limited. It is noteworthy, however, that both our study and Fanning's (1967) report that floor level and psychological strain are direct correlates, and Fanning's sample (the wives of British servicemen residing in a particular army base in Germany) is no less limited than ours. The fact that such specific but socially, culturally, geographically, and temporally different populations have produced similar findings adds to, rather than detracts from, the credibility of the findings.

Further research concerning the relationships among high floor level, sex, and psychological strain should not only include respondents who live in private housing, but respondents who are childless. All 442 respondents in our study were parents with children living at home. Whether childless women experience strain in conjunction with high living is unknown, and the answer to this question could provide important leads toward explaining the relationships found in this study.

Notes

1. Several journals (e.g., Sociological Symposium, American Behavioral Scientist) have recently had special editions on population density and crowding, and the American Sociological Association included environmental sociology as one of its fourteen subsections in 1975.

2. The proximity of others may be bothersome in a variety of ways (cf. Fischer et al. 1975). Two of these include stimulus overload and inhibition. That is, the presence of others may result in an "excessive" level of stimulus bombardment (Simmel 1950; Milgram 1970), and the presence of others may inhibit us from indulging in behaviors that are noisy or require a high degree of privacy (Keyfitz 1966; Raven 1967).

3. "Strain" and "stress" tend to be used interchangeably by social and life scientists to refer to a set of tension-related psycho-physiological symptoms. In this paper, "strain" rather than "stress" is used as the referent to these symptoms, since in the physical sciences, where the terms

were first used, "stress" refers to the *conditions* that produce strain (see Nettler 1976 for a more detailed discussion).

4. Unfortunately, Mitchell did not run separate analyses for men and women.

5. It should be noted that the public housing sample is in fact a sub-sample of a larger sample of housing funded under various sections of the National Housing Act.

6. Persons per acre, with the housing project as the unit of analysis.

7. The scale used by Indik et al. (1964) is a shorter version of the index developed by Gurin et al. (1960). The items are substantially similar to those in the more widely used, but longer scale constructed by Langner (1962).

Indik et al. report that all interitem correlations were positive, with 90 percent of them significant beyond the .10 level. The scale has an estimated split-half reliability of $+.85$ and was found by Indik et al. to discriminate on demographic variables among a sample of 8,234.

For my sample, all interitem correlations were positive with over 95 percent significant beyond the .05 level. A factor analysis of these items revealed a single factor "accounting" for 69 percent of the variance. This is consistent with the findings of Indik et al.

My use of this index differs slightly from the way it was employed by Indik et al. First, Indik et al. included a sixteenth item, containing nine subitems. Because of its length, this item was not included in my study. Second, Indik et al. coded some items (numbers 1 to 6) using five categories, and other items (numbers 7 to 15) using four categories. (Item 16 was coded with three categories.) I simplified matters by coding all fifteen items with five categories: never $= 1$, unsure $= 2$, occasionally $= 3$, frequently $= 4$, nearly always $= 5$. Thus, possible scores range from 15 (low strain) to 75 (high strain) and actual scores in our sample cover the full range. The mean score is 24.97 with a standard deviation of 8.57.

The items from the Indik et al. scale that I used in the present study are:

1. Do you have any trouble getting to sleep or staying asleep?
2. Have you ever been bothered by nervousness, feeling fidgety and tense?
3. Are you ever troubled by headaches or pains in the head?
4. Do you have loss of appetite?
5. How often are you bothered by having an upset stomach?
6. Do you find it difficult to get up in the morning?
7. Has any ill health affected the amount of work you do?
8. Have you ever been bothered by shortness of breath when you were not exercising or working hard?
9. Have you ever been bothered by your heart beating hard?
10. Have you ever had spells of dizziness?
11. Are you ever bothered by nightmares?

12. Do you tend to lose weight when you have something important bothering you?

13. Do your hands ever tremble enough to bother you?

14. Are you troubled by your hands sweating so that you feel damp and clammy?

15. Have there ever been times when you couldn't take care of things because you just couldn't get going?

8. These include the following: sex (women = 1, men = 0); marital status (married, common law = 0, single, separated, divorced, widowed = 1); ethnicity (Anglo origin = 0, non-Anglo = 1); religion (Protestant = 1, non-Protestant = 0); urban-rural background: pre 15 and post 15 (nonurban = 0, urban only = 1).

9. The log-linear models of Leo Goodman (1970, 1972) are less appropriate here because of the large number of ordinal and interval variables to be analyzed. Further, except in unusual circumstances, the log-linear and dummy variable regression approaches are analogous (Goodman 1975; Knoke 1975).

10. Neither the sample nor the population include people living in basement units.

11. It is noteworthy that family income is the only measure of socioeconomic status that is a positive correlate of psychological strain. This may be a result of the maximum income rule maintained by the Public Housing Authorities. That is, as family income increases, one is moved closer to eviction or the necessity of misreporting family income, and this may produce strain.

12. "Duration of present tenancy" was included here to control for the possibility that new tenants in public housing are both more likely to experience psychological strain and to be located in newer buildings, which tend to be high-rise structures. The other demographic variables are more commonly used by sociologists as standard control variables.

13. Although multicollinearity can affect the magnitude of partial *slope* estimates, *tests of significance* are unaffected since they derive from F ratios of "explained" variation in the dependent variable Y to the total variation in Y (Nie et al. 1975). This is why, for example, the partial slope of strain on family income is significant with $p \leq .05$ and the slope of strain on sex is not, though the former (.108) is less than half the magnitude of the latter ($-.242$).

14. It is also feasible that the higher levels of strain experienced by women on the ground floor result from the *design* of the structure they inhabit rather than their location in it. That is, it is possible that women residing in single-level structures (single, detached, semidetached, and the like) tend to suffer from higher rates of psychological strain than do women in multi-level structures. However, an examination of the patterns of strain among women inhabiting multi-level structures showed that women living

on the ground floor reported higher levels of psychological strain than did women on the second, third, or fourth floors.

    15. There is little evidence to support the notion that women more than men suffer from acrophobia. Royce et al. (1975) found a higher incidence of acrophobia among male mice, but Gray (1973) notes that the *direction* of sex differences in neurotic behavior among rodents typically differs from that for humans. The only study we were able to locate concerning acrophobia among humans involved thirty acrophobics who answered a newspaper advertisement. Twenty-one of these were women. Whether this is indicative of a pattern in the general population is unknown; female acrophobics may simply be more inclined than males to answer advertisements.

References

Althauser, 1971. "Multicollinearity and Non-additive Regression Models." In H. M. Blalock, Jr., ed., *Causal Models in the Social Sciences*, pp. 453–472. Chicago: Aldine-Atherton.

Baker, B. L., D. C. Cohen, and J. T. Saunders. 1973. "Self-Directed Desensitization for Acrophobia." *Behaviour Research and Therapy*, 11:79–89.

Blalock, H. M., Jr. 1963. "Correlated Independent Variables: The Problem of Multicollinearity." *American Journal of Sociology*, 42:233–237.

—— 1972. *Social Statistics*, 2d ed. New York: McGraw-Hill.

Booth, A. and J. Cowell. 1976. "Crowding and Health." *Journal of Health and Social Behavior*, 17:204–220.

Booth, A. and J. N. Edwards. 1976. "Crowding and Family Relations." *American Sociological Review*, 41:308–332.

Collette, J. and S. Webb. 1974. "Urban Density, Crowding and Stress Reactions." Presented to the Urban Ecology Section of the Annual Meeting of the Pacific Sociological Association.

Duncan, O. D. 1961. "A Socioeconomic Index for All Occupations." In A. J. Reiss, Jr., O. D. Duncan, P. Hatt, and C. C. North, eds., *Occupations and Social Status*. New York: Free Press.

Fanning, D. M. 1967. "Families in Flats." *British Medical Journal*, 18:382–386.

Faris, R. E. L. 1939. *An Ecological Study of Insanity in the City.* Chicago: University of Chicago Press.

Fischer, C. S. 1973. "Urban Malaise." *Social Forces* 52:221–235.

Fischer, C. S., M. Baldassare, and R. J. Ofshe. 1975. "Crowding Studies and Urban Life: A Critical Review." *Journal of the American Institute of Planners*, 41:406–475.

Fitch, J. M. 1972. "The Aesthetics of Function." In R. Guttman, ed., *People and Buildings*, pp. 3–16. New York: Basic Books.

Freedman, J. 1975. *Crowding and Behavior.* San Francisco: Freeman.

Freedman, J., A. Levy, R. W. Buchanan, and J. Price. 1972. "Crowding and Human Aggressiveness." *Journal of Experimental Social Psychology,* 8:528–548.

Gillis, A. R. 1974. "Population Density and Social Pathology: The Case of Building Type, Social Allowance and Juvenile Delinquency." *Social Forces,* 53:306–314.

Goodman, L. A. 1970. "The Multivariate Analysis of Qualitative Data: Interactions among Multiple Classifications." *Journal of the American Statistical Association,* 65:225–256.

—— 1972. "A Modified Multiple Regression Approach to the Analysis of Dichotomous Variables." *American Sociological Review,* 37:28–46.

—— 1975. "The Relationship Between Modified and Usual Multiple-Regression Approaches to the Analysis of Dichotomous Variables." In D. R. Heise, ed., *Sociological Methodology,* pp. 83–110. San Francisco: Jossey-Bass.

Gary, J. A. 1973. "Causal Theories of Personality and How to Test Them." In J. R. Royce, ed., *Multivariate Analysis and Psychological Theory,* pp. 409–463. New York: Academic Press.

Gurin, G., J. Veroff, and S. Feld. 1960. *Americans View Their Mental Health.* New York: Basic Books.

Guttman, R. 1975. "Architecture and Sociology." *The American Sociologist,* 10:219–228.

Hartnagel, T. F. 1974. "Measuring the Significance of Others: A Methodological Note." *American Journal of Sociology,* 80:397–401.

Indik, B., S. Seashore, and J. Slesinger. 1964. "Demographic Correlates of Psychological Strain." *Abnormal and Social Psychology,* 69:26–39.

Izumi, K. 1970. "Psychosocial Phenomena and Building Design." In H. M. Proshansky, W. Ittelson, and L. Rivlin, eds., *Environmental Psychology,* pp. 569–573. New York: Holt, Rinehart and Winston.

Jackson, E. and P. Burke. 1965. "Status and Symptoms of Stress: Additive and Interaction Effects." *American Sociological Review,* 30:556–564.

Kerlinger, F. N. and E. J. Pedhazur. 1973. *Multiple Regression in Behavioral Research.* New York: Holt, Rinehart and Winston.

Keyfitz, N. 1966. "Population Density and the Style of Social Life." *Bioscience,* 16:868–873.

Knoke, D. 1975. "A Comparison of Log-linear and Regression Models for Systems of Dichotomous Variables." *Sociological Methods and Research,* 3:416–435.

Kumove, L. 1966. "A Preliminary Study of the Social Implications of High Density Living Conditions." Mimeographed, Toronto: Social Planning Council of Metropolitan Toronto.

Langner, T. S. 1962. "A Twenty-two Item Screening Score of Psychosomatic Symptoms Indicating Impairment." *Journal of Health and Human Behavior,* 3:269–276.

Lemkau, P. 1955. *Mental Hygiene in Public Health*, 2d ed. New York: McGraw-Hill.

Loo, C. 1974. *Crowding and Human Behavior*. New York: MSS Information Corporation.

Maslow, A. and N. L. Mintz. 1972. "Effects of Esthetic Surroundings I. Initial Short-Term Effects of Three Esthetic Conditions Upon Perceiving 'Energy' and 'Well-Being' in Faces." In R. Guttman, ed., *People and Buildings*, pp. 212–219. New York: Basic Books.

Michelson, W. 1970. *Man and His Urban Environment: A Sociological Approach*. Don Mills: Addison-Wesley.

Milgram, S. 1970. "The Experience of Living in Cities." *Science*, 167:1461–1468.

Mintz, N. L. 1972. "Effects of Esthetic Surroundings II. Prolonged and Repeated Experience in a 'Beautiful' and an 'Ugly' Room." In R. Guttman, ed., *People and Buildings*, pp. 220–228. New York: Basic Books.

Mitchell, R. E. 1971. "Some Social Implications of High Density Housing." *American Sociological Review*, 36:18–29.

Namboodiri, N. K., L. E. Carter, and H. M. Blalock, Jr. 1975. *Applied Multivariate Analysis and Experimental Designs*. New York: McGraw-Hill.

Nettler, G. 1976. *Social Concerns*. New York: McGraw-Hill.

Newman, O. 1972. *Defensible Space*. New York: Macmillan.

Nie, N., C. Hull, J. Jenkins, K. Steinbrenner, and D. Bent. 1975. *Statistical Package for the Social Sciences*, 2d ed. New York: McGraw-Hill.

Rainwater, L. 1966. "Fear and the House-As-Haven in the Lower Class." *Journal of the American Institute of Planners*, 32:23–31.

—— 1970. *Behind Ghetto Walls*. Chicago: Aldine.

Raven, J. 1967. "Sociological Evidence on Housing (2: The Home Environment)." *The Architectural Review*, 142:382–386.

Rothblatt, D. M. 1971. "Housing and Human Needs." *Town Planning Review*, 42:130–144.

Royce, J. R., T. M. Nolmes, and W. Poley. 1975. "Behavior Genetic Analysis of Mouse Emotionality III. The Diallel Analysis." *Behavior Genetics*, 5:351–372.

Schorr, A. L. 1963. *Slums and Social Insecurity: An Appraisal of the Effectiveness of Housing Policies in Helping to Eliminate Poverty in the United States*. Washington, D.C.: U.S. Government Printing Office.

Simmel, G. 1950. *The Sociology of Georg Simmel*, K. H. Wolf, ed. New York: Macmillan.

U.S. Department of Health, Education, and Welfare. 1970. *Selected Symptoms of Psychological Distress*. Vital and Health Statistics, series II, number 37. Washington, D.C.: U.S. Government Printing Office.

U.S. Department of Housing and Urban Development. 1975. *Safety and Security*. Housing Management Technical Memoranda 1(1). Washington, D.C.: Office of Housing Management.

Wallace, A. F. C. 1952. "Housing and Social Structure: A Preliminary Survey with Particular Reference to Multi-Story, Low-Rent Public Housing Projects." Mimeograph. Philadelphia: Philadelphia Housing Authority.

Ward, S. 1975. "Methodology Considerations in the Study of Population Density and Social Pathology." *Human Ecology*, 3:275–283.

Welch, S. and A. Booth. 1975. "The Effect of Crowding on Aggression." Ottawa: Ministry of State for Urban Affairs.

Willis, 1955. *Living in High Flats*. London: London County Council, Architects Department, as cited in W. Michelson, *Man and His Urban Environment: A Sociological Approach*. Don Mills: Addison Wesley.

Yancey, W. 1972. "Architecture, Interaction, and Social Control: The Case of a Large-Scale Housing Project." In J. F. Wohlwill and D. H. Carson, eds., *Environment and the Social Sciences*, pp. 126–136. Washington, D.C.: American Psychological Association.

PART FIVE

Vulnerable Populations in the City

EDITOR'S NOTE:

ANTUNES ET AL. explores why the elderly, who are less crime-prone than others, are more fearful of crime. National surveys point to the importance of social context, especially the likelihood that crimes against the elderly occur near their homes and involve young male strangers. Strategies to reduce the availability, vulnerability, and desirability of elderly victims are discussed. Melville intensively interviewed women who have moved to the Houston area from Mexico. Loneliness, no knowledge of English, lack of transportation, strain due to changing sex roles, inability to use health services, and fears of deportation characterized this group. Nevertheless, improved living conditions lead most to remain and adapt through forming locally-based networks, becoming employed, learning English in schools, and frequently visiting the homeland. Farley et al. studied the causes of racial segregation through interviews with blacks and whites in Detroit. Neither economic status differences nor blacks' desire to segregate are important factors. White reluctance to move to integrated areas and to stay in neighborhoods which blacks move into appear to account for pervasive segregation.

11
Patterns of Personal Crime Against the Elderly: Findings from a National Survey

GEORGE E. ANTUNES, FAY LOMAX COOK, THOMAS D. COOK, AND WESLEY G. SKOGAN

CONCERN ABOUT THE criminal victimization of elderly Americans currently seems to be very high. A recent book by Goldsmith and Goldsmith (1976) suggests two reasons for this. First, elderly persons may be victimized more often than others or may suffer more serious consequences as a result of being victimized; second, many surveys show that elderly persons are more fearful of crime than younger persons. This concern with the victimization of elderly Americans is also reflected in the recent agreement between the Administration on Aging and the Law Enforcement and Assistance Administration to launch cooperative efforts aimed at understanding and alleviating problems associated with the criminal victimization of older Americans. Behind these efforts is the explicit assumption that criminal victimization of the elderly

Reprinted with permission from *The Gerontologist* (August 1977), vol. 17, no. 4. Tables and text references to tables omitted due to space constraints. These are available from the author.

is "special," but we do not yet know in which ways such victimization is indeed special.

We already know one way in which the criminal victimization of older Americans is not special. Evidence from national (Cook and Cook 1976) and citywide (Hindelang 1976) surveys shows that the elderly are less likely to be victimized than younger persons in all crime categories that have been studied to date. The only exception is personal larceny, for purse and wallet snatchings seem to be as frequently targeted against the elderly as against other age groups (Cook and Cook 1976; Hindelang 1976). But there is no indication that personal larceny affects older persons more than younger ones.

The evidence on crime rates has to be balanced against the fact that elderly persons' fear of crime is greater than younger persons'. This is one area where criminal victimization of the elderly is truly special (Clemente and Kleinman 1976). An important research task is to solve the apparent puzzle of why the elderly are more fearful of crime even though they are less likely than others to be victimized. In this paper, we shall investigate whether there is something special about *the social context* in which crimes against the elderly occur and whether any special features of the context might account for the elderly being especially afraid of crime.

Specifically, this paper addresses the following questions:

(1) Are elderly victims more likely than other victims to suffer from crimes of violence?

(2) Are elderly victims more likely than others to be in or near their homes when crimes are committed against them?

(3) Are elderly victims more likely than others to be attacked by gangs of youths rather than individuals, as Conklin (1976) has suggested?

(4) Are elderly victims more likely than others to be attacked by strangers rather than persons they know?

(5) Are elderly victims more likely than others to be attacked by persons with weapons?

Research Data and Design

A major problem in trying to answer questions about criminal victimization of the aged has been the absence of valid data on topics other than crime rates and fear of crime. Until recently, scholars interested in other questions had to rely on small-scale, localized victim surveys. The resulting studies about crime and the elderly were deficient in terms of both generalizability and the comprehensiveness and validity of the raw data (Skogan 1975, 1976).

The data for this report are based on self-reports of victimization gathered from individuals interviewed between February 1973 and July 1974 as part of a survey program financed by the Law Enforcement Assistance Administration. Each month the Census Bureau interviews all persons twelve years of age and older in a national panel sample of ten thousand households, asking them about their experiences with crime during the preceding six months. The data about crimes in 1973 thus are based on interviews with nearly 375,000 respondents. The sample is large because only a minority of persons have such experiences to report. During the interview, respondents who have been victimized are asked about those events, and detailed data are collected about the circumstances surrounding each. It is these data that form the basis for the present report. The survey is particularly useful because it provides information about crimes that were not reported to the police. These are often 50 percent of the total in some major categories. While the Crime Panel data are subject to some methodological limitations (National Academy of Sciences, 1976), they nonetheless provide rich and novel information about our national experience with crime and the process of victimization (for a further description of the survey, see Skogan 1976).

In the analysis that follows we categorize respondents to the survey in eight age categories, focusing our discussion on the oldest of these, persons over sixty-five years of age. These categories were assigned to reflect some major stages in the life-cycle and, more importantly, to balance the number of crime victims in each. Since victimization rates begin to drop markedly before middle age, older groups tend to span longer periods than those containing high-risk individuals.

The Context of Victimization

Any assessment of crimes against the elderly must begin with an analysis of how frequently crimes are committed against the elderly compared to other age groups. The appropriate data from the 1973 national survey were examined. *Assault* was the most frequent personal crime reported in the survey, with 1.4 percent of those interviewed reporting an attack of some type in the preceding six months. Assault victims, however, were concentrated in the younger age categories, and persons sixty-five and older were victimized least frequently of all. Indeed, their victimization rate was one-seventh that of the total sample and one-twenty-fourth that of persons aged seventeen to twenty. *Robbery* (theft with threat or use of force) was also concentrated in the youngest age categories. The proportion of the total sample reporting a robbery was 0.4 percent, while the figure for those sixty-five and older was half that. In contrast, the crime of *personal larceny* (purse snatchings and picked pockets—simple thefts involving personal contact) was less frequent than robbery and was distributed more or less evenly across age groups.[1] The proportion of the total sample reporting a personal larceny was 0.2 percent, the same as that reported by those age sixty-five and older. Finally, *rape* was the least frequent personal crime and was reported by only 0.1 percent of the total sample. Rape is a crime primarily afflicting the young, and almost none were reported by older respondents. There is in all these data about crime rates no indication that the elderly are special because they are victimized more frequently than others.

Age of Victim and Type of Victimization

An examination of persons in each age group who have reported a victimization will allow us to describe the "mix" of victimization experiences in each age category and whether that experience is different for elderly persons. In other words, *when they are victimized,* what types of crime are people in each age group most likely to experience?

The data show that the mix of crime inflicted on the aged is strikingly different from that affecting adolescents and younger adults. Elderly victims are less likely to be raped or assaulted than they are to be robbed or to suffer from personal larceny, while the reverse is true for adolescents. Robbery and larceny can be characterized as "predatory crimes" since their object is to obtain another's property with or without the threat of force. Rape and assault, on the other hand, are crimes that can be classified as "violent," since their purpose is to injure or harm another. The contrast between the victimization experiences of the aged and younger persons is most vividly seen where summary figures on "predatory" and "violent" victimizations are presented. Elderly victims are more likely to be preyed on than treated violently, while younger victims are more likely to be treated violently than preyed on.

Age of Victim and Location of Violent and Predatory Victimization

The relative safety or danger of various locations can have important effects on human behavior and the perceived quality of life. For instance, crimes committed in the home or near it (in doorways, alleys, or elevators that are functionally part of the building in which the home is located) may be especially disconcerting, for they represent a penetration of one's personal life space. This is a zone that most people believe should be a source of unquestioned safety (Rainwater 1966), especially from strangers. These are noteworthy differences between the aged and other adults in terms of the proportion of *violent crimes* committed in various locations. For elderly persons, over half the violent victimizations occurred in or near their homes, and less than 30 percent took place on the street. For other adults the percentages tended to be reversed, and younger adults were more likely to suffer from violent crimes on public streets and in commercial establishments than in or near their homes.

This age difference in the location of violent crimes may be very important. Many violent crimes are committed against persons who place themselves in potentially dangerous situations (such as bars), or who become involved in arguments with family members or close acquaintances (Curtis 1974). In contrast, the elderly typically live alone and so have fewer opportunities to become involved in rancorous intrafamilial disputes. When they do get into disputes, the elderly are also less likely than younger persons to resort to violence. In addition, the aged can (and presumably do) stay away from dangerous places, avoid neighborhood bars, and even restrict their use of the public streets. Whatever precautions one takes, however, one has to be at home at some time and use the doorways, elevators, and alleys of the building. It is precisely in such locations that the elderly tend to be victimized—their last refuge penetrated, despite their best precautions.

Concerning the location of *predatory crimes,* the data indicate that about half of all predatory victimizations took place on public streets, regardless of the age of the victim. The aged were somewhat less likely to be victimized in an office building or commercial establishment and were somewhat more likely to be victimized in or near their homes. The magnitude of these effects is rather small, however, and there seems to be little justification for claiming that the elderly are in any way special victims of predatory crime. Indeed, the only major locational difference in predatory crime involved adolescents, who tended to be victimized more often than others in schools and on the streets (this last category includes school grounds).

Age of Victim and Characteristics of Offenders
Who Commit Violent and Predatory Crimes

A variety of offender variables might give the victimization experiences of the aged a more fearful quality than the victimization experiences of other adults. We consider the extent to which violent and predatory crimes against persons of different age groups are committed by youths, by gangs, by offenders employing weapons, by assailants who are strangers, and by offenders who are black. (The phenomenon of whites attacking blacks will not be considered here. Blacks, who as a group suffer *higher* rates of victimization, almost never reported being victimized by whites.)

The data on violent crimes indicate that the elderly were no more likely than other age groups to be attacked by gangs. When compared to persons twenty-one to forty-nine, aged victims were more likely to have been attacked by youths than by older criminals. But the elderly were much less likely to have been attacked by youths when compared to persons under twenty-one. The data show that most violent crime was committed by youths and was inflicted on their peers.

The data, however, also indicate that violence against the elderly was more likely to be committed by strangers. In fact, almost three-quarters of the crimes against the elderly were committed by strangers. In addition, elderly whites were more likely to be attacked by black offenders than were white victims under fifty. Almost 30 percent of the white victims of violent crime over fifty years of age had black attackers, as opposed to between 17 and 20 percent of younger victims. However fear-inducing these attacks may have been, they were less likely to involve weapons than were attacks on younger victims.

The elderly were also more likely than others to be victimized by individuals as opposed to gangs, and elderly whites' assailants were more likely to be young, unarmed strangers of a different race.

Summary

The preceding analyses allow us to answer the five descriptive questions about victimization of the elderly that were listed in the introduction. First, the elderly were less likely than others to be victimized, and, when only victims are considered, they were less likely than others to be subjected to violent crimes but were more likely to suffer from predatory incidents. Second, while on the street, senior citizens were no more likely than others to be victims of predatory crimes and were less likely to be victims of violent incidents. Attacks on the elderly that involved violence were more likely to occur in or near the home than was the case for other age groups. Third, the elderly were no more likely than other age groups to be victimized by gangs. Fourth, they were more likely than younger victims to have been attacked by black youths acting alone who were strangers to them. And finally, their assailants were less likely to be armed than were the assailants of younger victims.

These findings may have implications for understanding why the elderly fear crime more than younger persons though they are victimized less frequently. Young black male strangers can be seen on the streets in many areas. Since this is the profile of persons who usually attack the elderly, each person who conforms to this physical profile may reinstate in elderly persons the fear of being victimized, even though the young black male stranger may be merely an innocent passerby. If it is true that the elderly stay at home more than younger persons, fear of meeting strangers on the street might be partly responsible for this. If so, our data suggest that the elderly are not likely to have *all* their fears stilled by staying at home, for when they are victimized they are more likely than others to be attacked in their homes or its immediate surroundings.

Alternative Solutions

What is to be done in order to prevent the elderly being victimized by young criminals engaged in unplanned low-skill endeavors, and thereby to reduce levels of fear among the elderly? Skogan and Klecka (1976) have suggested that it might be useful to consider victimization in terms of three factors, each of which may be positively related to victimization. These factors are *availability*, *vulnerability*, and *desirability*.

In terms of *availability*, we found that violent crimes were differently related to location for the elderly, while predatory crimes were not. Violent crimes were especially prevalent for the elderly in or near their homes, but less prevalent on the street than for other age groups. An obvious way to make the elderly less available for violent crimes would be to segregate them into security-intensive retirement communities or high-rise apartment buildings. This recommendation has been put forward by Sherman et al. (1975), who interviewed 169 residents of public housing projects in the Albany-Troy, New York, area. Their study suggested that residents of age-segregated housing may experience fewer crimes and have less fear of crime within their building than is the case with elderly residents of age-integrated housing or age-segregated housing within age-integrated projects. The policy of segregating the elderly, however, though seductively simple, may have many undesirable, unintended social consequences. First, it may increase the isolation of the elderly. Second, it may give no opportunity for age-related stereotypes to be disconfirmed in casual everyday encounters. Third, the effects are restricted to crimes and fear of crime *within the building*, for Sherman et al.'s findings suggested that residents in age-segregated housing were somewhat more fearful of crime in their neighborhoods than residents in age-integrated or mixed housing. And finally, the strategy of segregated housing is only relevant to crimes of violence from which the elderly are less likely to suffer than predatory crimes (see table 11-2).

The elderly would be victimized less often if they could be made less *desirable* as targets of crime. This could be accomplished by increasing the penalties for victimizing them. For instance, the desirability of victimizing the aged would decrease if there were an improvement in the system for detecting criminals and for sentencing them swiftly and harshly. We found, however, that the elderly are disproportionately victimized by young males acting alone who do not threaten with weapons or carry guns. According to some criminologists (Morris and Hawkins 1970), youths of this type should be prime targets for supervision or community-based treatment, for the fear is that prolonged contact with the social life of jails and prisons may confirm them as criminals and put them beyond "rehabilitation." Alternatively, the desirability of the elderly as victims might be reduced by decreasing the apparent profitability of the criminal venture. This might be achieved by encouraging elderly women not to carry their money in purses that can be easily snatched. The principle here is similar to the practice of taxicab drivers who prominently advertise that they do not carry more than five dollars in change.

Finally, the elderly can be made to appear less *vulnerable* as targets of crime. We found that elderly victims were easily intimidated. They were attacked, often successfully, by offenders without weapons, working alone. There are at least three general strategies for reducing this apparent vulnerability. The first would be to increase police surveillance of places the elderly frequent. It is not clear, however, whether this could be done to an extent that significantly reduces crime without depleting the treasury. A second strategy would be for the elderly to take self-defensive measures, including physical resistance to offenders. Hindelang's (1976) analysis, however, indicates that such measures may backfire and increase the chances of being injured during the course of the crime.[2] Finally, there are a set of self-help activities that may well be of some utility in reducing the victimization of the elderly. "Buddy systems" and other group activities, which make it more difficult to accost the elderly on the street, are in this category, as are "escort programs" that join the elderly with youths who accompany the elderly on their daily rounds.

A more general approach to breaking the present pattern of victimizations against the elderly involves finding employment for young males with low education, particularly in the cities. The aim is to get the young people off the streets and to give them money and a stake in the very social order that they threaten by their criminal acts. This strategy would not protect any one group of victims but rather would be targeted at the overall problem of criminal victimization. It is not clear whether this strategy, if implemented, would be effective. Nor is it clear whether the political will exists to finance the creation of millions of jobs for urban youths.

We do not yet know the policies that are most likely to reduce crimes against the elderly and to still some of their fears. None of the alternatives we have considered strikes us as being of sufficient scope or probability of success that we could confidently recommend it as a general policy. Some of the alternatives appear promising, however, especially those related to self-help activities including group support for the elderly, making it more difficult for offenders to accost them. What is needed now is research aimed at adding to the list of alternatives and at empirically deciding which is the most effective among them.

Notes

1. The distinction between robbery and personal larceny may be somewhat artificial. When someone takes property from another by force or the threat of force the crime is classified as a robbery. If there is no threat or use of force it is recorded as a personal larceny. As Repetto notes in his discussion of residential robbery (1974:29), however, the victims of personal larceny are predominantly women who are purse-snatch victims, whereas residential robbery victims are predominantly men who, having no purse to be snatched, must be threatened or forced to hand over their wallets.

2. Facing an unarmed assailant may work to the detriment of victims. Several studies have reported that those who fall victim to unarmed robbers are more likely to be injured than those robbed by an armed assailant (Conklin 1972; Hindelang 1976; Repetto 1974). The reasons for this are unclear, although the sources cited articulate several hypotheses. It should be noted, however, that victims are likely to suffer most of all if they offer resistance to armed attackers.

References

Clemente, F. and M. Kleinman. 1976. "Fear of Crime Among the Aged." *Gerontologist,* 16:207–210.

Conklin, J. E. 1972. *Robbery and the Criminal Justice System.* Philadelphia: Lippincott.

—— 1976. "Robbery, the Elderly and Fear: An Urban Problem in Search of a Solution." In J. Goldsmith and S. Goldsmith, eds., *Crime and the Elderly.* Lexington, Mass.: Lexington Books.

Cook, F. L. and T. D. Cook. 1976. "Evaluating the Rhetoric of Crisis: A Case Study of Criminal Victimization of the Elderly." *Social Service Review,* 50:632–646.

Curtis, L. A. 1974. "Victim Precipitation and Violent Crime." *Social Problems,* 21:594–605.

Goldsmith, J. and S. Goldsmith. 1976. *Crime and the Elderly.* Lexington, Mass.: Lexington Books.

Hindelang, M. 1976. *Criminal Victimization in Eight American Cities.* Cambridge, Mass.: Ballinger.

Morris, N. and G. Hawkins. 1970. *The Honest Politician's Guide to Crime Control.* Chicago: University of Chicago Press.

National Academy of Sciences. 1976. *Surveying Crime.* Washington, D.C.: Committee on National Statistics, National Academy of Sciences.

Rainwater, L. 1966. "Fear and the House-as-Haven in the Lower Class." *Journal of the American Institute of Planners,* 32:23–31.

Repetto, T. 1974. *Residential Crime.* Cambridge, Mass.: Ballinger.

Sherman, E., E. S. Newman, A. Nelson, and D. Van Buren. 1975. "Crimes against the Elderly in Public Housing: Policy Alternatives." School of Social Welfare, State University of New York at Albany.

Skogan, W. G. 1975. "Measurement Problems in Official and Survey Crime Rates." *Journal of Criminal Justice,* 3:17–31.

—— 1976. *Sample Surveys of the Victims of Crime.* Cambridge, Mass.: Ballinger.

Skogan, W. G. and W. R. Klecka. 1976. *The Fear of Crime.* Washington, D.C.: American Political Science Association.

12

Mexican Women Adapt to Migration

MARGARITA B. MELVILLE

INCREASING GOVERNMENTAL AND public concern with the Mexican "alien invasion" in the United States and its media coverage have contributed to the negative stereotyping of these migrants. Most of the studies, intended to clarify the reality of illegal Mexican aliens and thereby to aid in the formulation of public policy affecting them, have concentrated on male laborers who have been apprehended and are being held in detention centers awaiting deportation (Samora 1971:68, Cornelius 1977). As Samora and others have noted, however, data obtained under such circumstances are highly unreliable.

Precisely because of their unregistered status, there is no accurate count of the undocumented persons living in the United States today, nor of their family situation, their economic or social status, or whether they pay taxes, utilize public services, or take jobs from willing and available native-born workers. The estimates, however, tend to favor the assumption that the majority of them are males and that a sizable number of temporary residents who come one or more times without their families to earn some money, return to Mexico (Weaver and Downing 1976:55). Such an assumption

Reprinted with permission from *International Migration Review* (Summer 1978), vol. 12, no. 2, Center for Migration Studies of New York.

appears at least questionable if we can assume that there is any similarity between documented and undocumented workers, in view of the fact that since the 1950s, the male/female ratio of documented Mexican immigrants has narrowed until the present time, when men and women migrate in about equal numbers (Weaver and Downing 1976:55). This assumption of male dominance tends to deny the importance of undocumented women and children who accompany a male household head to the U.S. or, what seems to be more often the case, who come to join a husband, or father, who has managed to establish himself in this country.

In the pertinent literature on documented and undocumented immigrants the numbers and situation of female Mexican immigrants is often neglected. Although my interest lies mainly with the undocumented female immigrants, because of the many methodological problems involved in a study devoted exclusively to them, I decided to expand my investigation to include women of both documented and undocumented status. This had both its drawbacks and its advantages.

I include among its advantages the facility with which undocumented persons can be approached by overtly ignoring any interest in their legal status, as well as the end result that two subsets of the target population are researched and are therefore available for comparative purposes. In addition to this increased accessibility, in most interviews the subject revealed her status, as a matter of course, because of the importance this status played in her life. In this preliminary essay, however, I will not attempt to make any categorical comparisons between the documented and the undocumented groups, since the data need further analysis for such an undertaking and because I think there is enough similarity in the two groups to warrant a comprehensive exposition of my total data here.

The drawbacks to the approach of this study relate mainly to the question of the representativeness of the sample, since all individuals were contacted by means of informal networks, the originating point of which were six public-service institutions with agencies located in those sections of Houston with large Spanish-speaking populations. Although the representativeness of the sample may be questioned, the method used for contacting the sample unforeseenly may have provided results that could be considered indicative of the ratio of undocumented female immigrants to documented ones (21:11) in the larger population, at least here in Houston. This, of course, excludes U.S.-born citizens. I prefer to categorize this first summation of my findings as a qualitative study, however, deferring at this point from its quantitative significance.

Qualitative studies of migration cover a wide range of concerns. The research reported here deals primarily with the mental stress of acculturation that results from such migration. Numerous studies have attested to the presence of stress in the process of migration to a new cultural setting (Parker et al. 1969; Bagley 1967; Fried 1959). My purpose was to locate recent Mexican[1] female migrants to the city of Houston and to determine what strategies they used to cope with the stress of migration.[2] As has been mentioned, no effort was made to specify legal status in locating the women. The only stipulations were that they be Spanish-speaking and of Mexican background, having come either from Mexico or from a rural U.S. setting and that they be residents of Houston for two years or less.

Fieldwork was done during the summer and early fall of 1977. The forty-six women were interviewed[3] in their homes. Some women were accompanied on errands, such as visits to hospitals, to food stamp offices, to lawyers, and to schools. Interviews were open-ended and followed a minimum outline to allow each woman to introduce personal concerns. Thirty-two had come from Mexico and fourteen from rural United States. Both working-class and professional women were represented in a 36:10 ratio, respectively.

Problems Encountered

The sources of stress experienced by the Houston immigrants coincided on several salient issues with what other investigators have discovered among a variety of migrating peoples, particularly among those going from a rural to an urban setting. The outstanding source of stress is the loneliness caused by the separation from the extended family, support network, familiar and predictable neighbors, and well-known, culturally meaningful surroundings. Although all but six of the informants had come to Houston with some relative or acquaintance to welcome them, the separation from a customary social network and frequent and numerous social contacts created a strain. In addition, housing could not always be found in locations proximate to close relatives or friends. Loneliness is compounded for those migrant women who have to remain at home all day to take care of children. Their contacts are often limited to a neighbor or two, and for some it is difficult to find these. As one remarked: "Here people have air conditioning and leave their doors and windows closed." The loneliness is eased somewhat for those who have close relatives who live nearby and for those who get jobs and, as a result, have the opportunity to meet people outside their immediate household, generally nuclear, family.

A feeling of helplessness pervades those women who do not speak English. Out of forty-six interviewees, only four spoke English and seven others could use only a few simple English phrases. The higher educational background of middle-class women and the length of experience in the migrant farmworker stream provided the English knowledge. "It is like having arrived in a different world," said one. Another remarked: "It is like being a child again when I can't understand those who speak to me, or express myself." They found trying to read labels or signs a problem. The lack of a facility with English deterred women from seeking directions, information, or help from people presumed to be monolingual English-speaking Anglos, thus decreasing potential contact with Anglos.

The sense of dependence on husbands, or on relatives and neighbors, is exacerbated by the lack of mobility due to scarce or nonexistent transportation. For many, even household chores such as shopping and laundry have to be postponed until weekends when husbands could transport the women.

Of all the needs faced by migrants, health concerns are probably the most stressful, especially if they are emergencies. A case of illness causes tension in itself, but when the patient, or responsible relative (a mother or a wife), cannot explain what the ailment or problem is and cannot request the required aid, frustration and anxiety increase exponentially. Especially when giving birth, the women experienced extreme frustration, helplessness, and loneliness by not being able to communicate with attending nurses and doctors. For this reason, two returned to Mexico to give birth and one had her child at home with her mother to help her.

Two cases of nervous disorders were encountered among the interviewees. One woman attributed temporary facial paralysis to extreme tension caused by a comatose husband for whom she had to obtain emergency help when she had only been in the city two months. A second woman reported having seizures which she attributed to tension caused by divorce proceedings.

We found three additional sources of stress that have not been singled out by many investigators and therefore may not be as obvious as the foregoing. The first two are concomitant with the illegal residence status of the subjects. Forfeited expectations, the fear of deportation, and changing gender roles all caused varying degrees of anxiety for 26 of the women interviewed.

Women who come to a large urban setting in the United States have many expectations. Second only to the hope of a better paying job (or perhaps any job at all) for one's husband or oneself is the expectation of giving one's children better educational opportunities than they had in Mexico or in rural United States. All those interviewed had either completed or at least initiated the procedure to obtain legal residence, but for the parents who have as yet been unable to get residence permits for their children, this expectation of better schooling has been unrealized during 1976 and 1977. Seven husbands had legalized their own residence but had been unable to legalize that of their children or their wives. Because the Houston Independent School District has demanded proof of legal residence or between $90 and $130 tuition a month per child since 1976, these parents have been forced to keep their children out of school. They all hope that this situation will change soon; until then, however, they attempt to fill the educational gap with an untrained neighborhood tutor or an improvised school that has been locally organized. Nevertheless, a great deal of anxiety is generated by the situation and some entertain doubts regarding the advisability of remaining. Most, however, due to their economic situation, have little choice.

The women who do not have legal residence papers experience fear of being deported. Out of 46 interviewees, 21 were in this situation. Some had initiated the process of legalization as many as five years before coming to the U.S. These women are reluctant to request or utilize services, be they public or private. All but one mentioned living in constant fear. One attributed her frequent feelings of "nervousness"[4] to this. Denunciations leading to deportation often are believed to have come from Mexicans who know the tenuous legal situation of the individual and who for some personal reason develop a grudge and use this as a conflict-resolution mechanism. This increases the reluctance to establish new social contacts and augments the feelings of loneliness. Two interviewees, who now have legal residence, had previously been deported with their husbands and children. At least six others had experienced the deportation of their husbands one or more times. They were not deported with their husbands because the husbands claimed to be single when apprehended, demonstrating the lack of validity of data obtained from detainees.

The third source of serious emotional stress comes from changes that occur in the interpretation of rights and duties associated with gender roles. The drinking behavior of Cuban males has been related to this type of stress by Angela and Luis Rodriguez (1977:74). Their study does not relate the stress of gender role changes to female behavior, however.

Michael Whiteford (1977:12ff.) found that the female migrants he studied in Colombia assumed new gender roles in the city as a result of their active economic roles. My informants experienced the need to reinterpret their gender roles due to factors arising from two entirely different and subcontrary situations. At one extreme some find they are less capable of fulfilling traditional female duties such as shopping for food, preparing that food tastefully and economically, and doing the family laundry. This is due to the unavailability of fresh, traditional ingredients for meals, and/or their inaccessibility because of lack of transportation. As a result, such women entertain feelings of frustration and inadequacy. The 16 who were employed, on the other hand, found they were contributing a more or less equal share to the household income. All but three of the eleven who were married were still expected by their husbands to perform, unassisted by them, all of the household duties of a traditional housewife. A gradual change in the wives' attitudes toward strict traditional gender roles is evident, but corresponding changes in the husbands' attitudes have not occurred. Three of the women actually earned more than their husbands. This seemed to provoke feelings of inadequacy in the husbands, and friction between husband and wife. Four of the 34 married interviewees admitted that they were considering divorce attributable to such a cause.

Migration studies have generally indicated that tension is caused by the need to adapt to a new sociocultural environment (Fried 1959; Kemnitzer 1973). Immigration would not take place, however, or would be matched by a reverse migration, if there were no positive payoffs for the immigrants. Consequently, I found that the population that I researched felt that the stress and anxiety of acculturation were worth the effort for the most part.

The positive payoffs mainly consisted of improved housing conditions and the ability to provide more nutritious and abundant food for their children. Two said it was easy to get used to a "better life." Another remarked: "Aquí está a todo dar" (Things are great here). The type of work available in

Houston is an improvement over what most migrants are able
to obtain at their point of origin. The exceptions to this rule
were the professional women, a chemical analyst, a key-
puncher, four secretaries, two college graduates, and two
teachers. Because of language problems, only three of these
had been able to obtain work in Houston at the time of my
investigation. Their hopes for a positive payoff in the near
future must materialize, presumably, or they will become part
of the reverse stream.

Several social scientists have documented the negative
psychological effects of racial prejudice on migrants (Isaacs
1964; De Vos and Wagatsuma 1966; Berreman 1966). On the
other hand, Fried says that "the well-integrated ethnic community has long been recognized as a powerful aid to the
recent migrant in overcoming the first shocks of change"
(1959:129), including racial prejudice. My research confirms
Fried's thesis. It also confirms Dworkin's finding (1976) that
new Mexican migrants tend to have a better concept of Anglos than long-term residents. Most interviewees claimed to
have little or no contact with Anglos. "Most of the people I
deal with are Chicanos," was the common response. Gonzalez (1976:37) found that Dominican women could live in New
York for years and not learn English. The contacts our informants did have with Anglos were in a service setting (health
or education). Any evidence of belittling or derogatory attitudes were accepted, not as racial or ethnic prejudice, but as
a language problem or as an expression of class difference, to
which they are well accustomed in class-structured Mexico.
The stress generated is minimal since it comes from something that is expected and is not considered extraordinary.

Coping Strategies

Earlier, loneliness was mentioned as one of the principal
sources of stress. Although this loneliness is all-pervasive, it
is made somewhat bearable by the near presence of a relative,
even though the relationship may be distant. Social networks

for most are instrumental in their coming to the city. Gonzalez (1976:42) found that almost all the Dominican women she interviewed who had migrated to New York knew someone who had previously been to New York. Only five of my interviewees came accompanying their husbands and had no acquaintances or relatives in the city at the time. Ten came as single women to stay with relatives (siblings or parents) and one, a widow, came to work as a maid for a woman recommended by someone she knew in Mexico. Six came with their husbands but arrived at the home of relatives. The largest number, 24, came to join husbands who had been here anywhere from one to seven years. Thus, for the majority, although loneliness is present and burdensome, the transition is eased somewhat by the help of a husband or relative who introduces the migrant to her new setting.

The help of relatives includes such things as providing a home until the family can find their own, helping the husband and/or wife find work, introducing the family to shopping and laundry procedures, and recommending medical and school services.

Two of the women who came with their husbands and had no relatives in Houston previous to their arrival, have themselves encouraged several relatives to come. They have introduced them to a new life discovered during the fewer than two years since their own arrival.

The use of social networks eases the tension in proportion to the closeness of the relationship while never entirely eliminating it. Those whose parents were left behind are anxious for them. The situation is particularly stressful for those who have had to leave children behind. When the contact in Houston is limited to a woman's husband, who is out working all day, loneliness is greatest.

A second strategy, which eases the strain of migration, consists of frequent visits to and from relatives in Mexico or southern Texas. Fried (1959) found this to be true also of migrants to Lima. In many convenience stores or bakeries in the neighborhoods where these families live, one can find handwritten signs advertising noncommercial passenger cars that leave for Monterrey, Matamoros, or Laredo on Friday afternoon to return on Sunday afternoon. For a fee, a passenger is given a round-trip ride from his home address in Houston to his relatives' address in Mexico. One woman explained that during her first year here, she and her husband travelled to Matamoros (an eight- or ten-hour drive) one weekend every month. Those who have not been able to legalize their residential status, however, are deprived of this recourse. They do not want to risk detection.

Three other tension-easing mechanisms were encountered. One was assisting at English classes. These are provided by one community center and at least two churches. Those with residence papers can find other options. In addition to helping a person to do something about the feeling of language inadequacy, these classes provide a relaxed opportunity to interact with people outside the immediate family.

Employment releases some of the tension caused by loneliness and the feeling of dependency. Sixteen women were working. Several mentioned that employment allowed them to send economic help and gifts to parents, siblings, and children in Mexico, thus alleviating the sense of separation and of guilt at not being able to fulfill familial responsibilities. On the other hand, employment caused eight women—all married—much anxiety due to gender role changes. For them it became a cause of one type of stress while constituting relief for another.

According to the director of a social-service center that caters principally to Mexican Americans, women rarely if ever have recourse to alcohol, but do use tranquilizers to cope with strain. We found, however, that the persons using that center are predominantly those with more than three years residency in Houston. Among my informants only two had used drugs prescribed by a doctor for nervousness. Those who did rely on the use of a substance to relieve tension used a natural tea made from lettuce leaves, the medicinal effects of which I cannot substantiate. This difference between the clients of the social-service center and my informants may confirm what Gecas (1976) and Dworkin (1976) report, that is, that longer residence seems to increase awareness of discrimination and corresponding tension.

Two original hypotheses for this study proved to be null. One, that women would choose a church-centered network to replace absent familial support systems, was not confirmed by a single case. One family had been converted to a Protestant Church in Mexico, but they did not find their church in Houston particularly helpful. A social worker in a social-services office of a Catholic Church informed us that women often courteously declined help when they were notified that they had to give their names and addresses as part of the established procedure.

My other hypothesis stated that the role of motherhood would be embraced as the primary and most meaningful role available to a woman, and such role-involvement would be a tension-combating strategy used by a significant number. We found this to be true of only one woman interviewed. Of the 34 married women interviewed, she was the only one adverse to birth control. At least 6 had already availed themselves of sterilization and at least two were taking birth-control pills. Six young mothers with one or two children did not want more than three and intended to take steps to limit themselves to that number. All found that the economic burden of providing for many children prevented them from giving these children the kind of care for which they had immigrated.

Predicting Permanence of Residency in the United States

One of the respondents has returned to Mexico since my interview, accompanied by her children, but not her husband. The sister of another respondent has returned with her husband and children. In both cases, the needs of the children were said to be the primary determinants for the change. The first claimed she was dissatisfied with the "sexually immoral atmosphere" of the United States. She was unwilling to allow her children to receive what she considered to be much too explicit and early sex instruction. The second mother explained that her two sons (aged eight and ten) had both had convulsions when they came to Houston. She then returned them to Mexico and left them with her mother. This, however, was more than she could bear and decided to return to Mexico herself so that she could be with them.

If permanence could be predicted, I would suggest that it depends on job availability and children's well-being. Several women said that the worst thing that could happen to them was that their husbands lose their jobs. While there is work to be had, people will continue to immigrate. If some children have to be left behind in Mexico and cannot come to the United States, indications are that their mothers will not remain. If stress causes a divorce, the woman is likely to remain. Three respondents indicated that they would stay here and work to support their children, even should there be a divorce.

Finally, if there are other family members already living in the area, or who arrive subsequently, their supportive presence constitutes some assurance of permanence. One woman, whose relationship with her husband had deteriorated, declared that if her brother, her only relative here, should return to Mexico, she would leave her husband and return also. Permanent residence is desired particularly by those who migrate as a family. For those who find their living situation improved, and this is the majority, migration and the adaptation it demands are worth the mental stress the process produces.

Notes

1. The term "Mexican" is used in this paper to denote all those people who came to Houston from south Texas or Mexico, whose first language is Spanish, and whose culture has historical roots traceable to Mexico.

2. Random sampling was out of the question. Adequate representation was secured, however, through the variety of sources utilized, as well as variety in residential location and in socioeconomic status.

3. The author was assisted by two research assistants: Maria T. Rodriguez and Gilda Salazar.

4. The term *sentirse nerviosa* is used in Spanish to refer to tension or mental stress due to worry or distress.

References

Bagley, C. 1967. "Migration, Race and Mental Health: A Review of Some Recent Research." *Race* 9(3):343–356.

Berreman, G. D. 1966. "Concomitants of Caste Organization." In G. De Vos and H. Wagatsuma, eds., *Japan's Invisible Race*, pp. 308–324. Berkeley: University of California Press.

Clark, B. M. 1976. "Mexican Migration to the United States." In T. Weaver and T. Downing, eds., *Mexican Migration*, pp. 51–63. Tucson: University of Arizona Press.

Cornelius, W. A. 1977. "Report to President Carter." Quoted in *El espalda mojada*, no. 9, Mexico, D.F.

De Vos, G. and H. Wagatsuma. 1966. *Japan's Invisible Race: Caste in Culture and Personality*. Berkeley: University of California Press.

Dworkin, A. G. 1976. "National Origin and Ghetto Experience as Variables in Mexican American Stereotypy." In C. Hernández, M. Haug, and N. Wagner, eds., *Chicanos: Social and Psychological Perspectives*, pp. 136–139. St. Louis: Mosby.

Fried, J. 1959. "Acculturation and Mental Health Among Indian Migrants in Peru." In M. K. Opler, ed., *Culture and Mental Health: Cross-cultural Studies*, pp. 119–137. New York: Macmillan.

Gecas, V. 1976. "Self-Conceptions of Migrant and Settled Mexican Americans." In C. A. Hernández, M. J. Haug, and N. N. Wagner, eds., *Chicanos: Social and Psychological Perspectives*, pp. 140–151. St. Louis: Mosby.

Gonzalez, N. L. 1976. "Multiple Migratory Experiences of Dominican Women." *Anthropological Quarterly* (January), 49:36–44.

Goodman, M. E. 1971. *The Mexican American Population of Houston: A Monograph in Cultural Anthropology*. Houston: Rice University Press.

Isaacs, H. R. 1964. *India's Ex-untouchables*. New York: Day.

Kemnitzer, L. S. 1973. "Adjustment and Value Conflict in Urbanizing Dakota Indians." *American Anthropologist*, 75:687–707.

Parker, S., et al. 1969. "Migration and Mental Illness: Some Reconsiderations and Suggestions for Further Analysis," *Social Science and Medicine* 3:1–9.

Rodriguez, A. M. and L. J. Rodriquez. 1977. "Planning and Delivering Alcoholism Services to the Cubans in America." In R. T. Trotter and J. A. Chavira, eds., *El uso De alcohol*. Edinburgh, Tex.: Pan American University.

Salisbury, R. F. and M. E. Salisbury. 1972. "The Rural-oriented Strategy of Urban Adaptation: Siane Migrants in Port Moresby." In T. Weaver and

D. White, eds., *The Anthropology of Urban Environments*, pp. 59–68. Boulder, Col.: Society for Applied Anthropology.

Samora, J. 1971. *Los Mojados: The Wetback Story.* Notre Dame: University of Notre Dame Press.

Stoddard, E. R. 1976. "A Conceptual Analysis of the 'Alien Invasion': Institutionalized Support of Illegal Mexican Aliens in the U.S.." *International Migration Review*, 10(2):157–190.

Weaver, T. and T. Downing. 1976. *Mexican Migration.* Tucson: University of Arizona Press.

Whiteford, M. 1977. "Women, Migration and Social Change: A Colombian Case Study." Mimeographed, Iowa State University.

13
"Chocolate City, Vanilla Suburbs": Will the Trend Toward Racially Separate Communities Continue?

REYNOLDS FARLEY, HOWARD SCHUMAN, SUZANNE BIANCHI, DIANE COLASANTO, AND SHIRLEY HATCHETT

ALMOST A DECADE ago, the Kerner Commission warned that this country was moving toward two societies—one white and one black (U.S. National Advisory Commission on Civil Disorders, 1969:407). Recent data on patterns of residential segregation in large metropolitan areas (Sørensen et al. 1975; Long 1975; U.S. Bureau of the Census, 1975, table 1; Hermalin and Farley 1973) confirm this prophecy and indicate clear-cut boundaries for these two societies—large cities are becoming black and suburban areas are remaining white.

Reprinted with permission from *Social Science Research* (1978), vol. 7, Academic Press. Tables and figures and text references to tables and figures are omitted due to space constraints. They are available from the authors.

The Detroit metropolitan area is a case in point. About 45 percent of the central city's 1.5 million residents were black in 1970 but only 4 percent of the 2.5 million suburban residents were black (U.S. Bureau of the Census, 1971a, table 24). Since 1970, the city has become even more black. One indicator of this is the racial composition of the public schools. The proportion black in the city's schools rose from 64 percent in 1970 to 80 percent in 1976 (U.S. Office for Civil Rights, 1977).[1] In essence, it appears Detroit is becoming a black city imbedded in a white suburban ring, or as a pop tune describes it: a "chocolate city with vanilla suburbs" (Malbix/Ricks Music, BMI, 1976).

This situation led us, as investigators for the 1976 Detroit Area Study (DAS) of the University of Michigan, to try to understand better the nature and causes of residential segregation in Detroit. We believe that our results may be generalized to many of the nation's large metropolises.

We began by examining the three most common explanations for racial residential segregation. One view contends that racial differences in economic status account for residential segregation. This is not a satisfactory explanation. In recent years, racial differences in education have narrowed and the income of blacks has risen slightly faster than that of whites (Levitan et al. 1975). In the Detroit area, for example, the median income of black families as a proportion of that of white families rose from 59 percent in 1959 to 69 percent in 1969 (U.S. Bureau of the Census, 1962, tables 76 and 78; 1972a, table 198). Despite these changes in the economic position of blacks, racial residential segregation in the Detroit area hardly decreased (Van Valey et al. 1977, table 1; Sørensen et al. 1975, table 1).

Another explanation for residential segregation focuses on the prejudices of whites. Over time, however, whites appear to have become much more willing to accept black neighbors. The proportion of whites in national samples who said that they would not be upset if a black with an income and education similar to their own moved onto their block rose from 35 percent in 1942 to 84 percent in 1972 (Sheatsley

1966; National Opinion Research Center, 1972). Specifically, in the Detroit area, the proportion of whites saying they would not be disturbed if a black moved onto their block increased from 40 percent in 1958 to 79 percent in 1976. Although white responses to these standard questions have changed greatly, there have not been concomitant reductions in residential segregation.

A third popular view contends that neighborhoods are segregated because blacks prefer to live with other blacks and not with whites. Evidence does not support this explanation. A variety of national and local studies reveal that blacks would rather live in racially mixed than in segregated neighborhoods (Pettigrew 1973:43–58). Moreover, there has been an apparent increase in this preference in recent years. Between 1958 and 1971, the percentage of blacks in Detroit saying they preferred racially mixed areas rose from 56 to 62 percent (Duncan et al. 1973:108) and reached 83 percent in the 1976 study that we conducted.

Since these explanations, as tested in previous studies, do not account for the persistence of racially separate communities, our study of racial segregation included several innovations in measurement. We focused our concern on three specific topics.

Economic factors and knowledge of the housing market. We realize that economic variables do not account for residential segregation but we do not know how much information people have about the cost of housing and the financial capabilities of blacks. We wondered if blacks fail to seek suburban housing which they can afford because they overestimate its costs. We wondered if whites give liberal answers to the "black on your block" question because they believed that very few blacks can actually afford homes in white areas. We also wished to determine if blacks and whites had similar ideas about which areas are attractive and if they share the same views of the hostility blacks would face if they moved into the suburbs.

The residential preferences of blacks. Most previous investigations of the neighborhood preferences of blacks have used one question asking whether it is desirable to live in mixed or segregated neighborhoods. This provides insufficient information about the nature of black preferences and thus we presented black respondents with diagrams representing varying degrees of interracial neighborhoods, asked their preferences, and then determined why they selected such neighborhoods. We assessed their willingness to move into neighborhoods of each type and, if they were unwilling to enter an all-black or all-white neighborhood, we asked why.

The residential preferences of whites. We believe that the "black on your block" question that has traditionally been used in studies of the neighborhood preferences of whites provides too little information. As Levine noted, it does not assess how whites would react in a variety of real and potential settings and does not assist in understanding a complex issue (Levine 1971–1972:577). We presented white respondents with diagrams of a number of neighborhoods with different interracial mixtures. We asked if they would be uncomfortable in each of the neighborhoods and, if so, would they try to move away and why. We also determined their willingness to purchase a home in a racially mixed neighborhood.

Data were gathered in the spring and summer of 1976. The target population consisted of heads or coheads of households who lived in year-round housing units in the Detroit area in April to July of 1976. The DAS sample consisted of two components. One was a two-stage probability sample of housing units drawn from the three-county Detroit Standard Metropolitan Statistical Area (SMSA). The second component was an additional probability sample of housing units occupied by blacks and located within central-city census tracts at least 15 percent black in 1970. The purpose of this supplement was to increase the number of blacks available for analysis (Bianchi 1976).[2]

A total of 1,503 sample households was drawn from which 1,134 interviews were obtained from one person per household, either the head or spouse of head, chosen by a random process in multiperson households. A total of 734 whites and 400 blacks were interviewed, yielding response rates of 77.9 and 71.3 percent, respectively. Race of interviewer was controlled such that black respondents were always interviewed by blacks; white respondents, by white interviewers.

The geographic distribution of the sample mirrored that of the area. Eighty-five percent of 734 white respondents lived within the Detroit suburbs but only 11 of the 400 blacks were suburban residents. The mean age of respondents in the DAS was forty-five years for whites and forty-three years for blacks. On the average white household heads or their spouses completed 12.1 years of school while blacks completed about one year less. Median household income was about $18,500 for whites and $12,500 for blacks. Income levels are relatively high in Detroit and thus the average income of white households in the Detroit area exceeds the national average by about $4,000 while among blacks the Detroit advantage is $2,500.

We wished to determine if our sample overrepresented some groups of the population and underrepresented others. Fortunately, we were able to compare the demographic characteristics of DAS respondents to those of residents included in the Census Bureau's March, 1976, Current Population Survey. The data indicate that the DAS sample and that of the Census Bureau are very similar with regard to age, educational attainment, sex of household heads, and income. Excluding the supplemental sample of blacks we found that 18 percent of the household heads or their spouses were black while the Census Bureau's CPS found that 19 percent were black, which suggests that our sample did not underrepresent blacks.

Economic Factors and Knowledge of the Housing Market

To determine what knowledge people have about the housing market, we selected one area from the central city and four of the largest suburbs; colored each distinctively on a map of the Detroit SMSA and asked several questions about each area. If race were not salient in the selection of housing, we expect that many whites would like to live in the northwest area of the central city and that many blacks would live in the suburbs. The locations have very different reputations but in each area the dwelling units are primarily single-family homes. The locations we selected were the following.

Housing Locations

Northwest Detroit central city. This is the area within the city that has the most desirable and expensive homes. A large fraction of them were built in the 1920s but there was substantial construction in this area following World War II. This section of the city is quite far removed from the deteriorating inner core where crime rates are presumed to be much higher. Through the 1960s, this section of the city was almost exclusively white. During the 1970s, blacks entered but when the Census of 1970 was conducted, 99.14 percent of the residents were still white (U.S. Bureau of the Census, 1972b, table P-1) though there has probably been noticeable change since then.

Southfield. This large suburb shares a common boundary with the central city. It is primarily a dormitory suburb of expensive single-family homes and the average value of a house in 1970—$36,000—was almost double the average for the entire metropolis. Our survey results supported our belief that this suburb does not have a reputation for being antiblack although in 1970 only 100 of its 69,000 residents were black (U.S. Bureau of the Census, 1971b, table 24).

Warren. This is a large industrial and residential suburb which also shares a common boundary with Detroit. The average value of homes—$23,000 in 1970—was typical for the suburban ring. This suburb has a reputation for hostility to blacks and, in 1970, only 120 of its 180,000 inhabitants were black (U.S. Bureau of the Census, 1971b, table 24). However, more than 5,000 central-city black residents were working at jobs within Warren in 1970 (U.S. Bureau of the Census, 1973, table 2).

Dearborn. This suburb is surrounded on three sides by sections of the city of Detroit that are largely black. Houses in this suburb are also about average in value for the suburban ring—$22,000 in 1970. It is the home of the Ford Motor Company and about 79,000 people—including 11,000 central-city blacks—work in its shops and offices (U.S. Bureau of the Census, 1973, tables 1 and 2). Dearborn has a reputation as being vigorously antiblack and several of our respondents assured us that as long as Mr. Hubbard remained mayor, no black would live within this suburb. In 1970, the census found only 13 blacks among the suburb's 104,000 residents (U.S. Bureau of the Census, 1971b, table 24).

Taylor. Among the major Detroit suburbs, Taylor is the one with the least expensive homes. They averaged about $19,000 in 1970. This is not an area of employment but it is surrounded by the metropolitan airport and several unattractive industrial complexes. This suburb does not have a reputation for unusual hostility to blacks but, in 1970, only 20 of its 70,000 residents were black (U.S. Bureau of the Census, 1971b, table 24).

Housing Costs

We first wished to learn if blacks and whites accurately knew the cost of housing in these areas. We asked respondents their estimates of the average cost of homes in each area, and then asked them whether they thought that only a few, about half, many, or almost all black families in the Detroit area could afford to live within the designated area. We then compare our best estimate of the true cost of a single-family home in each area in 1976 with the mean estimate of black and white respondents. The "true estimates" were developed from tabulations of the 1970 Census of Housing and the 1974 Annual Housing Survey. This survey, conducted by the Bureau of the Census, gathered data about housing costs and conditions from fifteen thousand Detroit area households (U.S. Bureau of the Census, 1972b, table H-1; 1976, tables B-1, B-4, C-1, and C-4). Housing prices have been adjusted for inflation.

Both blacks and whites are quite knowledgeable about the costs of housing. They correctly differentiate the suburbs and perceive that suburban housing is least expensive in Taylor and most costly in Southfield. In general, the average estimates of blacks and whites are similar for each of the locations. The standard deviations of the estimates of suburban housing costs of black respondents are considerably larger than those of whites, perhaps reflecting a lack of familiarity with the suburban housing market on the part of blacks. The most serious mistake is the tendency of both races substantially to underestimate housing prices in Southfield. We conclude that blacks do not overestimate suburban housing costs and they identify accurately variations in the prices of suburban housing.

Do whites and blacks believe that many black families can afford to live within these areas? We examine the proportion of respondents who think that at least one-half of the Detroit area black families can afford to live in each location. There is a major city-suburban difference and about 90 percent of the respondents—white and black—believe that most blacks can afford the northwest section of the central city. Thus there is consensus that central-city housing is within the price range of Detroit blacks.

Respondents, however, perceived differences in the ability of blacks to afford homes in various suburbs. More than half the white and black respondents thought that most black families could pay for housing in two of the least expensive suburbs: Taylor and Warren. When considering the other suburbs, Southfield and Dearborn, respondents believed that fewer blacks could afford homes in these locations, though even in these cases at least a third of each racial group saw the suburb as financially accessible to half or more of the black population.

These data suggest that blacks are quite well informed about suburban housing costs and thus we reject the hypothesis that one reason blacks do not live in the suburbs is that they believe that all suburban housing is very expensive and therefore do not seek it. Blacks realize that the majority of blacks can afford to live in several of the suburbs we considered, and Detroit area whites are also cognizant of the financial capabilities of blacks. We infer that whites understand that the absence of blacks from the suburbs is not due to blacks being unable to afford suburban housing.

Do Blacks Wish to Live in Racially Mixed Neighborhoodds?

Previous studies (for a summary see Pettigrew 1973:43–58) found that a majority of blacks expressed a general preference for integrated neighborhoods. To analyze more adequately the nature of these preferences, we developed a graphic measure that provided black respondents with five diagrams of neighborhoods. Each diagram shows fifteen homes but the racial composition of the neighborhoods varies from one diagram to the next. We asked respondents to imagine that they are looking for a house and have found one that they can afford. This house is designated as the center of each of the neighborhoods pictured. In the first card, all fourteen other homes are occupied by blacks; while the fifth card represents a neighborhood that contains no black families. The other three cards show intermediate mixtures.

Black respondents were asked to rank the neighborhoods from the one most attractive to them through the neighborhood that was least attractive. A very clear preference pattern emerged. Sixty-two percent selected the half-black half-white neighborhood as their first choice and another 20 percent of the black respondents said it was their second choice. The second most popular was the area containing ten black and four white families. The neighborhoods with either two blacks or all blacks were favored by much lower percentages. The strongest aversion was to the all-white neighborhood, since only 5 percent placed it first and 63 percent ranked it as the least attractive area.

Respondents were asked to consider further the one neighborhood they found most attractive. Using an open-ended question we asked them to explain why they found it so. We anticipated that those choosing the 50/50 neighborhood would often state that city services were better or that physical conditions were more attractive in integrated areas, but only one-quarter of the black respondents gave these as their primary reasons for wanting to live in mixed neighborhoods. The most frequently espoused view had to do with getting along with whites. About two-thirds of those who preferred the 50/50 area gave reasons such as: "When you have different kinds of people around, children understand better," "I'd like my children to know different kinds of people," "I'd rather live in a neighborhood that is mixed—don't have any trouble, no hostility," "It might make it better to get along with white people." These results corroborate earlier findings which show that a majority of black respondents not only favor residential integration but they do so because of a belief in racial harmony rather than a belief that services are better in mixed neighborhoods (Campbell and Schuman 1968:16).

For each type of neighborhood, we asked respondents whether they would be willing to move into it provided they found a nice house they could afford. Almost all blacks claimed they would move into neighborhoods that contained ten, seven, or two other black residents. Opposition to all-black neighborhoods seemed strong, given the pervasive residential segregation of the Detroit area which leads most blacks to live in almost exclusively black areas. Thirty-one percent of the respondents said they would not move into a nice house in an all-black neighborhood. We also used an open-ended question to get at their reasons for this. About one-half of the respondents cited such problems as low property values, crime, vandalism, and difficulties with children in all-black neighborhoods.

Many blacks are apparently willing to be the third black family in a largely white area but are reluctant to be the first. The more than 300 blacks who would not move into an all-white area were also asked their reasons. Only a few gave ideological explanations concerning an explicit desire to live with other blacks. The majority—about 90 percent— expressed the opinion that whites in white areas would not welcome them. About one-sixth of the black respondents stated such views as "I might get burned out or never wake up," "They would probably blow my house up." A much more common view—given by more than 60 percent of those who would not enter on all-white area—was that whites would be unfriendly to the first black family, scrutinize their behavior, and make them feel out of place.

Our data from the residential segregation questions and from several other racial attitude questions suggest that there is no strong ideological support in the Detroit black community for separate black neighborhoods nor do most blacks express antiwhite attitudes. Freed of the fear of racial hostility, we believe that most Detroit area blacks would select neighborhoods that are about one-half white and one-half black. Their reasons for choosing such areas often involve learning to get along with whites. Almost all blacks are willing to move into integrated neighborhoods but there is considerable reluctance on the part of blacks to enter all-black areas and even greater reluctance to move into exclusively white neighborhoods.

The Openness of Areas to Blacks and Their Desirability

Blacks wish to live in racially mixed areas but many of them are fearful about moving into largely white neighborhoods. We wondered if blacks viewed all-white residential areas as equally hostile to them or if they differentiated the locations and realized that they might be welcome in some places but not in others.

We once again showed respondents the map of the Detroit area and asked them: If a black family moved into each area, would the family be welcome or would whites who already lived there be upset?

The one area that is experiencing racial transition is northwest Detroit. Blacks define it as the most "open" of the areas and believe that few whites would be upset if more blacks entered that area. They do not view the suburbs as an undifferentiated mass for they realize that blacks are more likely to receive a friendly welcome in Southfield—the most expensive suburb—or Taylor—the least expensive, than in Dearborn or Warren.

We wondered if views about the openness of areas to blacks were widely shared in the Detroit area or if blacks and whites had different information about this aspect of the housing market. Whites were asked their opinions about the reception blacks would receive. Almost all whites think that blacks who move into the northwest section of the city will be welcomed and that the white residents of Dearborn would be exceptionally inhospitable to blacks. This suggests that information about where blacks can live is widely known by both races.

We wished to determine if blacks who saw an area as "open" to them also tended to believe that it is a desirable place to live. Respondents were asked to look at the map and rank each location on a four-point scale ranging from very desirable to very undesirable.

Among both races, we find a strong correspondence between the perceived openness of an area to blacks and its desirability. Blacks see Dearborn as the most hostile location and rank it as the least desirable. Whites, on the other hand, see it as least open to blacks and rank it the most desirable place to live.

The most striking racial difference is the evaluation of the northwest section of the central city. Blacks view this as the area where they would experience little white hostility and rank it as most desirable but whites see it as very much less desirable than any of the suburbs. Recall that this area was more than 99 percent white in 1970 and, although some racial transition has occurred, it is still predominantly white. More than 80 percent of the respondents in our 1976 cross-sectional survey who lived in or near this area were white. We asked white respondents what they thought the racial composition of this area was and 85 percent believed that it was currently at least half black. Whites erroneously think of this section of the city as black and this probably explains their low evaluation of it.

Blacks and whites in the Detroit area share the same views of which areas will give blacks a friendly or hostile reception. They have very different opinions, however, about the desirability of various areas. Blacks tend to see as most desirable those locations that are open to them whereas whites see areas open to blacks as undesirable. The areas they think most desirable are those closed to black residents.

How Much Residential Integration Will Whites Accept?

Residential segregation depends not only on the willingness of blacks to enter largely white areas but also on the willingness of whites to remain in or enter neighborhoods where there are already black residents. The residential preferences of whites were studied in a manner similar but not exactly identical to that used with black respondents.

Each white respondent was presented with a series of five diagrams showing fifteen homes. We asked them to imagine that they lived in an all-white area similar to that shown on the first card, using the center house as theirs. Next, they were asked to imagine that a black family moved into the neighborhood. At this point, they were shown the second card, which indicates one home occupied by blacks and thirteen by whites. White respondents were asked how comfortable they would be in that neighborhood. They were then shown the third card, which indicated that three black families lived in the neighborhood; a fourth card with five black families; and, finally, a fifth card, which portrayed a neighborhood of eight black and six white families. In pretests, we experimented with cards showing even higher densities of blacks but almost no whites felt comfortable in such neighborhoods.

We examined the proportion of white respondents who said they would be uncomfortable in each neighborhood. White resistance to mixed neighborhoods is very evident.

Even in the situation of minimum integration—one black and fourteen white families—one-quarter of the whites claimed they would be uncomfortable. As the proportion black rose, so too did discomfort among whites. In a neighborhood that was half black, 72 percent of the whites said they would be uncomfortable.

We asked those white respondents who reported being uncomfortable in a neighborhood whether they would actually try to move out. This proportion is quite low for the neighborhood that contains one black family—only 7 percent of the whites would try to leave—but increases rapidly. Forty percent say they would move away from a neighborhood that is one-third black and 64 percent would leave the majority black area.

The more than 400 white respondents who said they would move away from one of the neighborhoods were asked why they would do so. The modal explanation focused on property values. That is, about 40 percent of the whites believed that the entry of blacks was tantamount to depreciating property values. The most common reasons were "They don't care about anything they own," and "Because if I stayed longer, my home wouldn't be worth anything." The next most common explanation had to do with crime and safety. Some white respondents contended that crime rates in any area are directly proportional to the black population and that if there were many blacks, they would fear for their personal safety. A related theme was reported by many whites who said they would feel out of place if they lived in a majority black neighborhood.

As a final question concerning residential preferences white respondents were asked to imagine they had been looking for a home and had found a nice one they could afford. The house could be located in the several types of neighborhoods shown on the cards presented to them. We asked them which neighborhoods they would consider moving into.

The willingness of whites to enter a neighborhood is, as

anticipated, inversely proportional to the representation of blacks in that area. However, there is some opposition to entering even the minimally integrated area. More than one-quarter of the whites said they would not consider a nice home they could afford if the area contained one black and thirteen whites. We observe that if there are three blacks in the neighborhood, more than 40 percent of the whites would be uncomfortable, about one-quarter would try to move out, and one-half of the whites would not consider moving into such an area.

Tipping Points and Neighborhood Transition

There is a good deal of variation in the neighborhood preferences of the white respondents. While the majority of whites would not remain in a neighborhood that is mostly black, there are many whites who are willing to tolerate some representation of blacks in their neighborhoods. In evaluating the consequences of the preferences of whites for future trends in residential integration, it is appropriate to consider the distribution of white preferences in greater detail.

We can consider the point where the curve representing the proportion of whites who would move out intersects with the curve representing the proportion of whites who would enter the neighborhood to be a "tipping point." That is, points to the left of this point have fewer whites willing to move in than who say they would move out. We conceptualize this as a tipping point because as the proportional representation of blacks in a neighborhood increases beyond this point, the transition to an all-black neighborhood is likely to accelerate. More whites begin to feel uncomfortable and try to move out and there are fewer and fewer whites who are willing to replace them in a neighborhood with such a large representation of blacks.[3]

According to our data, we can define a 70 percent white, 30 percent black neighborhood as the tipping point. This point represents the intersection of the "move out" and "move in" curves for whites. This seems to imply that neighborhoods with greater than 70 percent white will remain stably integrated. For example, consider the point on the horizontal axis that represents a neighborhood that is 93 percent white—one black and fourteen whites. We find that 76 percent of the whites would consider moving into such an area and only 7 percent would try to leave. We expect that such an area might remain racially mixed for there are many whites willing to move in and replace those other whites who would leave. We know, however, that stably integrated neighborhoods are rarely found in American cities (Taeuber and Taeuber 1965, chap. 5; Duncan and Duncan 1957:99, 120). Schelling (1971, 1972) determined through the use of mathematical models that if the residential preferences of the white residents of a neighborhood differ, the dynamics of the situation will drive the proportion black successively over each individual's maximum tolerance and the neighborhood will ultimately become a black residential area. That is, although there are more whites who would move into a 93 percent white neighborhood than move out, if any of the vacancies created by the exodus of whites are filled by blacks—and almost all Detroit area blacks would consider moving into that type of neighborhood—some additional whites who were comfortable will become uncomfortable with the new racial composition. They may move and create new vacancies which may be filled by blacks. Therefore the proportion black will rise and other whites may decide to leave. As Schelling has demonstrated theoretically, it is precisely the variance that we observe in the neighborhood preferences of whites that causes neighborhoods to change from all white to all black. Until the distribution of preferences by neighborhood is considered, however, it is difficult to determine if this pattern of neighborhood change is inevitable in Detroit.[4]

The Prospects for Residential Integration

When we consider the residential preferences of whites in the Detroit area, the prospects for residential integration seem quite slim. Many whites are willing to tolerate some degree of racial integration in their neighborhoods, but the variance in white preference indicates that stable neighborhood integration is unlikely to occur. While the neighborhood preferences of blacks are considerably more favorable to residential integration than the preferences of whites—the overwhelming majority of blacks chose an integrated neighborhood as the one that is most attractive to them—even these data must be interpreted with a certain amount of pessimism. Since neighborhoods with equal numbers of black and white residents are not widely available and because there is a strong aversion to all-white neighborhoods, many blacks who state a preference for integrated neighborhoods may actually choose to live in largely black areas.

Consideration of data about the knowledge that blacks and whites have of the Detroit area housing market also leads to the conclusion that the prospects for residential integration are not good. We speculate that both blacks and whites are very knowledgeable about where they and the other race "belong" and that real estate marketing practices reinforce these judgments primarily by steering blacks and whites to separate areas. For instance, our investigation finds that almost all Detroit area residents are aware of the antiblack reputation of Dearborn and, we presume, few blacks would try to enter that suburb. Whites, on the other hand, define the northwest corner of the central city as black and probably do not seek housing there even if it is readily available at an attractive price. We presented the following hypothetical situation to all respondents.

I'd like you to imagine that you're going to move. You have a choice of buying two houses that are identical, except that one is located in northwest Detroit and the other is located in a desirable suburb. The house in the suburb costs $8,000 more than the house in Detroit. Which of the two houses would you choose to move into?

Given these alternatives, 90 percent of the whites selected the suburban home while 75 percent of the blacks selected the one in the city. Although endorsing the ideal of residential integration and expressing some willingness to live in racially mixed areas, we believe that many whites would actually spend large sums of money to avoid living in an area that they believe "belongs" to blacks, such as the northwest section of the central city.

Blacks are equally knowledgeable about housing costs and the openness of various areas to them. They realize that whites in each of the suburbs would be more upset by their entry than whites in the central city. For these reasons many blacks who endorse the ideal of integrated housing may avoid the suburbs and seek homes in those parts of the city that are now undergoing racial transition.

These data indicate that the likelihood of achieving stably integrated neighborhoods in the Detroit area is small. Before issuing such a dismal pronouncement, however, it is appropriate to consider other factors that may reduce residential segregation. Whites vary in their tolerance for living with blacks and some blacks are more willing than others to enter white neighborhoods. We wondered if we could identify groups of the population who were favorable to integration and whether this might portend an eventual reduction in residential segregation. Perhaps young and well-educated blacks and whites have residential preferences that will lead to integration.

For each white respondent we defined a residential preference score based on his or her ordering of the cards, showing various interracial neighborhoods. Scores ranged from 0—low acceptance of racial residential integration—to 40—high acceptance of such integration. For blacks, a similar but not identical scoring system was devised with values ranging from 5—low acceptance of residential integration—to 40 (Colasanto 1977, chap. 4).

The racial residential preference score was the dependent variable while the independent variables are age, educational attainment, family income, and residential closeness to the other race. The analytic technique of multiple classification analysis (MCA) was used. For each category of every independent variable, the gross deviation from the overall mean was determined. That is, white respondents had an average racial residential preference score of 24.7; those under age thirty-one were slightly more favorable to integration and had a score averaging 0.2 points higher than the overall average. A net difference was also presented which was the deviation from the overall average once the effects of all other variables have been taken into account. The MCA model indicated the variance in racial residential preference accounted for singularly by each independent variable and by the entire collection of explanatory variables (Andrews et al. 1969).

Racial residential preferences are very weakly linked to these background variables. Among both races, age is inconsistently related to residential preferences and thus we cannot conclude that young people are more willing to live in mixed areas than are the old. Among both blacks and whites, education is positively related to the acceptance of residential integration but the differences are small. Among whites, family income appears inversely related to a tolerance of black neighbors whereas among blacks, it is the richer who have stronger preferences for mixed areas but the income differences are not significantly different from zero. We find that those who live on a block with members of the other race have somewhat higher scores on this measure of racial residential preferences but once again the differences are not significant.

We believe that residential preferences are not strongly or substantially related to these or to other background factors and thus we were unable to identify groups of the white or black population who have distinct residential preferences. There seems to be little hope that attitudes about neighborhood integration will change rapidly because of increases in educational attainment or because "conservative" older whites are replaced by "liberal" younger persons. It is possible, however, that the preferences of whites and blacks can change for other reasons. Just as the attitudes of whites about school integration and the integration of public facilities are much more liberal now than before the federal government began to take action against these types of segregation, so the attitudes of whites about neighborhood integration may change rapidly as blacks begin to be more dispersed in the metropolitan area. Until we know more about the sources of these preferences for whites and blacks, it is difficult to specify what kind of changes are likely to occur in the distribution of neighborhood preferences.

Summary and Conclusion

This study moved beyond previous investigations of the causes of racial residential segregation. By the use of improved measures of knowledge, beliefs, and attitudes, we addressed three questions:

(1) Is racial residential segregation largely the result of misperceptions about the ability of blacks to afford housing in the Detroit area?

(2) Is residential segregation mainly the result of black preferences for segregated neighborhoods?

(3) Is residential segregation mainly the result of white preferences for segregated neighborhoods?

Turning to the first question, our study analyzed a subjective version of the economic hypothesis. We discovered that both blacks and whites were quite knowledgeable about the costs of housing in various parts of the Detroit area. They also correctly perceive that many blacks can afford to live in attractive white areas. We reject the idea that ignorance of the housing market is responsible for racial residential segregation.

With regard to the second question, we find that black preferences as a cause of residential segregation finds credence only in the attributions of whites themselves. When asked why there was such extensive residential segregation, whites often said that "Birds of a feather flock together" or that "Blacks try to stick with their own kind." Most black respondents, however, expressed a preference for mixed neighborhoods. Whites dramatically underestimate the willingness of blacks to live in racially mixed areas, perhaps because they themselves seldom wish to live in such neighborhoods.

The preferences of whites for neighborhoods that do not include many blacks are one important source of the maintenance of high levels of residential segregation.[5] Through the use of carefully constructed sets of measures, this study demonstrates what other investigations of attitudes toward racial residential segregation have failed to show—that whites are not very accepting of residential integration. This investigation replicated two items that have been used in several studies of white attitude change, which show steady improvement in the acceptance of integration—the "black on your block" and "would you sell to a black" questions. If we had asked just these questions, we would have concluded that there was a widespread acceptance of residential integration on the part of Detroit area whites. This would have been contrary to the objective evidence. Our techniques—the use of diagrams of mixed neighborhoods—allowed respondents to go beyond reacting to general values and move toward how they would personally feel in specific situations, what they would actually do, and why. For this mode of inquiry, we obtained a different picture—one closer to the "reality" of high levels of racial residential segregation.

Notes

1. Another indication of the changing racial composition of the central city was obtained from the Census Bureau's March 1976 Current Population Survey (CPS). In 1970, the decennial census reported that 60 percent of the city's households and 96 percent of those in the suburbs were headed by whites. The 1976 CPS included a sample of 288 central-city and 547 suburban households and found that 50 percent of the city and 96 percent of the suburban households were headed by whites. If we assume there are no design effects, the standard error of estimate for the proportion of household heads white in the city in 1976 is approximately 3 percent,

suggesting that the chances are two out of three that the true proportion white among household heads was between 47 and 53 percent.

2. Of the 400 black respondents, 358 were in the area covered by the additional probability sample. Data presented in this paper are not weighted for the disproportionate sampling of blacks who lived in predominantly black census tracts. We experimented with the use of both weighted and unweighted data for blacks and concluded that the use of weights did not significantly alter our findings.

3. Of course, given the proportional representation of blacks and whites in the metropolitan area, the actual supply of whites who would move into many neighborhoods (even those that are less than 70 percent white) is likely to be larger than the supply of blacks. For this reason, the "tipping point" should more realistically be represented somewhat more to the left.

4. To get a realistic picture of the stability of neighborhoods it would also be necessary to take into account other factors that determine the operation of the housing market.

5. In this paper we have considered only those factors that relate to individual preferences and perceptions as causes for residential segregation. The fact that these preferences are important does not imply that other factors (i.e., structural factors, discrimination) are not important. In fact, it is quite likely that structural factors and individual factors may be associated and are jointly responsible for the high levels of segregation observed in urban areas.

References

Andrews, F., J. Morgan, and J. Sonquist. 1969. *Multiple Classification Analysis*. Ann Arbor: Institute for Social Research, University of Michigan.

Bianchi, S. M. 1976. "Sampling Report for the 1976 Detroit Area Study." Unpublished manuscript, Detroit Area Study, University of Michigan, Ann Arbor.

Campbell, A. and H. Schuman. 1968. *Racial Attitudes in Fifteen American Cities*. Ann Arbor: Institute for Social Research, University of Michigan.

Colasanto, D. 1977. "The Prospects for Racial Integration in Neighborhoods: An Analysis of Residential Preferences in the Detroit Metropolitan Area." Ph.D. dissertation, University of Michigan.

Duncan, O. D. and B. Duncan. 1957. *The Negro Population of Chicago*. Chicago: University of Chicago Press.

Duncan, O. D., H. Schuman, and B. Duncan. 1973. *Social Change in a Metropolitan Community*. New York: Russell Sage Foundation.

Hermalin, A. I. and R. Farley. 1973. "The Potential for Residential Integration in Cities and Suburbs: Implications for the Busing Controversy." *American Sociological Review*, 38:595–610.

Levine, R. A. 1971–1972. "The Silent Majority: Neither Simple nor Simple-Minded." *Public Opinion Quarterly*, 35:571–577.

Levitan, S. A., W. B. Johnston, and R. Taggart. 1975. *Still a Dream: The Changing Status of Blacks since 1960.* Cambridge, Mass.: Harvard University Press.

Long, L. H. 1975. "How the Racial Composition of Cities Changes." *Land Economics*, 51:258–267.

Mablix/Ricks Music, BMI. 1976. "Chocolate City." Available on Casablanca Records, NBLP 7014.

National Opinion Research Center. 1972. *National Data Program for the Social Sciences (General Social Survey).* Chicago: National Opinion Research Center, University of Chicago.

Pettigrew, T. F. 1973. "Attitudes on Race and Housing: A Social-psychological View." In A. H. Hawley and V. P. Rock, eds., *Segregation in Residential Areas*, pp. 21–84. Washington, D.C.: National Academy of Sciences.

Schelling, T. C. 1971. "Dynamic Models of Segregation." *Journal of Mathematical Sociology*, 1:148–186.

—— 1972. "A Process of Residential Segregation: Neighborhood Tipping." In A. H. Pascal, ed., *Racial Discrimination in Economic Life.* Boston: Heath.

Sheatsley, P. B. 1966. "White Attitudes Toward the Negro." *Daedalus*, 95:217–238.

Sørensen, A., K. E. Taeuber, and L. J. Hollingsworth, Jr. 1975. "Indexes of Racial Residential Segregation for 109 Cities in the United States, 1940 to 1970." *Sociological Focus*, 8:125–142.

Taeuber K. E. and A. F. Taeuber. 1965. *Negroes in Cities.* Chicago: Aldine.

U.S. Bureau of the Census. 1962. *Census of Population: 1960.* PC(1)-24C.

—— 1971a. *Census of Population: 1970.* PC(1)-B24.

—— 1971b. *Census of Housing: 1970.* HC(1)-A24.

—— 1972a. *Census of Population: 1970.* PC(1)-C24.

—— 1972b. *Census of Population and Housing: 1970.* PHC(1)-58.

—— 1973. *Census of Population: 1970.* PC(2)-60.

—— 1975. *Current Population Reports*, series P-20, no. 285.

—— 1976. *Annual Housing Survey: 1974.* Series H-170-74-5.

U.S. National Advisory Commission on Civil Disorders. 1969. *Report of the National Advisory Commission on Civil Disorders.* Washington, D.C.: Government Printing Office.

U.S. Office for Civil Rights. 1977. *Directory of Public Elementary and Secondary Schools in Selected Districts, Enrollment and Staff by Racial/Ethnic Groups.* Tape File.

Van Valey, T., W. C. Roof, and J. E. Wilcox. 1977. "Trends in Residential Segregation: 1960–1970." *American Journal of Sociology*, 82:826–844.

PART SIX

New Perspectives in Urban Sociology

EDITOR'S NOTE:

WALTON DOCUMENTS THE movement away from community studies and toward understanding the political-economic factors that affect cities. The inability of traditional sociology to explain "the urban crisis" largely accounts for this paradigm shift. A research agenda is presented, including examinations of social movements and state services, which should result in progressive policy alternatives. Molotch argues that growth is the political and economic purpose of every American city. This is because land-owning elites take control of local governments and ensure pro-growth policies to increase their profits. Few benefits and numerous costs are shared by average citizens, and collective opposition to growth is rare.

14
The New
Urban Sociology

JOHN WALTON

The Paradigm Shift

IN THE SHORT space of the last decade urban social science has undergone a revolution. What began in the late 1960s and early 1970s as a critical reaction to certain anomalies in received doctrines of urbanism has in the last few years culminated in a true paradigm shift.

The previous paradigm rested on an amalgam of ideas summed up in the terms of social organization (disorganization) and ecological succession—the master theme of community as it emerged from the market mechanisms of social differentiation and political pluralism. In genealogy the paradigm drew heavily on European theories of social integration (for example, Durkheim and Simmel) and reached its fullest development in the United States with the Chicago School of urban sociology (such as Wirth, Park, and Burgess). By the 1970s this paradigm had reached maturity and exhaustion. In contrast to the historical processes it was fashioned to address, such as primary urbanization, immigration and community formation, or the elaboration of spatial struc-

Reprinted with permission from *International Social Science Journal* (1981), vol. 33, no. 2.

ture, the paradigm was unequipped to deal with the new urban crisis.

Doubtless, this paradigm shift is gradual in some quarters and resisted in others. But the Kuhnian metaphor is apropos, as suggested by several indicators. Beginning in the
late 1960s anomalies multiplied as the urban crisis posed un-
answerable questions about increasing class and racial inequalities rather than social integration, urban decay rather
than ecological competition and succession, protest organization rather than anomic disorganization, and the politics of
domination and accumulation rather than pluralism. The
paradigm crisis was the social crisis and, characteristically,
the new approach combined fertility with answers (however
concise) to the now critical questions. The new approach re-
cruited rapidly from the ranks of younger scholars and related disciplines. A final and telltale sign is the fact that the
basic textbooks are being rewritten from the standpoint of the
new approach.

By now it seems safe to conclude that the revolution in
urban social science is nearing completion, that a new period
of "normal science" (with its own limitations) has set in, and
that the most compelling task is to indicate the critical and
progressive steps that must be taken next. In that connection
it is necessary at the outset to characterize the new approach.
Since particular labels incur the risks of reification and reaction, I prefer to call this simply the new urban social science
and to characterize it in the points that follow. From these I
hope to make clear that if the approach has "structural" emphases they are not at the expense of process; if it stresses the
economy it does not diminish the society and polity; if it al-
ludes to Marx it does so in the same forward-looking manner
that Weber would have. If there are to be demurs with the
perspective, let them concern the analytical issues.

The new urban social science has diverse origins in theory and practice. As I have suggested, it was partly a product
of the urban crisis that erupted internationally from Watts to
Paris in the late 1960s. The familiar ingredients of the crisis

that defied conventional interpretation and called for a new vision included social protest, declining city resources and services, the loss of jobs and industry, new responsibilities for enfeebled local governments, a changing population base and (migratory, casual) labor market, the socioeconomic polarization of the city and its surroundings (the suburbs and new cities), official efforts to pacify or suppress inner-city residents, and ultimately the signs of fiscal crisis.

The urban crisis had the ironic consequence of producing a great deal of descriptively useful conventional research, which nevertheless proved inadequate to the task of explaining these developments. Studies of riot participants and their targets, for example, produced some informative results that tended to refute theories of social disorganization and irrational alienation. Inquiries into local politics that revealed the power of business and governmental coalitions implied but never analyzed their connections to the class structure and national economy. Research that documented ecological segregation and political fragmentation stopped short of any explanation of how these transformations came about and what interests they served, once it became clear that the hidden hand of competition and equilibrium could not account for these crisis-provoking changes. The conventional approach in a deluge of empirical efficiency washed away its own quasi-theoretical foundations.

Coincident with this accumulation of anomalies about the urban crisis in the advanced societies, and particularly the United States, other approaches to urban development were maturing. Notably, research on dependent urbanism in the underdeveloped countries made rapid headway owing in part to the "advantage of backwardness"—the fact that it did not start out from the balkanized disciplinary views of urban sociology, economics, and political science. Urbanization and its consequences could be seen as cause and effect of societal transformation. Another key element was the development of assiduous empirical research in Europe that grew out of a more holistic theoretical tradition. This combination of anomaly, prescient yet theoretically uninterpreted research, and emergent holistic traditions combined to provide the foundation of the new urban social science.

As it has developed over the past decade the new urban social science embraces several characteristic premises. First, from a theoretical and historical standpoint it holds that urbanism itself requires definition and explanation rather than to be taken for granted or treated simply as a phenomenon of aggregation. Urbanism and urbanization must assume the status of "theoretical objects" in the sense of phenomena that arise (or do not) and take different forms under various modes of socioeconomic organization and political control (Castells 1978; Harvey 1973). Second, the approach is concerned with the interplay of relations of production, consumption, exchange, and the structure of power manifest in the state. None of these can be understood separately or as analytically prior except in the sense of a logical exercise (that is, *ceteris paribus*). Third, as in the case of urbanism generally, concrete urban processes (ecological patterns, community organization, economic activities, class and ethnic politics, local government) must be understood in terms of their structural bases or how they are conditioned by their connection with economic exigencies, political arrangements, and the sociocultural milieu. Fourth, the approach is fundamentally concerned with social change and conceives of this as growing out of conflicts (or contradictions) among classes and status groups. These conflicts are the basis of the political process, which increasingly is coincident with the arena of the state. Changes in the economy are socially and politically generated as well as mediated. Political and social changes are in no sense independent of the economy. Finally, the perspective is inextricably tied to the concerns of normative theory. It is concerned not only to draw out the ideological and distributive implications of alternative positions, but critically aware of its own premises and the dilemmas they too pose.

If the new urban social science has secured for itself a paradigmatic role more or less consistent with these premises, its work has just begun. At this juncture the challenge is to move beyond an elegant—and sometimes formalistic—critique of conventional urban sociology or economics and to demonstrate the value of the approach in research and explanation concerning the major transformations experienced by cities within the context of the national and international political economy. While this task is necessarily historical, particular importance attaches to an explanation of the dislocations at present being felt by cities as a result of the global economic crisis and attendant austerity politics that have succeeded the urban crisis of the 1970s as the fundamental problem of the urban milieu. This problem is experienced in different forms across urban settings depending on a host of circumstances including the location and resources of the national society within the global system, the local economy, population and class structure, distinctive political arrangements, and so forth. The challenges facing the new urban research consist precisely in determining the nature and significance of this local variation and relating it to the more general systemic trends. Briefly stated, this is the charge and the agenda for urban social science in the 1980s.

The historical conditions that give rise to the new urban social science and generate much of its subject matter can be described collectively, and without risk of hyperbole, in the theoretical terms of economic crisis. The word "crisis" is employed here in the concrete sense of a periodic imbalance in the development of advanced capitalism that forces a fundamental reorganization or rationalization of the economy and social policy. Crises occur at various levels and do not necessarily signal the dénouement. They may be partial, sectoral, or, as in this case, global (Harvey 1978) and represent normal, even necessary, interludes.

The contemporary global economic crisis is, of course, historically unprecedented. In scope it rivals the 1930s, but its substance and impact are different. The crisis that began in the advanced capitalist countries in 1973 is, at bottom, a crisis of overproduction (Mandel 1978). It comes at the close of a period of massive and fairly continuous expansion of the advanced industrial economies after the second World War.

That period witnessed the recovery of Western Europe and Japan as economic powers eventually rivaling the United States in world trade and investment—imperial competitors and occasional multinational corporate collaborators in the contest for Third World markets, themselves becoming increasingly resistant to denationalization. This core competition was responsible for the collapse of the Bretton Woods accord, the end of the dollar's convertibility to gold as an international currency, the adoption of floating exchange rates, and the general unpredictability of the current world financial system.

In the advanced capitalist societies, particularly the United States, the international crisis is reflected in reduced world trade (with the saving exception of agricultural exports), trade deficits, declining industrial production, declining rates of profit, increased idle capacity, rising unemployment, and, generally, the characteristic features of deep recession. In the United States the initial crisis of 1973 was followed by a temporary recovery as the result of accelerated consumption stimulated by an explosion of consumer credit, institutional borrowing, government borrowing and deficit spending, and steady expansion of the money supply. The result was an enormous acceleration of public and private debt that fueled inflation while only briefly stalling stagnation. Oil-price increases certainly contributed to this "stagflation," but their timing, relative amounts, recirculation (as in OPEC purchases), and differential effects across national economies all rule them out as primary causes. The interlude of recovery was brief (1975–1977), and by 1979 the recession had returned with a growing vengeance.

As we begin the 1980s the effects of the global crisis are plain to see. Rates of industrial production across the advanced capitalist countries continue to decline. World trade slumps further, with individual countries taking increasing recourse to protectionist measures (Strange 1979). Inflation continues its upward movement, to the point where countries like the United States are forced to abandon hopes of recovery through credit expansion or debt financing and turn instead to austerity measures to curb borrowing and balance the budget. The immediate impact is increasing unemployment, reduction in social expenditures, and the further depression of key industrial sectors such as housing, steel, automobiles, and so forth. Welfare-state policies that sealed the pact between capital and labor in periods of expansion are progressively eliminated while the labor force spared unemployment is chastened by reductions in real income. As the crisis unfolds we may anticipate the devaluation also of fixed capital (Harvey 1978) and generally a process of the "recapitalization of capital" (Miller 1978).

Proceeding from this very general characterization of the current economic crisis we may, for present purposes, indicate the links with urban issues or some of the more compelling ways in which the crisis shows up on a locality basis. At this level we are concerned to indicate the structural implications that require concrete comparative research and provide the theoretical basis of the new research agenda.

Beginning with the obvious, there is a sense in which the global economic crisis is identical with the urban crisis as the former takes shape in the highly urban industrial advanced countries. National problems such as unemployment and austerity policies are to a large extent the problems of cities that have historically been an essential requisite for capitalist development. Yet the urban effects of crisis are far more specific and exacting. The differential effects of unemployment, for example, are borne more heavily by central-city populations that include higher proportions of recent migrants, the elderly, minorities, and the less skilled working class. Austerity measures that concentrate on social expenditures are apt to be pursued more vigorously in the field of social consumption (versus social investment, compare O'Connor 1973), that is, with respect to projects and services that benefit labor (or reduce the costs of its reproduction) such as health, housing, transportation, and social insurance. The most volatile and immediately affected private industries, especially housing, are at once the most desperate problem areas of the city.

As we pursue the fallout of economic crisis the uniquely urban manifestations appear in greater relief. The "urban fiscal crisis" is prototypical. If we may take the example of New York as somewhat representative of situations common to other American and world cities, the origins of the local plight can be traced to broader structural dislocations such as over-production, the collapse of the postwar boom, competition in export markets, the loss of industry and jobs, and short-sighted financial solutions based on expanding debt (Edel 1977). In a closely related vein, the central cities are most prone to devaluation of fixed capital in housing and rental stock, commercial buildings, and public lands and invest-ments that may be sold off to meet other pressing govern-mental obligations (see Harvey 1978 for historical examples and Cleveland for contemporary ones). Once adequately de-valued, the repurchase of these properties or infrastructural systems is sometimes hailed as evidence of an urban renais-sance (Edel 1977). What this optimism fails to reckon with is who has won and lost in the process. In the case of both re-financing the urban fiscal crisis and reinvesting in deval-uated urban properties, the costs have been shifted heavily onto pension-fund members, taxpayers, homeowners, and small business.

To a large extent big capital does not suffer these bur-dens, by virtue of its mobility and possession of money cap-ital (that, too, a product of overaccumulation). Devalued fixed capital becomes a tax advantage in reinvestment strategies that have increasingly taken capital and jobs abroad (Walton 1980) or to more inviting domestic regions such as the "Sun-belt" of the United States (Perry and Watkins, 1977). These "switching crises" (Harvey 1978) are doubly disadvanta-geous to older urban areas since they involve both geo-graphic and sectoral shifts. Investment not only abandons the older industrial, working-class cities, but also moves domes-tically into new product lines in which previous workers would have no special advantage should they migrate with capital. Typically their jobs have been exported to the Third World, the poorer European countries (Ireland, Spain, Portugal), or enclave economies (such as Taiwan, Hong Kong, Singapore).

Finally, it should be noted that where austerity and fiscal crisis evenhandedly produce reductions in public expenditures, the burdens are still disproportionately shouldered by the urban working class. For example, while cuts in public employment may at a given moment take place across the board, the historical significance of public-sector expansion has in some considerable part involved the absorption of workers displaced by capital-intensive industrial growth. Moreover, the various forms of collective consumption mentioned previously serve not only to augment the social wage, but also to provide the entire wage for many of the least privileged strata of the urban labor force (especially women and minorities, since these jobs have been the most progressive in affirmative action).

Before us, then, are a number of issues that relate to the broader course of contemporary history, yet are at a more tractable level of immediate concern. From these rather loosely and casually organized themes the new urban researcher could move in a variety of directions. Obviously, no such initiative is to be discouraged. Nevertheless, recent developments in urban social science have taken some important steps in specific directions, guided at once by characteristic theoretical sensitivities and by the informative contributions of earlier traditions in urban research. In short, certain foci may now be especially strategic and fruitful. In what follows I shall list and comment critically on a set of these, which is offered as one research agenda. Numerous limitations, which I shall conveniently attribute to space, prevent detailed discussion of these points. For the moment they are presented as a vehicle to move our considerations forward.

A Research Agenda

The Integration of Levels

The first general issue on this research agenda concerns the integration of levels within holistic analyses. It has become almost platitudinous in criticism of conventional research to insist on the recognition of "broader structural forces" that are at the "roots" of changes on the urban scene—to lament the spurious character of research that catches a piece of an important development but misconstrues it for want of an adequate causal analysis. Despite the near-axiomatic status of such criticisms, there is a dearth of exemplary analyses that actually trace global processes to urban effects in systematic (as opposed to contextual) ways through all of the socially specific detours along the way and back again in the sense of what those concrete deviations may mean for the general theory. This lacuna is ironic since some of the most elegant and compelling theory is addressed precisely at "the structural links we need to understand the urban process under capitalism" (Harvey 1978:114; see also Lojkine 1976, and Lamarche 1976).

Naturally, there are some instructive exceptions. As suggested previously, it has been in the study of Third World urbanization that the most elaborate research has traced the determinate and varied impact of capitalist development on urban structure (for example, Castells 1978; Slater 1978; Quijano 1968; Hardoy 1975; Lubeck and Walton 1979). With respect to the advanced countries some heuristic efforts include Edel's analysis (1977) of the New York fiscal crisis in the context of the global economy and Gordon's (1978) treatment of periods in American urban development that correspond to stages in the changing modes of production and labor control. A recent piece of my own dealing with the internationalization of capital and class structures of the advanced countries attempts to trace the effects of the export of capital and jobs to urban and regional transformations (Portes and Walton 1981; see also Cohen 1977).

An excellent and timely illustration of global-urban linkage in Mingione's analysis (1978) of "capitalist crisis, neo-dualism, and marginalization" Mingione conceives the global crisis of the advanced countries in terms of not overproduction but a decrease in the rate of accumulation and the increase of surplus labor. Previously successful responses to this recurrent problem through the capture of new markets or technological innovation are now unlikely due to the over-exploitation of the Third World (as well as competition from the socialist countries) and technological stagnation, itself partly owing to underaccumulation. These and other conditions combine to suggest an "internal solution" whereby the large numbers of underemployed and unemployed are converted to a new kind of informal economy within the advanced countries: "One option is for capitalism to expand these marginal sectors whose features are low wages, irregular employment and super-exploitation of labor, by diverting some of the economic activities which were previously carried out in the great industrial concerns" (1978:215). The potential consequences of this change are then traced to urban and regional struggles. Although the analysis is quite brief, it is loaded with fascinating implications and research issues given the tremendous consequences of the informal economy demonstrated in work on Third World urban social organization (Portes and Walton 1981) and the growing importance of this phenomenon in the advanced countries.

Yet these, and some related efforts, are very modest beginnings given the theoretical (not to mention the rhetorical) significance of the problem. Urban effects of the present economic crisis are pervasive, not only in the export of jobs and capital, fiscal crises, and the informal economy, but also in the basic domestic sectors of production, in private and collective consumption, and in a panorama of state measures designed to cope with austerity. Much remains to be done in the systematic and researchable linkage of these levels.

Alternative Responses

Second on this agenda is the broad question of alternative responses to the exigencies or crises in the economy and polity. Clearly, the fundamental, and frequently valid, criticism of research within the new paradigm is its penchant for lapses into functionalism, teleology, or ex *post facto* determinism—in retrospect a particular development is "explained" as the necessary outcome of a particular constellation of economic and political forces. As certain writers (Marx included) are fond of saying, "how could it be otherwise." In a moment of candor Marx (1857) once wrote to Engels about his analysis of the Asiatic mode of production, "I might be wrong but if so I can always get out of it by using a little dialectic. I have set myself up in order to be right even in the opposite case." Although crude functionalism (as opposed to studied formulations à la Stinchcombe 1968) is objectionable irrespective of the particular theory it serves, it is by no means an endemic feature of the approach under consideration—as many overeager critics have charged. On the contrary, sophisticated analyses frequently indicate the alternative ways in which a given crisis, or mere conundrum, may be resolved in light of available political and economic stratagems.

Illustrations come to mind drawn from the theoretical literature alluded to previously. For example, O'Connor's (1973) schematic analysis of the fiscal crisis of the state poses for resolution in the short-to-middle run: managed recession, wage and price controls, and increased productivity in the service sector, that is, the "social-industrial complex." Harvey's treatment (1978) of overaccumulation and the urban process considers the possibilities of renewed accumulation and devaluation with respect to production and consumption in the three "circuits of capital" as well as the struggles these are apt to engender.

Historical and empirical inquiries have attempted to explain the variety of contemporary adaptations to the exigencies of urban development and what they portend for the future. Hill's analysis (1978) of capital accumulation and urbanization in the United States gives three responses to fiscal collapse, the pariah, socialist, and state capitalist city, with elements of all in evidence despite the growing dominance of the latter. In parallel analyses of the conditions that once favored expansion toward the suburbs and the Sunbelt, Markusen (1978) and Perry and Watkins (1977) indicate the circumstances under which older urban centers are likely to experience a revival. European research in this area has concentrated on the circumstances in which capital is invested in various forms of urban development, construction, and housing (such as Ascher and Lévy 1973; Duclos 1973; Pickvance 1976; Preteceille 1973).

Nevertheless, these illustrations are exceptions to the general preference for imperious explanation, and even the exceptions are too often hedged with vagueness and escape clauses. What is most needed are theoretical, informed explanations that arrive at the point of enumerating a delimited set of likely alternatives and then indicating the conditions under which one or another will ensue. This is not an appeal for mechanism—itself a double-edged sword. It is, rather, an appeal for the replacement of smug assurances with consequential and researchable hypotheses. Moreover, it is precisely at this juncture that the oft-lamented (too often unfairly) tendency for "economistic" explanations can be most effectively addressed—the juncture at which the more elegantly derivable economic contradictions can be located on the grid of political possibility.

Political Struggles and Social Movements

This leads to the third point concerning the status of research on political struggles and social movements. In my view there is a proclivity in some of this work for contentious assertions about class struggle—its unexamined character and portent reflected in the habit of labeling all forms of political activity as class conflict. Following the Weberian lead, it is essential that we distinguish among political actions based on considerations of status and social honor and those based on class. Efforts to merge these in a denatured notion of social class produce analytic muddles and unwieldy schemes (such as Giddens 1973) that only detract from the incisiveness that recommended the concepts in the first place. Particularly, we need to identify the springs of action in class and status and to understand change. It has been theoretically linked to all manner of contradiction, and on its career ride the fortunes of any foreseeable progress. Obviously, very little progressive change is to be expected in the absence of social movements. But their origins, careers, and ultimate results need to be determined by reference to the broader institutional setting that changes in some ways independently of the movements themselves, while at the same time presenting the opportunities for their differential success. The research that stands the best chance of providing flesh for these reflections will depend on more demanding comparative methods that introduce and control for different institutional settings and movement types.

Assuming that we are clear about the diverse bases of political action in class and status considerations and the complex features of social movements, the study of class struggle may proceed unencumbered. It is encouraging to witness the eclipse of atheoretical and, therefore, irreconcilable polemics about the nature and distribution of political power that has resulted from new theoretical formulations that allow of more or less definitive solution. Articulate models informed by class analysis have proved their explanatory value by contrast to others based on pluralism or elitism in comparative case studies in the United States on urban issues such as transportation (Whitt 1979), corporate power in cities (Friedland 1977) and states (Hicks et al. 1978), and in imaginative work combining case-study and comparative methods in the study of environmental problems (such as Crenson 1971). Starting under fewer handicaps, European research on corporate and business dominance of urban politics has produced some intriguing work including the classic book of Castells and Godard (1974) on *Monopolville* and the recent comparative study by Lojkine of local politics in Lille and Marseille. Were it ever seriously doubted, the proposition that the interests of corporate capital predominate in urban politics is now supported by the best empirical research.

Although this is a necessary result painfully arrived at, it is nevertheless a fairly basic proposition. It has paved the way for current and more challenging work that focuses on the political conditions and consequences of class divisions and coalitions. One avenue of approach has been the nature of intraclass division, particularly for capital. For example, several writers (such as Castells 1978; Harvey 1976; Mingione 1977) have analyzed the manner in which expenditures on collective consumption (housing being prototypical) tend to divide fractions of capital, with those dependent on land, construction, or rentals favoring greater profit in housing while industrial capital opposes such upward pressure on wages. Under these circumstances capital "in general" (Harvey 1976) and the state may side with industrial capital at the same time benefiting labor. The example, obviously, serves mainly to indicate how this approach opens up the possibility for analyses of more complex and realistic situations.

Mollenkopf's analysis (1978) of the diverse pro-growth coalitions that dominated American cities in the postwar period is a choice illustration of the fruitfulness of this approach. There he shows that while the pro-growth coalitions temporarily embraced many elements (for example, corporate capital, local officials and boosters, middle-class workers) at the expense of the urban poor dispossessed by redevelopment and suburbanization strategies, the coalition eventually fell apart, opening the opportunity for disadvantaged classes to join in a potential new alignment with local officials and the urban middle class to reinvest in the city. Environmental issues are particularly fascinating in this regard, since they seem to provide opportunities for both middle- and working-class coalitions in favor of environmental reform as well as capital and working-class alignments opposed to their expense (compare Schnaiberg 1979, and the recent work of Duclos).

Just as political struggles combine elements of class and status action, they typically cross lines as they become more intensive. With the maturation of class analysis it is now possible to become more exacting about class-based coalitions—the conditons under which these emerge, their varied configurations across time and issues, and their fates. It is in connection with these conditions of inter- and intra-class alignment and their associated social movements that the real consequences of political action are to be found. Fortunately, we are now at the point where they can be pursued on a firm theoretical footing and with some valuable empirical precedents.

The State and Public Services

The fourth area of research for our consideration concerns the state and public services. Analysis of the state logically follows from considerations of class, since the key questions about the state—its "functions" across time and issues—depend on first establishing the coordinates of class and class-based political action. That is, if the main concern of various theories of the state is the extent to which it acts in certain class interests or in a relatively autonomous fashion, any assessment of that issue depends on prior clarity about what the classes and their interests are. The same holds where we are concerned with the impact of class-based social movements on the state. These analytic directions, however, should not obscure the fact that in addition to its partial determination by class action, the state also participates historically in the very determination of class structure. These distinct "sides of the causal chain" should be kept in mind as we focus on the more immediate problems of state functions and class interests.

During the past decade the emergence of a new urban social science has coincided with renewed interest in a theory of the state. Since developments in the latter field cannot be reviewed here (and have been summarized often, for example in Wolfe 1974; Girardin 1974; Bridges 1974; Gold et al. 1975), let me simply assert that most of those who have considered the question subscribe to the view that the state is something more than the "executive committee of the bourgeoisie" (no one seems really to admit to being an "instrumentalist") and that the state possesses "relative autonomy." Yet the exact sense of this phrase is elusive. One can imagine several senses of relative autonomy: as a compromise, stalemate, or higher synthesis of competing class interests; as the occasion of a fluid or inchoate class situation; as the occasion of centralized executive power such as Marx (1963:122) described in the *Eighteenth Brumaire* as a "completely independent" state; or as some combination of the above wherein a distinctive set of bureaucratic interests exist independently. Which of these senses may be useful or valid is as much an empirical question as a theoretical one. For the moment all we need observe on this question is that concrete research at the urban level may give us some idea of the different kinds of autonomy and the conditions under which they arise.

Returning to our theme of economic crisis and urban austerity, the role of the state is usefully illustrated in three areas. The first is the matter of state administrative structure with particular reference to taxation and finance. In a paper on the state response to the fiscal crisis in American cities Friedland et al. (1977) argue that different forms of state intervention (such as those that benefit capital and those that provide social services) are differentially vulnerable to political pressures. As Friedland (1978:573) elsewhere succinctly puts it:

in the United States, social services tend to be noncentrally financed through investment-sensitive and non-progressive property taxes, while state interventions which are critical to production (defense contracting, public capital projects, tax incentives for capital investment) are centrally financed through potentially more progressive income taxes. First, this makes it extraordinarily difficult to conjoin a politics of the social wage with a politics of social capital. Second, locally financed welfare and education expansions often pit unionized working-class home-owners against unemployed and low-paid workers and surplus populations. Third, labor unions are encouraged to secure health, day care, transportation and other benefits through intra-corporate collective bargaining. Fourth, social wage ex-

penditures tend to be financed out of more visible forms of taxation and thus highly politicized, while social capital expenditures tend to be financed through less visible taxes and thereby
depoliticized.

Under conditions of economic crisis, of course, this arrange-
ment implies that necessary austerity measures are most likely
to come at the cost of social services and the social wage. But
the more insightful point here is that they come through the
seemingly even-handed operation of the political process by
virtue of the manner in which the state is organized to serve
"all" classes. The interests of legitimacy are served at the same
time, as the least advantaged classes bear the heaviest costs
of austerity policies. In this case the autonomy of the state is
a fiction constituted mainly by the apparatus that camou-
flages a class mechanism.

At the present moment the opportunities for research on
this question are, regrettably, abundant with the appearance
of service-reducing measures and the tax revolt movement.
One wonders, for example, under what conditions does the
fever for tax revolt get arrested by perceived and consequential reductions in services (Miller 1979); what classes and positions become politicized around these issues; what services
are more and less vulnerable; under what circumstances may
the structure itself become transparent?

These questions suggest a second area illustrating the role
of the state, namely the mix of crisis policies directed at production and consumption. As we have seen, policies in each
sphere have important and differential urban consequences.
State responses to the initial crisis of 1973 attempted to aid
production through greatly expanded consumer credit, which
might have benefited cities, save for its inflationary effects.
Similarly, state policy ultimately assists the relocation of production in more profitable regional and international climes.
If, as some suggest, the present economic crisis is one in
which overproduction is a key problem, it would be expected
that state policy will focus increasingly on the consumption
sphere. For example, collective consumption may increasingly be opened up to private accumulation, as O'Connor

(1973) forecasts with the "social-industrial complex" notion or, more concretely, as Harvey hypothesizes (1978:129): "Investment in working class housing or in a national health service can thus be transformed into a vehicle for accumulation via commodity production for these sectors." In short, a vital area for new research concerns the extent to which present conditions may lead to state policies that completely transform the organization of service provision in a manner of rescuing capital.

Third, these hypothetical and real changes that portend austerity in social services have deep implications for the welfare state. At the most obvious level they suggest that the welfare state is not in the business of enhancing people's welfare, but of attempting to maintain a viable economy in a one-sided pact between capital and the more privileged (and organized) sectors of labor. Again, in research stemming from the perspective under review, this point has been made innumerable times in connection with the themes of cooptation, super-exploitation, social control, and all of the seemingly beneficent measures of the state that can be interpreted as subtly accomplishing the extraction of greater profit and conformity (Marcuse 1978). Assuming, as is doubtless the case, that these liberal and radical criticisms of the welfare state capture some truth, the question becomes what will happen to this structure of social control with the transformation of the welfare state as we know it? If the welfare state has bought social peace at the expense of capital and the general public or, from a more extreme stance, if it has been a mechanism of repression, what will happen to the stability it has engineered once its services must be directly purchased? Although this question is formulated here in a doubly hypothetical manner, it is not without empirical precedent (for example, in health and education) and stating it in this way may help to convert a heavily ideological debate into a tractable research problem.

Progressive Policy Alternatives

The final point on this research agenda is implicit in everything that has been said so far and can be summarized briefly. In connection with its normative stance and commitment to practice, the new urban social science is deeply concerned with research on public policy. Despite this orientation in its research, there is a conspicuous lack of discussion of progressive policy alternatives. Virtually all policy research from a critical standpoint ends up in sweeping condemnations of the regressive or repressive character of occasionally well-intended programs, including ones the same parties may have looked upon with general favor earlier on (such as the notion of citizen participation). To the extent that "constructive" ideas are offered they tend to rhapsodize on socialism in the abstract or on reforms adopted in China or Cuba under entirely different circumstances—and sometimes of dubious merit.

Of course, there may be good reason for this general persuasion. But, if there is no conceivable policy that researchers can endorse short of the destruction of the capitalist system or the promotion of regressive policies that heighten contradiction as a prelude to the dénouement, then this needs to be admitted and the professed practice of policy research (with its associated status) abandoned for other pursuits. Conversely, if there are policies, or even realistic preconditions for policy making, then these should be laid out in terms of the research they are based on and lead toward.

This is simply to restate the observation that the critics of conventional urban social science and urban development have so far failed to present an attractive alternative. As Miller (1978:211) says in other terms:

> Currently, the recapitulization approach is aided by the absence of politically appealing, economically attractive, short-run left strategy. Can the left in capitalist nations provide more than a critique of current policies and offer a viable program which can cope with the immediate short-run economic problems of capitalism in ways that lead to attractive socialist conditions?

Naturally, the objectives of our deliberations go beyond the formulation of discrete policy ideas. Policy tends to reflect the level of understanding on which it rests and that is at least one reason why so much of it is so bad. Yet, a genuine understanding of our problems is certain to imply avenues for their remedy. Ideally these would be the fruit of our efforts.

References

Ascher, F. and D. Lévy. 1973. "Logement et construction: La crise et les solutions du Programme Commun." Économie et politique (May), 226:51–76.

Bendix, R. 1974. "Inequality and Social Structure: A Comparison of Marx and Weber." American Sociological Review (April), 39:149–161.

Bridges, A. B. 1974. "Nicos Poulantzas and the Marxist Theory of the State." Politics and Society (Winter), 4:161–190.

Castells, M. (1973) 1978. The Urban Question: A Marxist Approach. Cambridge, Mass.: MIT Press.

Castells, M. and F. Godard. 1974. Monopolville: L'Entreprise, l'État, l'Urbain. Paris: Mouton.

Cohen R. 1977. "Urban Effects of the Internationalization of Capital and Labor." Conservation of Human Resources Program, Columbia University. Unpublished.

Crenson, M. A. 1971. The Un-politics of Air Pollution: A Study of Nondecisionmaking in Cities. Baltimore: Johns Hopkins University Press.

Dowd, D. 1978. "Continuity, Change, and Tension in Global Capitalism." In B. H. Kaplan, ed., Social Change in the Capitalist World Economy, pp. 177–195. Beverly Hills, Calif.: Sage.

Duclos, D. 1973. Propriété foncier et processus d'urbanisation. Paris: CSU.

Edel, M. 1977. "The New York Crisis as Economic History." In R. E. Alcaly and D. Mermelstein, eds., The Fiscal Crisis of American Cities: Essays on the Political Economy of Urban America with Special Reference to New York, pp. 228–245. New York: Vintage.

Friedland, R. 1977. "Class Power and Social Control: The Case of the War on Poverty." Politics and Society, 7:459–489.

—— 1978. "Space, Society, and the State: A Critique of the Urban Question." International Journal of Urban and Regional Research (October), 2:569–576.

Friedland, R., F. F. Piven, and R. R. Alford. 1977. "Political Conflict, Urban Structure, and the Fiscal Crisis." In D. Ashford, ed., Comparative Public Policy: New Approaches and Methods, pp. 197–225. Beverly Hills, Calif.: Sage.

Giddens, A. 1973. *The Class Structures of the Advanced Societies*. New York: Barnes and Noble.

Girardin, J.-C. 1974. "On the Marxist Theory of the State." *Politics and Society* (Winter), 4:193–223.

Gold, D. A., C. Y. H. Lo, and E. O. Wright. 1975. "Recent Developments in Marxist Theories of the Capitalist State, Parts I and II." *Monthly Review* (October–November), 27:29–43, 36–51.

Gordon, D. 1978. "Capitalist Development and the History of American Cities." In W. K. Tabb and L. Sawers, eds., *Marxism and the Metropolis: New Perspectives in Urban Political Economy*, pp. 25–63. New York: Oxford University Press.

Hardoy, J. 1975. *Urbanization in Latin America: Approaches and Issues*. Garden City, N.Y.: Doubleday.

Harvey, D. 1973. *Social Justice and the City*. Baltimore: Johns Hopkins University Press.

—— 1976. "Labor, Capital, and Class Struggle Around the Built Environment in Advanced Capitalist Countries." *Politics and Society*, 3:265–295.

—— 1978. "The Urban Process Under Capitalism: A Framework for Analysis." *International Journal of Urban and Regional Research* (March), 2:101–131.

Hicks, A., R. Friedland, and E. D. Johnson. 1978. "Class Power and State Policy: The Case of Large Business Corporations, Labor Unions and Governmental Redistribution in the American States." *American Sociological Review* (June), 43:302–315.

Hill, R. C. 1978. "Fiscal Collapse and Political Struggle in Decaying Central Cities in the United States." In W. K. Tabb and L. Sawers, eds., *Marxism and the Metropolis: New Perspectives in Urban Political Economy*, pp. 213–240. New York: Oxford University Press.

Kornblum, W. 1974. *Blue Collar Community*. Chicago: University of Chicago Press.

Lamarche, F. 1976. "Property Development and the Economic Foundations of the Urban Question." In C. G. Pickvance, ed., *Urban Sociology: Critical Essays*, pp. 85–119. New York: St. Martin's.

Lojkine, J. 1976. "Contribution to a Marxist Theory of Capitalist Urbanization." In C. G. Pickvance, ed., *Urban Sociology: Critical Essays*, pp. 119–146. New York: St. Martin's.

Lubeck, P. and J. Walton. 1979. "Urban Class Conflict in Africa and Latin America: Comparative Analyses from a World Systems Perspective." *International Journal of Urban and Regional Research* (March), 3:3–28.

Mandel, E. 1978. *The Second Slump: A Marxist Analysis of Recession in the Seventies*. London: NLB.

Marcuse, P. 1978. "Housing Policy and the Myth of the Benevolent State." *Social Policy* (January–February).

Markusen, A. R. 1978. "Class and Urban Social Expenditure: A Marxist

Theory of Metropolitan Government." In W. K. Tabb and L. Sawers, eds., *Marxism and the Metropolis: New Perspectives in Urban Political Economy*, pp. 90–111. New York: Oxford University Press.

Marx, K. (1857) 1927–1935. "Letter to Engels Dated August 15." In *Karl Marx, Friedrich Engels; historisch-kritische Gesamtausgabe, Werke, Schriften, Briefe*, D. Rjazanov, ed. Moscow: Marx–Engels, Institut.

—— (1852) 1963. *The Eighteenth Brumaire of Louis Bonaparte*. New York: International Publishers.

Miller, S. M. 1978. "The Recapitalization of Capitalism." *International Journal of Urban and Regional Research* (June), 2:202–212.

—— 1979. "Proposition 13's Meaning and Implications." Paper presented at the annual meeting of the American Sociological Association, Boston.

Mingione, E. 1977. "Sociological Approach to Regional and Urban Development: Some Methodological and Theoretical Issues." *Comparative Urban Research*, 4:21–38.

—— 1978. "Capitalist Crisis, Neo-dualism, and Marginalization." *International Journal of Urban and Regional Research* (June), 2:213–221.

Mollenkopf, J. 1978. "The Postwar Politics of Urban Development." *Politics and Society*, 5:247–295.

O'Connor, J. 1973. *The Fiscal Crisis of the State*. New York: St. Martin's.

Perry, D. C. and A. J. Watkins. 1977. *The Rise of the Sunbelt Cities*. Beverly Hills, Calif.: Sage.

Pickvance, C. G. 1976. "Housing: Reproduction of Capital and Production of Labour: Some Recent French Work." In J. Walton and L. H. Masotti, eds., *The City in Comparative Perspective: Cross-national Research and New Directions in Theory*, pp. 271–289. Beverly Hills, Calif.: Sage.

Piven, F. F. and R. Cloward. 1977. *Poor People's Movements: Why They Succeed, How They Fail*. New York: Vintage.

Portes, A. and J. Walton. 1981. *Labor, Class, and the International System*. New York: Academic Press.

Preteceille, E. 1973. *La production des grands ensembles*. Paris: Mouton.

Quijano, A. 1968. "Dependencia, cambio social, y urbanización en América Latina." *Revista mexicana de sociologia* (July–September).

Schnaiberg, A. 1979. *The Environment: From Surplus to Scarcity*. New York: Oxford University Press.

Slater, D. 1978. "Towards a Political Economy of Urbanization in Peripheral Capitalist Societies: Problems of Theory and Method with Illustrations from Latin America." *International Journal of Urban and Regional Research* (March), 2:26–52.

Stinchcombe, A. L. 1968. *Constructing Social Theories*. New York: Harcourt, Brace.

Strange, S. 1979. "The Management of Surplus Capacity: Or How Does Theory Stand up to Protectionism 1970's Style?" *International Organization* (Summer), 33:303–333.

Whitt, J. A. 1979. "Toward a Class-Dialectic Model of Power: An Empirical

Assessment of Three Competing Models of Political Power." *American Sociological Review,* (February), 44:81–99.

Wolfe, A. 1974. "New Directions in the Marxist Theory of the State." *Politics and Society* (Winter), 4:131–159.

Yancey, W. L., E. P. Ericksen, and R. N. Juliani. 1976. "Emergent Ethnicity: A Review and Reformulation." *American Sociological Review,* 41:391–403.

15

The City
as a Growth Machine:
Toward a Political
Economy of Place

HARVEY MOLOTCH

CONVENTIONAL DEFINITIONS OF "city," "urban place,"
or "metropolis" have led to conventional analyses of urban
systems and urban-based social problems. Usually traceable
to Wirth's classic and highly plausible formulation of "numbers, density and heterogeneity," (1938), there has been a
continuing tendency, even in more recent formulations (such
as Davis 1965), to conceive of place quite apart from a crucial
dimension of social structure: power and social class hier-
archy. Consequently, sociological research based on the traditional definitions of what an urban place is has had very
little relevance to the actual, day-to-day activities of those at
the top of local power structure whose priorities set the limits within which decisions affecting land use, the public
budget, and urban social life come to be made. It has not
been very apparent from the scholarship of urban social science that land, the basic stuff of place, is a market commod-

Reprinted with permission from *American Journal of Sociology* (1975), vol. 87, no. 2,
University of Chicago Press. Tables and text references to tables were omitted because of space constraints.

ity providing wealth and power, and that some very important people consequently take a keen interest in it. Thus,
although there are extensive literatures on community power
as well as on how to define and conceptualize a city or urban
place, there are few notions available to link the two issues
coherently, focusing on the urban settlement as a political
economy.

This paper aims toward filling this need. I speculate that
the political and economic essence of virtually any given locality, in the present American context, is *growth*. I further
argue that the desire for growth provides the key operative
motivation toward consensus for members of politically mo-
bilized local elites, however split they might be on other issues, and that a common interest in growth is the overriding
commonality among important people is a given locale—at
least insofar as they have any important local goals at all.
Further, this growth imperative is the most important constraint upon available options for local initiative in social and
economic reform. It is thus that I argue that the very essence
of a locality is its operation as a growth machine.

The clearest indication of success at growth is a constantly rising urban-area population—a symptom of a pattern
ordinarily comprising an initial expansion of basic industries
followed by an expanded labor force, a rising scale of retail
and wholesale commerce, more far-flung and increasingly intensive land development, higher population density, and increased levels of financial activity. Although throughout this
paper I index growth by the variable population growth, it is
this entire syndrome of associated events that is meant by the
general term "growth."[1] I argue that the means of achieving
this growth, of setting off this chain of phenomena, constitute the central issue for those serious people who care about
their locality and who have the resources to make their caring felt as a political force. The city is, for those who count,
a growth machine.

The Human Ecology: Maps as Interest Mosaics

I have argued elsewhere (Molotch 1967, 1973) that any given parcel of land represents an interest and than any given locality is thus an aggregate of land-based interests. That is, each landowner (or person who otherwise has some interest in the prospective use of a particular piece of land) has in mind a certain future for that parcel which is linked somehow with his or her own well-being. If there is a simple ownership, the relationship is straightforward: to the degree to which the land's profit potential is enhanced, one's own wealth is increased. In other cases, the relationship may be more subtle: one has interest in an adjacent parcel, and if a noxious use should appear, one's own parcel may be harmed. More subtle still is the emergence of concern for an aggregate of parcels: one sees that one's future is bound to the future of a larger area, that the future enjoyment of financial benefit flowing from a given parcel will derive from the general future of the proximate aggregate of parcels. When this occurs, there is that "we feeling" (McKenzie 1922) which bespeaks community. We need to see each geographical map—whether of a small group of land parcels, a whole city, a region, or a nation—not merely as a demarcation of legal, political, or topographical features, but as a mosaic of competing land interests capable of strategic coalition and action.

Each unit of a community strives, at the expense of the others, to enhance the land-use potential of the parcels with which it is associated. Thus, for example, shopkeepers at both ends of a block may compete with one another to determine in front of which building the bus stop will be placed. Or, hotel owners on the north side of a city may compete with those on the south to get a convention center built nearby (see Banfield 1961). Likewise, area units fight over highway routes, airport locations, campus developments, defense contracts, traffic lights, one-way street designations, and park developments. The intensity of group consciousness and activity waxes and wanes as opportunities for and challenges to the collective good rise and fall; but when these coalitions are of sufficiently enduring quality, they constitute identifiable, ongoing communities. Each member of a community is simultaneously the member of a number of others; hence, communities exist in a nested fashion (for example, neighborhood within city within region), with salience of community level varying over both time and circumstance. Because of this nested nature of communities, subunits that are competitive with one another at one level (say, in an interblock dispute over where the bus stop should go) will be in coalition at a higher level (say, in an intercity rivalry over where the new port should go). Obviously, the anticipation of potential coalition acts to constrain the intensity of conflict at more local loci of growth competition.

Hence, to the degree to which otherwise competing land-interest groups collude to achieve a common land-enhancement scheme, there is community—whether at the level of a residential block club, a neighborhood association, a city or metropolitan chamber of commerce, a state development agency, or a regional association. Such aggregates, whether constituted formally or informally, whether governmental political institutions or voluntary associations, typically operate in the following way: an attempt is made to use government to gain those resources that will enhance the growth potential of the area unit in question. Often, the governmental level where action is needed is at least one level higher than the community from which the activism springs. Thus, individual landowners aggregate to extract neighborhood gains from the city government; a cluster of cities may coalesce to have an effective impact on the state government; and so on. Each locality, in striving to make these gains, is in competition with other localities because the degree of growth, at least at any given moment, is finite. The scarcity of developmental resources means that government becomes the arena in which land-use interest groups compete for public money and attempt to mold those decisions that will determine the land-use outcomes. Localities thus compete with one another to gain the *preconditions* of growth. Historically, U.S. cities were created and sustained largely through this process;[2] it continues to be the significant dynamic of contemporary local political economy and is critical to the allocation of public resources and the ordering of local issue agendas.

Government decisions are not the only kinds of social activities that affect local growth chances; decisions made by private corporations also have major impact. When a national corporation decides to locate a branch plant in a given locale, it sets the conditions for the surrounding land-use pattern. But even here, government decisions are involved: plant-location decisions are made with reference to such issues as labor costs, tax rates, and the costs of obtaining raw materials and transporting goods to markets. It is government decisions (at whatever level) that help determine the cost of access to markets and raw materials. This is especially so in the present era of raw material subsidies (such as the mineral depletion allowance) and reliance on government-approved or -subsidized air transport, highways, railways, pipelines, and port developments. Government decisions influence the cost of overhead expenses (such as pollution abatement requirements, employee safety standards), and government decisions affect the costs of labor through indirect manipulation of unemployment rates, through the use of police to constrain or enhance union organizing, and through the legislation and administration of welfare laws (see Piven and Cloward 1972).

Localities are generally mindful of these governmental powers and, in addition to creating the sorts of physical conditions that can best serve industrial growth, also attempt to maintain the kind of "business climate" that attracts industry: for example, favorable taxation, vocational training, law enforcement, and "good" labor relations. To promote growth, taxes should be "reasonable," the police force should be oriented toward protection of property, and overt social conflict should be minimized (see Rubin 1972:123; Agger et al. 1964:649).[3] Increased utility and government costs caused by new development should be borne (and they usually are—see, for example, Ann Arbor City Planning Department [1972])

by the public at large, rather than by those responsible for
the "excess" demand on the urban infrastructure. Virtually
any issue of a major business magazine is replete with ads
from localities of all types (including whole countries) trum-
peting their virtues in just these terms to prospective industrial settlers.[4] In addition, a key role of elected and appointed
officials becomes that of "ambassador" to industry, to communicate, usually with appropriate ceremony, these advantages to potential investors (see Wyner 1967).[5]

I aim to make the extreme statement that this organized
effort to affect the outcome of growth distribution is the essence of local government as a dynamic political force. It is
not the only function of government, but it is the key one
and, ironically, the one most ignored. Growth is not, in the
present analysis, merely one among a number of equally important concerns of political process (compare Adrian and
Williams 1963). Among contemporary social scientists, perhaps only Murray Edelman (1964) has provided appropriate
conceptual preparation for viewing government in such terms.
Edelman contrasts two kinds of politics. First there is the
"symbolic" politics, which comprises the "big issues" of
public morality and the symbolic reforms featured in the
headlines and editorials of the daily press. The other politics
is the process through which goods and services actually
come to be distributed in the society. Largely unseen, and
relegated to negotiations within committees (when it occurs
at all within a formal government body), this is the politics
that determines who, in material terms, gets what, where, and
how (Lasswell 1936). This is the kind of politics we must talk
about at the local level: it is the politics of distribution, and
land is the crucial (but not the only) variable in this system.

The people who participate with their energies, and particularly their fortunes, in local affairs are the sorts of persons
who—at least in vast disproportion to their representation in
the population—have the most to gain or lose in land-use
decisions. Prominent in terms of numbers have long been the
local businessmen (see Walton 1970),[6] particularly property
owners and investors in locally oriented financial institutions

(see Spaulding 1951; Mumford 1961:536), who need local government in their daily money-making routines. Also prominent are lawyers, syndicators, and realtors (see Bouma 1962) who need to put themselves in situations where they can be most useful to those with the land and property resources.[7] Finally, there are those who, although not directly involved in land use, have their futures tied to growth of the metropolis as a whole. At least, when the local market becomes saturated one of the few possible avenues for business expansion is sometimes the expansion of the surrounding community itself (see Adrian and Williams 1963:24).[8]

This is the general outline of the coalition that actively generates the community "we feeling" (or perhaps more aptly, the "our feeling")[9] that comes to be an influence in the politics of a given locality. It becomes manifest through a wide variety of techniques. Government funds support "boosterism" of various sorts: the Chamber of Commerce, locality-promotion ads in business journals and travel publications, city-sponsored parade floats, and stadia and other forms of support for professional sports teams carrying the locality name. The athletic teams in particular are an extraordinary mechanism for instilling a spirit of civic jingoism regarding the "progress" of the locality. A stadium filled with thousands (joined by thousands more at home before the TV) screaming for Cleveland or Baltimore (or whatever) is a scene difficult to fashion otherwise. This enthusiasm can be drawn on, with a glossy claim of creating a "greater Cleveland," "greater Baltimore," and so on, in order to gain general acceptance for local growth-oriented programs. Similarly, public school curricula, children's essay contests, soapbox derbies, spelling contests, beauty pageants, and the like, help build an ideological base for local boosterism and the acceptance of growth. My conception of the territorial bond among humans differs from those cast in terms of primordial instincts: instead, I see this bond as socially organized and sustained, at least in part, by those who have a use for it (compare Suttles 1972:111–139). I do not claim that there are no other sources of civic jingoism and growth enthusiasm in

American communities, only that the growth-machine coalition mobilizes what is there, legitimizes and sustains it, and
channels it as a political force into particular kinds of policy
decisions.

The local institution that seems to take prime responsibility for the sustenance of these civic resources—the metropolitan newspaper—is also the most important example of a
business that has its interest anchored in the aggregate growth
of the locality. Increasingly, American cities are one-news-
paper (metropolitan daily) town (or one-newspaper-company
towns), and the newspaper business seems to be one kind of
enterprise for which expansion to other locales is especially
difficult. The financial loss suffered by the New York Times
in its futile effort to establish a California edition is an important case in point. A paper's financial status (and that of
other media to a lesser extent) tends to be wed to the size of
the locality.[10] As the metropolis expands, a larger number of
ad lines can be sold on the basis of the increasing circulation
base. The local newspaper thus tends to occupy a rather
unique position: like many other local businesses, it has an
interest in growth, but unlike most, its critical interest is not
in the specific geographical pattern of that growth. That is,
the crucial matter to a newspaper is not whether the additional population comes to reside on the north side or south
side, or whether the money is made through a new convention center or a new olive factory. The newspaper has no axe
to grind, except the one axe that holds the community elite
together: growth. It is for this reason that the newspaper tends
to achieve a statesman-like attitude in the community and is
deferred to as something other than a special interest by the
special interests. Competing interests often regard the publisher or editor as a general community leader, as an om-
budsman and arbiter of internal bickering, and, at times, as
an enlightened third party who can restrain the short-term
profiteers in the interest of more stable, long-term, and properly planned growth.[11] The paper becomes the reformist influence, the "voice of the community," restraining the competing subunits, especially the small-scale, arriviste "fast-buck

artists" among them. The papers are variously successful in their continuous battle with the targeted special interests.[12] The media attempt to attain these goals not only through the kind of coverage they develop and editorials they write but also through the kinds of candidates they support for local office. The present point is not that the papers control the politics of the city, but rather that one of the sources of their special influence is their commitment to growth per se, and growth is a goal around which all important groups can rally.

Thus it is that, although newspaper editorialists have typically been in the forefront expressing sentiment in favor of "the ecology," they tend nevertheless to support growth-inducing investments for their regions. The *New York Times* likes office towers and additional industrial installations in the city even more than it loves the environment. The *Los Angeles Times* editorializes against narrow-minded profiteer-ing at the expense of the environment but has also favored the development of the supersonic transport because of the "jobs" it would lure to Southern California. The papers do tend to support "good planning principles" in some form be-cause such good planning is a long-term force that makes for even more potential future growth. If the roads are not planned wide enough, their narrowness will eventually strangle the increasingly intense uses to which the land will be put. It just makes good sense to plan, and good planning for "sound growth" thus is the key "environmental policy" of the nation's local media and their statesmen allies. Such policies of "good planning" should not be confused with limited growth or conservation: they more typically represent the opposite sort of goal.

Often leaders of public or quasi-public agencies (such as universities, utilities) achieve a role similar to that of the newspaper publisher: they become growth "statesmen" rather than advocates for a certain type or intralocal distribution of growth. A university may require an increase in the local ur-ban population pool to sustain its own expansion plans and, in addition, it may be induced to defer to others in the growth machine (bankers, newspapers) on whom it depends for the favorable financial and public-opinion environment necessary for institutional enhancement.

There are certain persons, ordinarily conceived of as members of the elite, who have much less, if any, interest in local growth. Thus, for example, there are branch executives of corporations headquartered elsewhere who, although perhaps emotionally sympathetic with pro-growth outlooks, work for corporations that have no vested interest in the growth of the locality in question. Their indirect interest is perhaps in the existence of the growth ideology rather than growth itself. It is that ideology which in fact helps make them revered people in the area (social worth is often defined in terms of number of people one employs) and which provides the rationale for the kind of local governmental policies most consistent with low business operating costs. Nonetheless, this interest is not nearly as strong as the direct growth interests of developers, mortgage bankers, and the like, and thus we find, as Schulze (1961) has observed, that there is a tendency for such executives to play a lesser local role than the parochial, homegrown businessmen whom they often replace.

Thus, because the city is a growth machine, it draws a special sort of person into its politics. These people—whether acting on their own or on behalf of the constituency which financed their rise to power—tend to be businessmen and, among businessmen, the more parochial sort. Typically, they come to politics not to save or destroy the environment, not to repress or liberate the blacks, not to eliminate civil liberties or enhance them. They may end up doing any or all of these things once they have achieved access to authority, perhaps as an inadvertent consequence of making decisions in other realms. But these types of symbolic positions are derived from the fact of having power—they are typically not the dynamics that bring people to power in the first place. Thus, people often become "involved" in government, especially in the local party structure and fund raising, for reasons of land business and related processes of resource distribution. Some are "statesmen" who think in terms of the growth of the whole community rather than that of a more narrow geographical delimitation. But they are there to wheel and deal to affect resource distribution through local government. As a result of their position, and in part to develop the symbolic issues that will enable them (in lieu of one of their opponents or colleagues) to maintain that position of power, they get interested in such things as welfare cheating, busing, street crime, and the price of meat. This interest in the symbolic issues (see Edelman 1964) is thus substantially an aftereffect of a need for power for other purposes. This is not to say that such people don't "feel strongly" about these matters—they do sometimes. It is also the case that certain moral zealots and "concerned citizens" go into politics to right symbolic wrongs; but the money and other supports that make them viable as politicians is usually nonsymbolic money.

Those who come to the forefront of local government (and those to whom they are directly responsive), therefore, are not statistically representative of the local population as a whole, nor even representative of the social classes that produce them. The issues they introduce into public discourse are not representative either. As noted by Edelman, the distributive issues, the matters that bring people to power, are more or less deliberately dropped from public discourse (see Schattschneider 1960). The issues that are permissible to discuss and the positions that the politicians take on them derive from the world views of those who come from certain sectors of the business and professional class and the need they have to whip up public sentiment without allowing distributive issues to become part of public discussion. It follows that any political change that succeeded in replacing the land business as the key determinant of the local political dynamic would simultaneously weaken the power of one of the more reactionary political forces in the society, thereby affecting outcomes with respect to those other symbolic issues that manage to gain so much attention. Thus, should such a change occur, there would likely be more progressive

positions taken on civil liberties, and less harassment of welfare recipients, social "deviants," and other defenseless victims.

Liabilities of the Growth Machine

Emerging trends are tending to enervate the locality growth
machines. First is the increasing suspicion that in many areas,
at many historical moments, growth benefits only a small
proportion of local residents. Growth almost always brings
with it the obvious problems of increased air and water pollution, traffic congestion, and overtaxing of natural amenities. These dysfunctions become increasingly important and
visible as increased consumer income fulfills people's other
needs and as the natural cleansing capacities of the environment are progressively overcome with deleterious material.
While it is by no means certain that growth and increased
density inevitably bring about social pathologies (see Fischer
et al. 1974), growth does make such pathologies more difficult to deal with. For example, the larger the jurisdiction, the
more difficult it becomes to achieve the goal of school integration without massive busing schemes. As increasing experience with busing makes clear, small towns can more easily have interracial schools, whether fortuitously through
spatial proximity or through managed programs.

In addition, the weight of research evidence is that
growth often costs existing residents more money. Evidently,
at various population levels, points of diminishing returns
are crossed such that additional increments lead to net revenue losses. A 1970 study for the city of Palo Alto, California,
indicated that it was substantially cheaper for that city to acquire at full market value its foothill open space than to allow it to become an "addition" to the tax base (Livingston
and Blayney 1971). A study of Santa Barbara, California,
demonstrated that additional population growth would require higher property taxes, as well as higher utility costs

(Appelbaum et al. 1974). Similar results on the costs of growth have been obtained in studies of Boulder, Colorado (cited in Finkler 1972), and Ann Arbor, Michigan (Ann Arbor City Planning Department, 1972).[13] Systematic analyses of government costs as a function of city size and growth have been carried out under a number of methodologies, but the use of the units of analysis most appropriate for comparison (urban areas) yields the finding that the cost is directly related to both size of place and rate of growth, at least for middle-size cities (see Follett 1976; Appelbaum 1976). Especially significant are per capita police costs, which virtually all studies show to be positively related to both city size and rate of growth (see Appelbaum et al. 1974; Appelbaum 1976).

Although damage to the physical environment and costs of utilities and governmental services may rise with size of settlement, "optimal" size is obviously determined by the sorts of values that are to be maximized (see Duncan 1957). It may indeed be necessary to sacrifice clean air to accumulate a population base large enough to support a major opera company. But the essential point remains that growth is certainly less of a financial advantage to the taxpayer than is conventionally depicted, and that most people's values are, according to the survey evidence (Hoch 1972:280; Finkler 1972:2, 23; Parke and Westoff 1972; Mazie and Rowlings 1973; Appelbaum et al. 1974:4.2–4.6), more consistent with small places than large. Indeed, it is rather clear that some substantial portion of the migrations to the great metropolitan areas of the last decade has been more in spite of people's values than because of them. In the recent words of Sundquist:

> The notion commonly expressed that Americans have "voted with their feet" in favor of the great cities is, on the basis of every available sampling, so much nonsense. . . . What is called "freedom of choice" is, in sum, freedom of employer choice or, more precisely, freedom of choice for that segment of the corporate world that operates mobile enterprises. The real question, then, is whether freedom of corporate choice should be automatically honored by government policy at the expense of freedom of individual choice where those conflict. (1975:258)

Taking all the evidence together, it is certainly a rather conservative statement to make that under many circumstances growth is a liability financially and in quality of life for the majority of local residents. Under such circumstances, local growth is a transfer of quality of life and wealth from the local general public to a certain segment of the local elite. To raise the question of wisdom of growth in regard to any specific locality is hence potentially to threaten such a wealth transfer and the interests of those who profit by it.

The Problems of Jobs

Perhaps the key ideological prop for the growth machine, especially in terms of sustaining support from the working-class majority (Levison 1974), is the claim that growth "makes jobs." This claim is aggressively promulgated by developers, builders, and chambers of commerce; it becomes a part of the statesman talk of editorialists and political officials. Such people do not speak of growth as useful to profits—rather, they speak of it as necessary for making jobs. But local growth does not, of course, make jobs: it distributes jobs. The United States will see next year the construction of a certain number of new factories, office units, and highways—regardless of where they are put. Similarly, a given number of automobiles, missiles, and lampshades will be made, regardless of where they are manufactured. Thus, the number of jobs in this society, whether in the building trades or any other economic sector, will be determined by rates of investment return, federal decisions affecting the money supply, and other factors having very little to do with local decision making. All that a locality can do is to attempt to guarantee that a certain proportion of newly created jobs will be in the locality in question. Aggregate employment is thus unaffected by the outcome of this competition among localities to "make" jobs.

The labor force is essentially a single national pool; workers are mobile and generally capable of taking advantage of employment opportunities emerging at geographically distant points.[14] As jobs develop in a fast-growing area, the unemployed will be attracted from other areas in sufficient numbers not only to fill those developing vacancies but also to form a work-force sector that is continuously unemployed. Thus, just as local growth does not affect aggregate employment, it likely has very little long-term impact on the local rate of unemployment. Again, the systematic evidence fails to show any advantage to growth: there is no tendency for either larger places or more rapidly growing ones to have lower unemployment rates than other kinds of urban areas. In fact, the tendency is for rapid growth to be associated with higher rates of unemployment (for general documentation, see Follett 1976; Appelbaum 1976; Hadden and Borgatta 1965:108; Samuelson 1942; Sierra Club of San Diego, 1973).[15]

This pattern of findings is vividly illustrated through inspection of relevant data on the most extreme cases of urban growth: those SMSAs that experienced the most rapid rates of population increase over the last two intercensus decades. In the case of both decade comparisons, half of the urban areas had unemployment rates above the national figure for all SMSAs.

Even the twenty-five slowest growing (1960–1970) SMSAs failed to experience particularly high rates of unemployment. Less than half of the SMSAs of this group had unemployment rates above the national mean at the decade's end.

Just as striking is the comparison of growth and unemployment rates for all SMSAs in California during the 1960–1966 period—a time of general boom in the state. Among all California metropolitan areas there is no significant relationship ($r = -17$, $z - .569$) between 1960 and 1966 growth rates and the 1966 unemployment rate. While there is a wide divergence in growth rates across metropolitan areas, there is no comparable variation in the unemployment rates, all of which cluster within the relatively narrow range of 4.3 percent to 6.5 percent. Consistent with my previous argument, I take this as evidence that the mobility of labor tends to flatten

out cross-SMSA unemployment rates, regardless of widely
diverging rates of locality growth. Taken together, the data
indicate that local population growth is no solution to the
problem of local unemployment.

It remains possible that for some reason certain specific
rates of growth may be peculiarly related to lower rates of
unemployment and that the measures used in this and cited
studies are insensitive to these patterns. Similarly, growth in
certain types of industries may be more likely than growth in
others to stimulate employment without attracting migrants.
It may also be possible that certain population groups, by reason of cultural milieu, are less responsive to mobility options
than others and thus provide bases for exceptions to the general argument I am advancing. The present analysis does not
preclude such future findings but does assert, minimally, that
the argument that growth makes jobs is contradicted by the
weight of evidence that is available.[16]

I conclude that for the average worker in a fast-growing
region job security has much the same status as for a worker
in a slower-growing region: there is a surplus of workers over
jobs, generating continuous anxiety over unemployment[17] and
the effective depressant on wages which any lumpenproletar-
iat of unemployed and marginally employed tends to exact
(see, for example, Bonacich 1975). Indigenous workers likely
receive little benefit from the growth machine in terms of jobs;
their "native" status gives them little edge over the "foreign"
migrants seeking the additional jobs which may develop. Instead, they are interchangeable parts of the labor pool, and
the degree of their job insecurity is expressed in the local
unemployment rate, just as is the case for the nonnative
worker. Ironically, it is probably this very anxiety that often
leads workers, or at least their union spokespeople, to support enthusiastically employers' preferred policies of growth.
It is the case that an actual decline in local job opportunities,
or economic growth not in proportion to natural increase,
might induce the hardship of migration. But this price is not
the same as, and is less severe than, the price of simple unemployment. It could also rather easily be compensated

through a relocation subsidy for mobile workers, as is now commonly provided for high-salaried executives by private corporations and in a limited way generally by the federal tax deduction for job-related moving expenses.

Workers' anxiety and its ideological consequences emerge from the larger fact that the United States is a society of constant substantial joblessness, with unemployment rates conservatively estimated by the Department of Commerce at 4 to 8 percent of that portion of the work force defined as ordinarily active. There is thus a game of musical chairs being played at all times, with workers circulating around the country, hoping to land in an empty chair at the moment the music stops. Increasing the stock of jobs in any one place neither causes the music to stop more frequently nor increases the number of chairs relative to the number of players. The only way effectively to ameliorate this circumstance is to create a full-employment economy, a comprehensive system of drastically increased unemployment insurance, or some other device that breaks the connection between a person's having a livelihood and the remote decisions of corporate executives. Without such a development, the fear of unemployment acts to make workers politically passive (if not downright supportive) with respect to land-use policies, taxation programs, and antipollution nonenforcement schemes which, in effect, represent income transfers from the general public to various sectors of the elite (see Whitt 1975). Thus, for many reasons, workers and their leaders should organize their political might more consistently not as part of the growth coalitions of the localities in which they are situated, but rather as part of national movements that aim to provide full employment, income security, and programs for taxation, land use, and the environment that benefit the vast majority of the population. They tend not to be doing this at present.

The Problem of Natural Increase

Localities grow in population not simply as a function of migration but also because of the fecundity of the existing population. Some means are obviously needed to provide jobs and housing to accommodate such growth—either in the immediate area or at some distant location. There are ways of handling this without compounding the environmental and budgetary problems of existing settlements. First, there are some localities that are, by many criteria, not overpopulated. Their atmospheres are clean, water supplies plentiful, and traffic congestion nonexistent. In fact, in certain places increased increments of population may spread the costs of existing road and sewer systems over a larger number of citizens or bring an increase in quality of public education by making rudimentary specialization possible. In the state of California, for example, the great bulk of the population lives on a narrow coastal belt in the southern two-thirds of the state. Thus the northern third of the state consists of a large unpopulated region rich in natural resources, including electric power and potable water. The option chosen in California, as evidenced by the state aqueduct, was to move the water from the uncrowded north to the dense, semiarid south, thus lowering the environmental qualities of both regions, and at a substantial long-term cost to the public budget. The opposite course of action was clearly an option.

The point is that there are relatively underpopulated areas in this country that do not have "natural" problems of inaccessibility, ugliness, or lack of population-support resources. Indeed, the nation's most severely depopulated areas, the towns of Appalachia, are in locales of sufficient resources and are widely regarded as aesthetically appealing; population outmigration likely decreased the aesthetic resources of both the migrants to and residents of Chicago and Detroit, while resulting in the desertion of a housing stock and utility infrastructure designed to serve a larger population. Following from my more general perspective, I see lack of population in a given area as resulting from the political economic decisions made to populate other areas instead. If the process were rendered more rational, the same investments in roads, airports, defense plants, etc., could be made to effect a very different land-use outcome. Indeed, utilization of such delib-

erate planning strategies is the practice in some other societies and shows some evidence of success (see Sundquist 1975);
perhaps it could be made to work in the United States as
well.

As a long-term problem, natural increase may well be
phased out. American birth rates have been steadily decreasing for the last several years, and we are on the verge of a
rate providing for zero population growth. If a stable population actually is achieved, a continuation of the present in-
terlocal competitive system will result in the proliferation of
ghost towns and unused capital stocks as the price paid for
the growth of the successful competing units. This will be an
even more clearly preposterous situation than the current one,
which is given to produce ghost towns only on occasion.

The Emerging Countercoalition

Although growth has been the dominant ideology in most
localities in the United States, there has always been a sub-
versive thread of resistance. Treated as romantic, or as somehow irrational (see White and White 1962), this minority long
was ignored, even in the face of accumulating journalistic
portrayals of the evils of bigness. But certainly it was an easy
observation to make that increased size was related to high
levels of pollution, traffic congestion, and other disadvantages. Similarly, it was easy enough to observe that tax rates
in large places were not generally less than those in small
places; although it received little attention, evidence that per-
capita government costs rise with population size was provided a generation ago (see Hawley 1951). But few took note,
though the very rich, somehow sensing these facts to be the
case, managed to reserve for themselves small, exclusive
meccas of low density by tightly imposing population ceilings (such as Beverly Hills, Sands Point, West Palm Beach,
Lake Forest).

In recent years, however, the base of the anti-growth
movement has become much broader and in some localities

has reached sufficient strength to achieve at least toeholds of political power. The most prominent cases seem to be certain university cities (Palo Alto, Santa Barbara, Boulder, Ann Arbor), all of which have sponsored impact studies documenting the costs of additional growth. Other localities that have imposed growth controls tend also to be places of high amenity value (such as Ramapo, N.Y.; Petaluma, Calif.; Boca Raton, Fla.). The anti-growth sentiment has become an important part of the politics of a few large cities (for example, San Diego) and has been the basis of important political careers at the state level (including the governorship) in Oregon, Colorado, and Vermont. Given the objective importance of the issue and the evidence on the general costs of growth, there is nothing to prevent anti-growth coalitions from similarly gaining power elsewhere—including those areas of the country that are generally considered to possess lower levels of amenity. Nor is there any reason, based on the facts of the matter, for these coalitions not to further broaden their base to include the great majority of the working class in the localities in which they appear.

But, like all political movements that attempt to rely on volunteer labor to supplant political powers institutionalized through a system of vested economic interest, anti-growth movements are probably more likely to succeed in those places where volunteer reform movements have a realistic constituency—a leisured and sophisticated middle class with a tradition of broad-based activism, free from an entrenched machine. At least, this appears to be an accurate profile of those places in which the anti-growth coalitions have already matured.

Systematic studies of the social makeup of the anti-growth activists are only now in progress (for example, Fitts 1976), but it seems that the emerging countercoalition is rooted in the recent environmental movements and relies on a mixture of young activists (some are veterans of the peace and civil rights movements), middle-class professionals, and workers, all of whom see their own tax rates as well as lifestyles in conflict with growth. Important in leadership roles are government employees and those who work for organizations not dependent on local expansion for profit, either directly or indirectly. In the Santa Barbara anti-growth movements, for example, much support is provided by professionals from research and electronics firms, as well as branch managers of small "high-technology" corporations. Cosmopolitan in outlook and pecuniary interest, they use the local community only as a setting for life and work, rather than as an exploitable resource. Related to this constituency are certain very wealthy people (particularly those whose wealth derives from the exploitation of nonlocal environments) who continue a tradition (with some modifications) of aristocratic conservation.[18]

The changes which the death of the growth machine will bring, should it occur, seem clear enough with respect to land-use policy. Local governments will establish holding capacities for their regions and then legislate, directly or indirectly, to limit population to those levels. The direction of any future development will tend to be planned to minimize negative environmental impacts. The so-called natural process (see Burgess 1925; Hoyt 1939) of land development, which has given American cities their present shape, will end as the political and economic foundations of such processes are undermined. Perhaps most important, industrial and business land users and their representatives will lose, at least to some extent, the effectiveness of their threat to locate elsewhere should public policies endanger the profitability they desire. As the growth machine is destroyed in many places, increasingly it will be the business interests who will be forced to make do with local policies, rather than the local populations having to bow to business wishes. New options for taxation, creative land-use programs, and new forms of urban services may thus emerge as city government comes to resemble an agency that asks what it can do for its people rather than what it can do to attract more people. More specifically, a particular industrial project will perhaps be evaluated in terms of its social utility—the usefulness of the product manufactured—either to the locality or to the society at large. Production, merely for the sake of local expansion, will be less likely to occur. Hence, there will be some pressure to increase the use value of the country's production apparatus and for external costs of production to be borne internally.

When growth ceases to be an issue, some of the investments made in the political system to influence and enhance growth will no longer make sense, thus changing the basis on which people get involved in government. We can expect that the local business elites—led by land developers and other growth-coalition forces—will tend to withdraw from local politics. This vacuum may then be filled by a more representative and, likely, less reactionary activist constituency. It is noteworthy that where anti-growth forces have established beachheads of power, their programs and policies have tended to be more progressive than their predecessors'—on all issues, not just on growth. In Colorado, for example, the environmentalist who led the successful fight against the Winter Olympics also successfuly sponsored abortion reform and other important progressive causes. The environmentally based Santa Barbara "Citizens Coalition" (with city government majority control) represents a fusion of the city's traditional left and counterculture with other environmental activists. The result of the no-growth influence on localities may thus be a tendency for an increasing progressiveness in local politics. To whatever degree local politics is the bedrock upon which the national political structure rests (and there is much debate here), there may follow reforms at the national level as well. Perhaps it will then become possible to utilize national institutions to effect other policies, which both solidify the death of the growth machine at the local level and create national priorities consistent with the new opportunities for urban civic life. These are speculations based on the questionable thesis that a reform-oriented, issue-based citizens' politics can be sustained over a long period. The historical record is not consistent with this thesis; it is only emerging political trends in the most affected localities and the general irrationality of the present urban system that suggest that the alternative possibility is an authentic future.

Notes

1. This association of related phenomena is the common conceptualization that students of the economic development of cities ordinarily utilize in their analyses (see, e.g., Alonso 1964; Leven 1964; Brown 1974:48–51; and Durr 1971:174–180). As Sundquist remarks in the context of his study of population policies in Western Europe:

> "The key to population distribution is, of course, job availability. A few persons—retired, notably, and some independent professionals such as artists, writers and inventors—may be free to live in any locality they choose but, for the rest, people are compelled to distribute themselves in whatever pattern is dictated by the distribution of employment opportunities. Some investors may locate their investment in areas of surplus labor voluntarily, and so check the migration flow, and others may be induced by government assistance to do so. But if neither of these happens—if the jobs do not go where the workers are—the workers must go to the jobs, if they are not to accept welfare as a way of life. When population distribution is an end, then, job distribution is inevitably the means" (1975:13).

2. For accounts of how "boosterism" worked in this manner, see Wade (1969) and Harris (1976).

3. Agger et al. remark, on the basis of their comparative study of four U.S. cities:

> "Members of the local elites value highly harmony and unity—"pulling together." They regard local community affairs as essentially nonpolitical, and tend to associate controversy with "politics." An additional factor reinforcing the value of harmony in many communities . . . is the nationwide competition among communities for new industries. Conflict is thought to create a highly unfavorable image to outsiders, an image that might well repel any prospective industry" (1964:649).

4. See, e.g., the May 19, 1974, issue of *Forbes*, which had the following ad placed by the State of Pennsylvania: "Q: [banner headline] Which state could possibly cut taxes at a time like this? A: Pennsylvania [same large type]. Pennsylvania intends to keep showing businessmen that it means business. Pennsylvania. Where business has a lot growing for it. . . ." The state of Maryland ran this ad in the same issue: "Maryland Finances the Training. . . In short, we can finance practically everything you need to establish a manufacturing plant. . . ."

5. The City of Los Angeles maintains an office, headed by a former key business executive, with this "liaison" role as its specific task (see "L.A.'s Business Envoy Speaks Softly and Sits at a Big Desk," *Los Angeles Times* [August 26, 1974]).

6. The literature on community power is vast and controversial but has been summarized by Walton: he indicates, on the basis of 39 studies of 61 communities, that "the proportion of businessmen found in the lead-

ership group is high irrespective of the type of power structure found"
(1970:446). It is my argument, of course, that this high level of participation does indeed indicate the exercise of power on behalf of at least a portion of the elite. My analysis does not assume that this portion of the elite
is necessarily always united with others of high status on the concrete
issues of local land use and the uses of local government.

7. Descriptions of some tactics typically employed in land-use politics
are contained in McConnell (1966), Tolchin and Tolchin (1971), and Makielski (1966), but a sophisticated relevant body of literature does not yet
exist.

8. Thus the stance taken by civic business groups toward growth and
land-use matters affecting growth is consistently positive, although the *intensity* of commitment to that goal varies. In his study of New York City
zoning, Makielski indicates that "the general business groups . . . approached zoning from an economic viewpoint, although this often led them
to share the Reformer's ideology. Their economic interest in the city gave
them a stake in a "healthy," "growing community" where tax rates were
not prohibitive, where city government was "efficient," and where some of
the problems of the urban environment—a constricting labor force, congestion, and lack of space—were being attacked." (1966:141)

A similar dynamic has been observed in a medium-size Mexican city:
"Despite many other differences, basic agreement on the primacy of stability and growth provides a basis for a dialogue between government and
business (Fagen and Tuohy 1972:56).

9. Bruce Pringle suggested the latter phrase to me.

10. Papers can expand into other industries, such as book publishing
and wood harvesting. The point is that, compared with most other industries, they cannot easily replicate themselves across geographical boundaries through chains, branch plants, and franchises.

11. In some cities (e.g., Chicago) it is the political machine that performs this function and thus can "get things done." Political scientists (e.g.,
Edward Banfield) often identify success in performing this function as evidence of effective local government.

12. In his study of the history of zoning in New York City, Makielski
remarks: "While the newspapers in the city are large landholders, the role
of the press was not quite like that of any of the other nongovernmental
actors. The press was in part one of the referees of the rules of the game,
especially the informal rules—calling attention to what it considered violations" (1966:189).

13. A useful bibliography of growth evaluation studies is Agelasto and
Perry (undated). A study with findings contrary to those reported here
(Gruen and Gruen Associates, 1972) limits cost evaluation to only three
municipal services and was carried out in a city that had already made
major capital expenditures that provided it with huge unused capacities in
water, schools, and sewage.

14. I am not arguing that the labor force is perfectly mobile, as indeed there is strong evidence that mobility is limited by imperfect information, skill limitations, and cultural and family ties. The argument is rather that the essential mobility of the labor force is sufficiently pronounced to make programs of local job creation largely irrelevant to long-term rates of unemployment.

15. This lack of relationship between local population change and unemployment has led others to conclusions similar to my own: "Economists unanimously have agreed that the only jurisdiction that should be concerned with the effects of its policies on the level of employment is the Federal government. Small jurisdictions do not have the power to effect significant changes in the level of unemployment" (Levy and Arnold 1972:95).

16. It is also true that this evidence is based on federal data, accumulated through the work of socially and geographically disparate persons who had purposes at hand different from mine. This important reservation can only be dealt with by noting that the findings were consistent with the author's theoretical expectations, rather than antecedents of them. At a minimum, the results throw the burden of proof on those who would argue the opposite hypothesis.

17. For an insightful treatment of joblessness with respect to the majority of the American work force, see Levison (1974).

18. Descriptions of the social makeup of American environmentalists (who coincide as a group only roughly with the no-growth activists) and of their increasing militancy are contained in Nash (1967), Bartell (1974), Dunlap and Gale (1972), and Faich and Gale (1971). For a journalistic survey of no-growth activities, see Robert Cahn, "Mr. Developer, Someone Is Watching You" (*Christian Science Monitor* [May 21, 1973]:9). A more comprehensive description is contained in Reilly (1973).

References

Adrian, C. R. and O. P. Williams. 1963. *Four Cities: A Study in Comparative Policy Making*. Philadelphia: University of Pennsylvania Press.

Agelasto, M. A., II, and P. R. Perry. Undated. "The No Growth Controversy." Mimeographed, Exchange Bibliography no. 519. Box 229, Monticello, Ill.: Council of Planning Libraries.

Agger, R., D. Goldrich, and B. E. Swanson. 1964. *The Rulers and the Ruled: Political Power and Impotence in American Communities*. New York: Wiley.

Alonso, W. 1964. "Location Theory." In J. Friedman and W. Alonso, eds., *Regional Development and Planning*, pp. 79–81. Cambridge, Mass.: M.I.T. Press.

Ann Arbor City Planning Department. 1972. *The Ann Arbor Growth Study.* Ann Arbor, Mich.: City Planning Department.

Appelbaum, R. 1976. "City Size and Urban Life: A Preliminary Inquiry Into Some Consequences of Growth in American Cities." *Urban Affairs Quarterly* (Spring), 12(2):139–169.

Appelbaum, R., J. Bigelow, H. Kramer, H. Molotch, and P. Relis. 1974. *Santa Barbara: The Impacts of Growth: A Report of the Santa Barbara Planning Task Force to the City of Santa Barbara.* Santa Barbara, Calif.: Office of the City Clerk. Forthcoming in abridged form as *The Effects of Urban Growth: A Population Impact Analysis.* New York: Praeger.

Banfield, E. 1961. *Political Influence.* New York: Macmillan.

Bartell, T. 1974. "Compositional Change and Attitude Change among Sierra Club Members." Mimeographed, Los Angeles: UCLA Survey Research Center.

Bonacich, E. 1975. "Advanced Capitalism and Black/White Race Relations in the U.S." Mimeographed, Riverside, Calif.: Department of Sociology, University of California.

Bouma, D. 1962. "Analysis of the Social Power Position of a Real Estate Board." *Social Problems* (Fall), 10:121–132.

Brown, D. 1974. *Introduction to Urban Economics.* New York: Academic Press.

Burgess, E. W. 1925. *The Growth of the City: An Introduction to a Research Project.* Chicago: University of Chicago Press.

Davis, K. 1965. "The Urbanization of the Human Population." *Scientific American* (September), 212:41–53.

Duncan, O. D. 1957. "Optimum Size of Cities." In P. Hatt and A. Reiss, Jr., eds., *Cities and Societies,* pp. 759–772. New York: Free Press.

Dunlap, R. E. and R. P. Gale. 1972. "Politics and Ecology: A Political Profile of Student Eco-Activists." *Youth and Society* (June), 3:379–397.

Durr, F. 1971. *The Urban Economy.* Scranton, Penn.: Intext.

Edelman, M. 1964. *The Symbolic Uses of Politics.* Urbana: University of Illinois Press.

Fagen, R. R. and W. S. Tuohy. 1972. *Politics and Privilege in a Mexican City.* Stanford, Calif.: Stanford University Press.

Faich, R. G. and R. Gale. 1971. "Environmental Movement: From Recreation to Politics." *Pacific Sociological Review* (July), 14:270–287.

Finkler, E. 1972. "No-growth as a Planning Alternative." Planning Advisory Report no. 283. Chicago: American Society of Planning Officials.

Fischer, C. S., M. Baldassare, and R. J. Ofshe. 1974. "Crowding Studies and Urban Life: A Critical Review." Working Paper no. 242. Institute of Urban and Regional Development, University of California, Berkeley.

Fitts, A. 1976. "No-Growth as a Political Issue." Ph.D. dissertation, University of California, Los Angeles.

Follett, R. 1976. "Social Consequences of Urban Size and Growth: An

Analysis of Middle-Size U.S. Urban Areas." Ph.D. dissertation, Department of Sociology, University of California, Santa Barbara.

Gruen and Gruen Associates. 1972. *Impacts of Growth: An Analytical Framework and Fiscal Examples.* Berkeley: California Better Housing Foundation.

Hadden, J. K. and E. F. Borgatta. 1965. *American Cities: Their Social Characteristics.* Chicago: Rand-McNally.

Harris, C. V. 1976. *Political Power in Birmingham, 1871–1921.* Memphis: University of Tennessee Press.

Hawley, A. 1951. "Metropolitan Population and Municipal Government Expenditures in Central Cities." *Journal of Social Issues* (January), 7:100–108.

Hoch, I. 1972. "Urban Scale and Environmental Quality." In U.S. Commission on Population Growth and the American Future Research Reports, Ronald Ridker, ed., *Population, Resources and the Environment,* vol. 3, pp. 231–284. Washington, D.C.: Government Printing Office.

Hoyt, H. 1939. *The Structure and Growth of Residential Neighborhoods in American Cities.* Washington, D.C.: Federal Housing Administration.

Lasswell, H. 1936. *Politics: Who Gets What, When, How.* New York: McGraw-Hill.

Leven, C. 1964. "Regional and Interregional Accounts in Perspective." *Papers, Regional Science Association,* 13:140–144.

Levison, A. 1974. *The Working Class Majority.* New York: Coward, McCann and Geoghegan.

Levy, S. and R. K. Arnold. 1972. "An Evaluation of Four Growth Alternatives in the City of Milpitas, 1972–1977." Technical Memorandum Report. Palo Alto, Calif.: Institute of Regional and Urban Studies.

Livingston, L. and J. A. Blayney. 1971. "Foothill Environmental Design Study: Open Space vs. Development." Final report to the City of Palo Alto. San Francisco: Livingston and Blayney.

McConnell, G. 1966. *Private Power and American Democracy.* New York: Knopf.

McKenzie, R. D. 1922. "The Neighborhood: A Study of Local Life in the City of Columbus, Ohio—Conclusion." *American Journal of Sociology* (May), 27:780–799.

Makielski, S. J., Jr. 1966. *The Politics of Zoning: The New York Experience.* New York: Columbia University Press.

Mazie, S. M. and S. Rowlings. 1973. "Public Attitude Toward Population Distribution Issues." In S. M. Mazie, ed., *Population Distribution and Policy,* pp. 603–615. Washington, D.C.: Commission on Population Growth and the American Future.

Molotch, H. L. 1967. "Toward a More Human Ecology." *Land Economics* (August), 43:336–341.

—— 1973. *Managed Integration: Dilemmas of Doing Good in the City.* Berkeley: University of California Press.

Mumford, L. 1961. *The City in History*. New York: Harcourt Brace Jovanov-ich.

Nash, R. 1967. *Wilderness and the American Mind*. New Haven, Conn.: Yale University Press.

Parke, R., Jr. and C. Westoff, eds. 1972. "Aspects of Population Growth Policy." Report of the U.S. Commission of Population Growth and the American Future, vol. 6. Washington, D.C.: Commission on Population Growth and the American Future.

Piven, F. F. and R. Cloward. 1972. *Regulating the Poor*. New York: Random House.

Reilly, W. K., ed. 1973. *The Use of Land: A Citizens' Policy Guide to Urban Growth*. New York: Crowell.

Rubin, L. 1972. *Busing and Backlash*. Berkeley: University of California Press.

Samuelson, P. 1942. "The Business Cycle and Urban Development." In G. Greer, ed., *The Problem of the Cities and Towns*, pp. 6–17. Cambridge, Mass.: Harvard University Press.

Schattschneider, E. E. 1960. *The Semisovereign People*. New York: Holt, Rinehart and Winston.

Schulze, R. O. 1961. "The Bifurcation of Power in a Satellite City." In M. Janowitz, ed., *Community Political Systems*, pp. 19–80. New York: Macmillan.

Sierra Club of San Diego. 1973. "Economy, Ecology, and Rapid Population Growth." Mimeographed, San Diego: Sierra Club.

Spaulding, C. 1951. "Occupational Affiliations of Councilmen in Small Cities." *Sociology and Social Research*, 35(3):194–200.

State of California. 1970. *California Statistical Abstract, 1970*. Sacramento: State of California.

Sundquist, J. 1975. *Dispersing Population: What America Can Learn from Europe*. Washington, D.C.: Brookings.

Suttles, G. 1972. *The Social Construction of Communities*. Chicago: University of Chicago Press.

Tolchin, M. and S. Tolchin. 1971. *To the Victor*. New York: Random House.

U.S. Bureau of the Census. 1962. *Census of Population*, vol. 1, pt. 1. Washington, D.C.: Government Printing Office.

—— 1969. *Population Estimates and Projections*. Current Population Reports, series P-25, no. 427 (July 31). Washington, D.C.: Government Printing Office.

—— 1972. *County and City Data Book*. Washington, D.C.: Government Printing Office.

Wade, R. 1969. *The Urban Frontier: The Rise of Western Cities*. Cambridge, Mass.: Harvard University Press.

Walton, J. 1970. "A Systematic Survey of Community Power Research." In M. Aiken and P. Mott, eds., *The Structure of Community Power*, pp. 443–464. New York: Random House.

White, M. and L. White. 1962. *The Intellectual Versus the City*. Cambridge, Mass.: Harvard and M.I.T. University Presses.

Whitt, J. A. 1975. "Means of Movement: The Politics of Modern Transportation Systems." Ph.D. dissertation, Department of Sociology, University of California, Santa Barbara.

Wirth, L. 1938. "Urbanism as a Way of Life." *American Journal of Sociology* (July), 44:1–14.

Wyner, A. 1967. "Governor—Salesman." *National Civic Review* (February), 61:81–86.

Index